FLAWED CHURCH, FAITHFUL GOD

Flawed Church, Faithful God

A Reformed Ecclesiology for the Real World

Joseph D. Small

WILLIAM B. EERDMANS PUBLISHING COMPANY
GRAND RAPIDS, MICHIGAN

Wm. B. Eerdmans Publishing Co.
2140 Oak Industrial Drive NE, Grand Rapids, Michigan 49505
www.eerdmans.com

27 26 25 24 23 22 21 20 19 18   1 2 3 4 5 6 7 8 9 10

ISBN 978-0-8028-7612-6

Library of Congress Cataloging-in-Publication Data

Names: Small, Joseph D., author.
Title: Flawed church, faithful God : a reformed ecclesiology for the real world /
    Joseph D. Small.
Description: Grand Rapids : Eerdmans Publishing Co., 2018. |
    Includes bibliographical references and index.
Identifiers: LCCN 2017059258 | ISBN 9780802876126 (pbk. : alk. paper)
Subjects: LCSH: Church.
Classification: LCC BV600.3 .S629 2018 | DDC 262/.042—dc23
    LC record available at https://lccn.loc.gov/2017059258

For Kalen and Barrie

Doug, Dalen, and Bennett

Carly and Blake

Jennifer, Rashana, and Selena

One generation shall laud your works to another. . . .

Psalm 145:4

A company of believers is like a prisonful of criminals: their intimacy and solidarity are based on what about themselves they can least justify.

John Updike, *In the Beauty of the Lilies*

Contents

Foreword by Craig Dykstra   ix

Preface   xiii

1. What (in the World) Is the Church?   1

2. We Believe?   22

3. Church of the Word and Sacrament   42

4. Communion of the Holy Spirit   62

5. Body Language   85

6. Call and Response   104

7. People of God   124

8. In Our Time   145

9. Professing the Faith   167

10. One, Holy, Catholic, and Apostolic Church   188

11. Hope for the Church   209

Bibliography   220

Index of Authors   229

Index of Subjects   232

Index of Scripture References   240

Foreword

Joseph D. Small is exactly the kind of person the church desperately needs among its leadership, as he has proven throughout his distinguished career as a local church pastor and as the longtime director of Theology, Worship, and Educational Ministries for the Presbyterian Church (USA). In those contexts, he has served the whole church (not just the Presbyterians) as one of its most influential theological educators and as a prominent leader in worldwide ecumenical dialogue. The church—its character, its life, its meaning, its faith, its ministry, its creation in and through the love of God made manifest in Jesus Christ—has been the passionate focus of Joe Small's attention throughout the course of his ministry. And the fruits of his endeavors have been both plentiful and welcome. Joe Small has written eight previous books and numerous monographs, book chapters, journal articles, and theological papers. But this may be his *summa*.

Small is deeply troubled about the condition of the church in our time and culture. He is also profoundly hopeful.

In a consumerist society riven by competition, the church, Small says, has a hard time resisting becoming a consumer commodity in competition with all manner of other goods and services. Religious beliefs, practices, programs, and institutions all become items in a religious marketplace from among which consumers can choose their favorites or ignore them altogether. "As purveyors of religious goods and services in a consumer-driven market economy," says Small, "churches are susceptible to the short leaps from the commodification of the church to the commodification of faith to the commodification of God. The progression from choosing beliefs, to choosing a church, to choosing a god, leads directly to 'I determine what God is'"(21).

This, of course, is idolatry. When we become the makers of "gods," we abandon the God who in love created the universe itself and who in Jesus Christ came to save us and all the world—perhaps without even knowing we have done so. We also abandon the church when we assume or decide that we are the ones who choose what the church is and how it is to be shaped and formed and made what we want it to be. No, says Small: the church is not created by human artifice; it is "born of the Word of God" (42). It is a gift created and given to us by God. This fundamental conviction is the truth upon which our faith and hope and life together as church is founded. The church is given to us by God and we are both invited and called to grow into the life-giving life that God makes possible for us in and through the church. This is the deep, everlasting source of hope for the life of the church—not only in our time and culture, but in every age and context.

"At the core of the church's life," says Small, "is the church's shared faith . . . certain core affirmations that identify Christian churches as Christian." What Christians all share is "a language used within the churches to describe their apprehension of the presence of God" (23). Throughout its history, the church has found its identity and shaped its life by telling, singing, and enacting the narrative that enables us to "say who we are as the people of God, the body of Christ, the communion of the Holy Spirit" and to tell the story "of God and ourselves, the story of redemption and new life" (34). Without this shared language, without this long, deep, theological inheritance, constantly drawn upon afresh in ever-unfolding new times and places, the faith we have been given cannot be sustained. And neither can the church.

Some years ago, the Lilly Endowment, a charitable foundation where I worked for many years, funded a research project that surveyed pastors of congregations from many denominations all across the United States. In his book, Small lifts up one of the key findings from this survey, which is that while most pastors regard their ministries to be quite satisfying, a large majority of them said that the most frustrating aspect of their ministry was the difficulty they experience in "reaching people with the gospel today." Small comments that the fundamental problem here is likely to be "the absence of clarity about the gospel itself" (41).

This is the problem that this book seeks to help remedy. Small provides a brief but comprehensive theological portrait of what it truly means to be the church and what it means for the gospel to be embodied in the lived faith of the people of God. The Nicene Creed provides the overarching

defined + connected

framework for a rich contemporary discussion of "the memory and the hope of the church as it strives to live out a clear and communal identity that is capable of proclaiming the gospel, nurturing the faithful, worshiping in Spirit and in Truth, fostering justice in church and society, and displaying to the world the coming reign of God" (40).

Chapter by chapter, Small describes for us what it means to be a church of Word and sacrament; a communion of the Holy Spirit; the body of Christ (and, indeed, the wounded body of Christ); a community that lives in deep, intimate, abiding mutuality; a people of God. At every point along the way, Small unpacks the significance and crucial nuances of all the essential dimensions of being "one holy, catholic, apostolic church." In the process, Small calls on a wide, rich body of theological literature, both ancient and contemporary. His task, as his subtitle suggests, is to provide a portrait of a Reformed ecclesiology, and he very much succeeds in that endeavor. A rich ecumenical conversation takes place on these pages, and the bibliography on which he draws is robust and comprehensive. The significance of key ecumenical discussions and debates in which Small has been involved is clearly articulated and the resources brought to bear are consistently apt. Of special interest are Small's two chapters, "People of God" and "In Our Time," which describe contemporary theological work on Jewish-Christian relations. Here he tackles what he calls "the ecclesiological deficit that results from failing to know both Christians and Jews *as people of God*" (126). The fruit of Small's long involvement in dialogues among Jews and Christians is harvested here in his statement: "That Christians and Jews are, together, the people of God is a conviction of Christian theology" (158). Working out the implications of this conviction for what it means for Christians to be the "people of God together with the Jewish people of God" is a profoundly important task for the church at every level to engage in our time.

Small is convinced that a serious effort to recover a practical-theological ecclesiology in the church as a whole at every level is essential both for the character and quality of its shared life and for its capacity to foster among its people and the larger culture a way of life that is truly life-giving. As Jesus said, "I came that you might have life and have it abundantly" (John 10:10). But an ecclesiology, however rich, that lives only in words on paper is no ecclesiology at all. When the words truly live, they live in the lives of people who live by the Word of God. As Small says of the early Christians living in a pagan society, they lived "a shared life distinguished by community practices centered in the One God" (179). It was a way of life together

that contrasted significantly from that of the larger society. And that is
what this book is ultimately all about. It is about believing in a way that is
consistent with the wisdom of the ancient creeds and draws deeply from
the wells of historic Christian faith and life. Even more, it is about living a
way of life in community with one another—a way of life that is born of the
Word of God and is shared as a gift of love to all who are in need.

Flawed Church, Faithful God is a rich and valuable primer, both com-
pact and comprehensive. This is a book that needs to be taught in theological seminaries, read and discussed in groups of pastors, and engaged
by lay leaders in congregations who are eager to think more deeply and
comprehensively about the substance of their faith and their vocations
in the world. People who are shaping and leading a wide variety of other
religious institutions—church-related colleges and universities, faith-based
social service and community development organizations, denominational
judicatories, and ecumenical and interfaith organizations among others—
will find this to be a valuable resource for helping them to diagnose the
religious and spiritual consequences of living in our secular age and com-
modified culture as well as to imagine possible alternative ways of being
in light of the presence and power of God's inexhaustible love and grace.

Open the book. Turn the pages. Dig in deeply. Draw on the riches you
will find here.

CRAIG DYKSTRA

Preface

Remind them of this, and warn them before God that they are
to avoid wrangling over words, which does no good but only
ruins those who are listening.

2 Timothy 2:14

The English language becomes ugly and inaccurate because
our thoughts are foolish, but the slovenliness of our language
makes it easier to have foolish thoughts. . . . If thought corrupts
language, language can also corrupt thought. A bad usage can
spread by tradition and imitation, even among people who
should and do know better.

George Orwell, "Politics and the English Language"

In John Updike's novel *In the Beauty of the Lilies*, he writes, "A company
of believers is like a prisonful of criminals: their intimacy and solidarity
are based on what about themselves they can least justify."[1] His comment
reminds me of familiar images for the church such as "hospital for the
sick" or even the old saw, "The church is like Noah's ark; if it weren't for
the storm outside you wouldn't be able to stand the smell inside." To play
with Updike's image and think of the church as a company of criminals
is to think of the church as a communion of persons, not just of persons within the church. This company of criminals is not the uniformly
good church—an always effective hospital for others out there who are

1. John Updike, *In the Beauty of the Lilies* (New York: Knopf, 1996), 416.

sick—but the church as a flawed company that nevertheless receives and witnesses to the grace of Christ, the love of God, and the communion of the Holy Spirit.

Thinking of the church as a company of criminals is not a cynical denigration of the church, but a counter to the church's proclivity to justify itself, to promote itself as a virtuous, holy enclave in a sinful world. Churches justify themselves theologically by heralding their existence as "a provisional demonstration of what God intends for the world," or they validate themselves culturally by promoting their capacity to provide religious goods and services. The church's genuine intimacy and solidarity are not based on self-justification but on the recognition that God alone justifies. The church is a communion of intimacy and solidarity because of what it cannot justify about itself coupled with recognition that its justification lies in the grace of God. Only as the church knows that its life is not self-generated and maintained can it witness faithfully to the God who generates and maintains it. This book is an ecclesiology that sees the church in that light.

It attempts to do so in a way that is not only Reformed but ecumenical. I am a minister in the Presbyterian Church (USA), the denomination that brought me to faith, nurtured and educated me, called me to ministry, and provided opportunities for service. I have been exposed to more Calvin than Aquinas, Luther, Hooker, or Wesley, although I have learned a great deal from them and many others. I read more Barth than Rahner or Pannenberg or Zizioulas, although I do read them and many others from a range of traditions. I am more familiar with conciliar than with episcopal or congregational church polities, although I find that aspects of both supplement and correct Presbyterian perspectives.

I would not claim that Reformed perspectives on the church's faith and life are the correct and faithful ones; exploring Reformed perspectives is a way into far broader ecumenical territory. My work through the Faith and Order commissions of the World and National Councils of Churches, the theology office of the World Communion of Reformed Churches, and the international Reformed-Pentecostal Dialogue has shaped me as surely as my own tradition has, and so I hope that my thinking about ecclesiology will resonate in circles beyond my own tradition. I also hope that my approach to ecclesiology will expand and deepen Reformed thinking about the "who, what, when, where, why, and how" of the church.

Finally, I write as a North American, which means that many of my references to specific historical and sociological characteristics of the church will indicate that context. However, I trust that my observations, even the most explicitly contextual, are not germane to North America alone. Similarly, my placement in a mainline denomination does not restrict my thinking to historic, white churches. We are all contextual, which simply means that we look at the church and the world from a particular social location. But we are not prisoners of context, unable to see beyond ourselves or to communicate to others what we see. My own thinking has been enriched and corrected by reading widely and by having conversations with church leaders in Africa, Asia, and Latin America. I hope that my approach to ecclesiology will resonate in contexts beyond my own, and that those who share my context will have their thinking about the church expanded and deepened.

THEOLOGY AND SCRIPTURE

Theology cannot be done faithfully apart from close attention to Scripture, as well as to the history of doctrine, ecclesiastical history, sociology, and other "non-theological" areas. I am not an expert in any of those fields. However, their separation into discrete areas of specialization is lamentable, arising from their confinement to distinct departments in theological education and religious studies. Edward Farley has critiqued the fourfold pattern—Scripture, church history, dogmatics, and practical theology—noting their isolation from one another. He observes that what was once a unified inquiry seeking sapiential knowledge "has dispersed not only into the independent sciences of the fourfold pattern, but into a great many subspecialities which have lost contact with the disciplines of the pattern itself."[2]

Separations and distinctions that result in the compartmentalization of self-referential disciplines, each with its own experts, is an unfortunate development that has a deleterious effect on theology, on theological education, on the intellectual life of pastors, and on the capacity of congregations to think the faith. Theologians do not know what Bible scholars are doing, New Testament and Old Testament studies have become strangers, New Testament has separated into Gospel and Pauline fields. A professor of New Testament, recently invited to address a conference

---

2. Edward Farley, *Theologia: The Fragmentation and Unity of Theological Education* (Philadelphia: Fortress, 1983), 142.

on the ascension, declined, saying, "Ascension is Luke, I'm John." The recent appearance of theological commentaries is a welcome development that aims to bring theology and biblical studies into conversation. Serious, sustained attention to Scripture in theological work will also be welcomed.

Although I am not a New Testament scholar or an Old Testament expert, I try to pay special attention to Scripture. To paraphrase Karl Barth, "the theologian cannot evade Scripture. Theologians cannot appeal past it directly to God, to Christ or the Holy Spirit."[3] Neither can theologians speak about the church directly, apart from Scripture's witness to the *ecclesia*, to the people of God, the body of Christ, the communion of the Holy Spirit.

NOTES ON LANGUAGE

The English language sometimes employs masculine nouns and pronouns to refer to all people. This usage produces what we now call gender exclusivity. Most churches recognize this problem and acknowledge that the diversity present in both church and world is not always reflected in the language of the church. Many churches have adopted policies or followed practices that encourage every effort to use inclusive language with respect to the people of God. In those churches, inclusive language for people is no longer controvertible. The churches' clear commitment has even helped us to understand that the original inclusivity of some biblical, creedal, and liturgical texts has been masked by gender-exclusive English translations. As with everything that I write, this book intends to be fully gender-inclusive in every reference to God's people. (Language for God presents a more difficult problem; hence the discussions of pronouns and of Trinity below.) I do not, however, alter the language of historical texts. Gender exclusivity was standard practice until a generation or two ago, and I do not attempt to "correct" Augustine or Calvin or Barth (or their translators). In retaining the language as I find it, I follow the lead of a prominent feminist theologian who once remarked that "we are not the Soviet Union so we do not airbrush history."

---

3. Karl Barth, *Church Dogmatics* I/1 (Edinburgh: T&T Clark, 1956), 544. Barth speaks of the church rather than the theologian.

Pronouns

The problem of language for God becomes particularly difficult with pronouns. The singular third-person pronoun options in English are *he*, *she*, and *it*. Use of *it* and *itself* for God would be unsuitably impersonal, so we are left with a choice between masculine and feminine pronouns. In recognizing the problem, some suggest the use of nouns rather than pronouns—"God shows God's love" rather than "God shows his love," for example. Other strategies substitute passive for active voice, as in "God's love is shown," or eliminate the pronoun, as in "God shows love."

The English language does not lend itself to natural solutions, however. The church's legitimate concern for inclusive language sometimes has the unintended consequence of depersonalizing our talk about God and each other. Use of the passive voice removes God as an active, personal presence in the world: "God's love is shown" . . . by whom? Eliminating the pronoun leads to abstraction: "God shows love" . . . a free-standing generic quality? The mechanical substitution of "God" for "he," and "God's" for "his," leads to abstract, impersonal, tedious language that renders God abstract, impersonal, and tedious.

The weakness of the pronoun-to-noun strategy would be obvious if non-theological writing employed it. At the beginning of Michael Ondaatje's novel *In the Skin of a Lion*, Ondaatje describes the thoughts of a young boy, Nicholas, as he wakes up on a cold winter morning—"He longs for the summer nights, for the moment when he turns out the lights, turns out even the small cream funnel in the hall near the room where his father sleeps." Imagine instead, "Nicholas longs for the summer nights, for the moment when Nicholas turns out the lights, turns out even the small cream funnel near the room where Nicholas's father sleeps." Or consider what would happen to a passage from Anne Tyler's novel *The Accidental Tourist* if the character Macon's name were substituted for every use of the third-person masculine pronoun: "Still, Macon noticed Macon had a tendency to hold Macon's arms close to Macon's body, to walk past furniture sideways, as if Macon imagined the house could barely accommodate Macon. Macon felt too tall. Macon's long, clumsy feet seemed unusually distant. Macon ducked Macon's head in doorways." The depersonalized drumbeat repetition of "God" and "God's" is especially problematic in worship, where impersonal abstraction suggests a distant, merely generic deity.

I confess that I do not have a good solution, particularly in the case of pronouns. Although I try to work around the limitations of English grammar and syntax, at times, especially when indicating God's active engagement in the world, the use of masculine pronouns seems unavoidable. At those points I can only trust that we all know God is beyond gender. God is neither male nor female, but rather the One who declares, "I am God, and not a human being—the Holy One among you" (Hos 11:9, TNIV).

Trinity

Many contemporary Christians have difficulty with the gender specificity of *Father* and *Son*. The church uses *Father-Son* language because it is scriptural and creedal. Scripture bears witness to Jesus, who is identified by the very voice of God: "You are my Son, the Beloved." Scripture bears witness to God who is identified by Jesus as "my Father." Moreover, the relationship is characterized in terms of mutual knowledge: "no one knows who the Son is except the Father, or who the Father is except the Son and anyone to whom the Son chooses to reveal him" (Luke 10:22). Throughout the centuries the creeds of the church have made consistent confession of one God—Father, Son, and Holy Spirit. Setting aside Scripture and creeds—and, perhaps more important, setting aside the words of Jesus whom we confess to be God-with-us—is not something to be done lightly, however admirable the motivation.

The more important reason for the church's retention of *Father-Son-Holy Spirit* language—and the reason that occasioned its revelation in the first place—is that the language is both relational and personal. Unlike, for example, "Creator, Redeemer, and Sustainer," *Father-Son-Spirit* language is relational. Fathers have sons, sons have fathers, fathers and sons have and are bound in commonality. On the other hand, creators do not have redeemers, redeemers do not have creators, creators and redeemers do not have sustainers. Language for the Trinity must be relational, not merely functional. Similarly, language for the Trinity must be personal.

Trinitarian language is not confined to *Father-Son-Spirit* language, however. A theological statement on the doctrine of the Trinity, received by the Presbyterian Church (USA), affirms *Father-Son-and Holy Spirit* as foundational, an indispensable anchor, the root from which all language about God grows. But the theological statement also acknowledges other faithful articulations that come from the deep tradition of the church: Speaker-Word-Breath, Sun-Ray-Warmth, Giver-Gift-Giving. None of these is adequate in itself, however; none is a replacement for Father, Son, and Holy Spirit; and none is intended as a form of address to God. All are helpful only as supplements to the fully personal, fully relational language of Scripture and tradition.

One final observation is in order. *Father-Son-Spirit* is explicitly Trinitarian language, language that expresses Trinitarian relationships. It is not intended as pervasive and exclusive language for God. It is as inappropriate to address God exclusively as "Father" as it is to refer to the Trinity as "Creator-Redeemer-Sustainer." "Father" is the name used in relation to the Son and in relation to our adoption through the Son, not a generic title for God. When we speak of the one triune God, rather than of the trinitarian relations, we are free to use language that expresses the full range of biblical images. Long before inclusive language became an issue in the church, John Calvin noted that "[God] did not satisfy himself with proposing the example of a father, but in order to express his very strong affection, he chose to liken himself to a mother, and calls [the people of Israel] not merely 'children,' but *the fruit of the womb*, towards which there is usually a warmer affection."[4] Scripture displays a wealth of language for God. Some of the scriptural language is central while other language is peripheral. The biblical witness to God employs rich metaphors, straightforward similes, and simple images as well as the central language of name and narrative. Christian use of language for God should be as full as the Scriptures and should distinguish between language that is central and pervasive and language that is occasional and peripheral.

Church and Denomination

Some Christian communities—notably Orthodox, Catholic, and Anglican—refer to themselves as *Church*, sometimes reserving that appellation to themselves. Protestant and Pentecostal communities also refer to themselves as *churches*, although in a far broader sense. All currently share an aversion to *denomination*, once simply a term that indicated the name of a religious entity that united congregations in a designated ecclesial body. At certain points, I try to recognize this linguistic thicket by referring to "world communions and denominations," but at other points I simply use "denominations" to refer to the totality of organized Christian ecclesial

---

4. John Calvin, *Commentary on the Book of the Prophet Isaiah*, vol. 4 (Grand Rapids: Eerdmans, 1956), Is. 49:15; 30.

bodies, not as a distinctively Protestant category. I trust that those who consider *denomination* to be a negative term will forgive me when I employ it simply as a non-theological generic designation.

GRATITUDE

I am grateful to four theological institutions whose invitations to lecture provided the opportunity to develop some of the material in this book. The Westervelt Lectures at Austin Presbyterian Theological Seminary helped me to develop material that has found its way throughout, but especially in chapter 6, "Call and Response." I am indebted to President Ted Wardlaw and the faculty, students, and alumni whose comments and questions have sharpened my thinking. The Warren Lectures on Church and Culture at the University of Dubuque Theological Seminary were the occasion for me to think through the material in chapter 10, "One, Holy, Catholic, and Apostolic Church," and elsewhere. I am grateful to President Jeffrey Bullock and Dean Bradley Longfield, and to faculty, students, and alumni whose response encouraged me to further develop my thinking about the church's place in American society. The Washington Theological Consortium's Figel Lecture on Ecumenism contributed to material in chapter 1, "What (in the World) Is the Church?" as well as elsewhere throughout the book. Consortium executive director Larry Golemon and students from member schools provided me the opportunity to talk about ecumenism to an ecumenical audience. An invitation from codirectors Victor Austin and Gregory Fryer to lecture at the Center for Catholic and Evangelical Theology's Pro Ecclesia Conference provided the opportunity to develop some of the material in chapter 9, "Professing the Faith."

Finally, I am indebted to many friends who slogged through drafts of chapters. Rabbis Gilbert Rosenthal and David Sandmell provided close readings of chapters 8 and 9, leading to sharpened terminology and focus. I am especially thankful to Jim Goodloe for the great care he took in reading and commenting on the whole, including footnotes! I thank Bill Eerdmans for his encouragement throughout the drafting of a manuscript. James Ernest and Kelsey Kaemingk of Eerdmans Publishing provided substantive suggestions and identified technical deficiencies, sharpening my focus and correcting my errors. Readers have made this a better book, but, of course, they are not responsible for any of its infelicities.

Chapter 1

WHAT (IN THE WORLD) IS THE CHURCH?

> But you are a chosen race, a royal priesthood, a holy nation, God's own people, in order that you may proclaim the mighty acts of him who called you out of darkness into his marvelous light.
>
> 1 Peter 2:9

> In general, the churches . . . bore for me the same relation to God that billboards did to Coca-Cola: they promoted thirst without quenching it.
>
> John Updike, *A Month of Sundays*

What in the world do we mean by *church*? Everyday speech encompasses a variety of meanings that are maintained kaleidoscopically, with ever-shifting changes in pattern and hue: buildings, people, congregations, denominations, organizations, Christians everywhere—each with innumerable variations. The situation is only marginally better when *church* is used theologically, necessitating qualifiers to specify what we mean: local, universal, visible and invisible, congregational, synodical, episcopal, ecclesial communities, denominations, communities of faith, and para-church organizations. We are usually able to determine what *church* means by the context in which it is used, but dependence on context to determine meaning indicates the indeterminate nature of the word itself.

Confusion about *church* is exacerbated by the English language. Unlike many others, English does not distinguish among realities as diverse as buildings, congregations, denominations, and global institutions. Problems with the word *church* are not new or confined to English, however.

Martin Luther lamented the use of "this meaningless and obscure word . . . *Kirche* is not German," he complained, "and does not convey the sense or meaning that should be taken."[1] Efforts have been made to overcome English limitation, such as the once-common distinction between uppercase *Church* when referring to the whole body of Christians across time and space and lower case *church* when referring to a particular body of Christians. But even this modest attempt at clarity was applied ambiguously and inconsistently, and has been generally discarded. The linguistic problem is compounded by the regular use of *church* to refer to non-Christian religious bodies. Christian churches are now seen as belonging to the same genre as the "church" of Scientology and even, according to a local television news reporter, the Buddhist "church." In ordinary usage, *church* has become simply synonymous with "religious institution."

The fundamental problem is more theological than linguistic, however. What we mean by *church* is important because churches are central in the reception, preservation, and transmission of Christian faith and faithfulness. Few of us become Christians, learn the substance of Christian faith, and begin to live patterns of Christian faithfulness on our own. We come to know Christian faith and to learn the shape of Christian life through the witness of Christian communities. "For I handed on to you as of first importance what I in turn had received," Paul wrote to the church in Corinth (1 Cor 15:3). We become Christ's disciples through the life and witness of churches.

Because of the centrality of ecclesial witness, John Calvin, following Cyprian and Augustine, spoke of the church as "the common mother of the godly."[2] "There is no other way to enter into life," said Calvin, "unless this mother conceive us in her womb, give us birth, nourish us at her breast, and lastly, unless she keep us under her care and guidance . . . until we have been pupils all our lives."[3] Because the church is our "common mother," the shape of the church was a central point of sixteenth-century disputes between reformers and the Catholic Church on the one hand, and between magisterial reformers and Anabaptists on the other. And that is why eccle-

---

1. Martin Luther, "On the Councils of the Church," in *Martin Luther's Theological Writings*, ed. Timothy F. Lull, 2nd ed. (Minneapolis: Fortress, 2005), 363.

2. John Calvin, *Commentaries on the Epistles of Paul to the Galatians and Ephesians* (Grand Rapids: Eerdmans, 1957), Eph 4:13; 282.

3. John Calvin, *Institutes of the Christian Religion*, ed. John T. McNeill, trans. Ford Lewis Battles (Philadelphia: Westminster, 1960) 4.1.4, 1016.

siology remains an ecumenical impasse among episcopal, conciliar, and congregationally ordered churches.

Dissimilar understandings of *church* are also at the root of current clashes between Pentecostals and classical Protestant churches, and between evangelical and mainline denominations. Perhaps most distressing is that disparate conceptions of *church* are at the heart of current fragmentation within denominations. Underlying both ecumenical and denominational tensions are differences in understanding the essential meaning, nature, purpose, and structure of the church. Before he was Benedict XVI, Cardinal Ratzinger acknowledged that "the difference in the ways in which Church is understood . . . has proved to be an insurmountable barrier."[4]

THINKING ABOUT THE CHURCH

It is surprising, then, that ecclesiology—the doctrine of the church—is often a theological afterthought. To the extent that basic questions about the shape of the church are asked, they are generally left to sociologists (or worse, to branders, marketers, and fundraisers). When theologians deal with the church, they regularly present an abstraction that bears only a vague resemblance to what we experience in actual congregations, judicatories, and denominations. We are presented with lovely portraits of the church, ideal paradigms meant to show us that there is more than meets the eye when we look at actual churches: "In the power of the Holy Spirit the church experiences itself as the messianic fellowship of service for the kingdom of God in the world";[5] "The Spiritual Community as the dynamic essence of the churches makes them existing communities of faith and love in which the ambiguities of religion are not eliminated but conquered in principle";[6] "As God in Christ and the Spirit are one, the many parts of the church are gathered together through one divine action as the sign of the coming household of God."[7] Really?

4. Joseph Ratzinger and Vittorio Messori, *The Ratzinger Report* (San Francisco: Ignatius Press, 1985), 160.

5. Jürgen Moltmann, *The Church in the Power of the Spirit* (New York: Harper & Row, 1977), 289.

6. Paul Tillich, *Systematic Theology*, vol. 3 (Chicago: University of Chicago Press, 1963), 172.

7. Letty Russell, *Church in the Round: Feminist Interpretation of the Church* (Louisville: Westminster John Knox, 1993), 132.

Idealized portraits of an abstract church bear scant resemblance to the actual churches we find in Pittsburgh, Pretoria, and Palau. Or, for that matter, the churches we encounter in Corinth, Galatia, and Thessalonica. Idealized theological descriptions of the church lead to the notion that what we experience is not the real church, for the real church is said to be purer than the actual, ambiguous churches we experience. The inescapable consequence of a theological disjunction between the ideal church and actual churches is disparagement or even contempt for actual churches. To the extent that the ideal church is presented as the ecclesiological norm, actual churches are reduced to flawed imitations of an immaculate concept. To the extent that actual congregations and denominations claim qualities of the ideal church, they are likely to be scorned as shams.

Unlike theologians, sociologists—both academic and amateur—generally show a documentary film of the flawed church. Sometimes they are designed merely to deconstruct, but they are often meant to suggest strategies that can produce the church that should be: "Trends show that congregations are shaped by the same cultural, social, and economic pressures affecting American life and institutions more generally";[8] "The denomination, then, is an ecclesiastical creature of modernity, a social form emerging with and closely akin to the political party, the free press, and free enterprise";[9] "Whether churches serve primarily as communities of memory, as denominations that help people to act locally while thinking globally, or as support groups that nurture the in-depth work required to reshape one's identity, they will need to provide role models and turn those role models into characters in the stories we all tell ourselves."[10] Is that all there is?

When actual churches are understood as the Christian species of the genus religion of the family organization, they are reduced to malleable human constructions. Like all human constructions, churches are then analyzed as organizations altered by environmental forces without and by remodeling efforts within. Scholarly sociologists such as Robert Wuthnow, Wade Clark Roof, and Robert Putnam have illuminated the church's situation within contemporary American culture, applying rigorous social

8. Mark Chaves, *American Religion: Contemporary Trends* (Princeton: Princeton University Press, 2011), 56.

9. Russell E. Richey, *Denominationalism Illustrated and Explained* (Eugene, OR: Cascade, 2013), 3.

10. Robert Wuthnow, *Christianity in the Twenty-first Century* (New York: Oxford University Press, 1993), 54.

analysis to religious organizations. They have been joined by innumerable pop sociologists who have created a cottage industry of publications purporting to show that churches can use sociological data such as generational cohorts in order to grow and prosper.

Both theological and sociological constructs are instances of what Nicholas Healy calls "blueprint ecclesiologies,"[11] two-dimensional templates that either display normative theological construals in the guise of description or description as the basis for normative sociological prescription. In both cases, ecclesiology is more about what should or could be than theological engagement with what is. Dietrich Bonhoeffer put the matter plainly more than eighty years ago: "There are basically two ways to misunderstand the church, one historicizing and the other religious; the former confuses the church with the religious community, the latter with the Realm of God."[12] Neither sociology nor theology alone is adequate to understand the reality of the church, which is simultaneously a historical-sociological phenomenon and a Christ/Spirit-created communion of faith. Theological talk apart from the concrete reality of actual churches easily becomes irrelevant to *lived* faith; sociological examination apart from faithful attention to the one, holy, catholic, apostolic church easily becomes irrelevant to lived *faith*.

Ecclesiology is not simply the backyard of sociologists or the playground of theologians. Understanding the church is a critical, although generally neglected, theological task of pastors, who bear significant responsibility for shaping patterns of congregational faith and life. While most pastors hope that their ministry will deepen a congregation's faith and broaden its mission, the basic given-ness of *church* is habitually assumed. Pastors may assess its spiritual health, evaluate its missional fidelity, and improve its management, but what "it" is remains elusive. Pastoral attention to improving what is will always be susceptible to religious market forces unless accompanied by sustained attention to the fundamental nature and purpose of the people of God. Similarly, apart from an understanding of who, what, when, where, why, and how the church is, members will be left to an endless round of evaluating and comparing congregations, assessing their capacity to provide appealing and satisfying religious goods and services.

11. Nicholas Healy, *Church, World and the Christian Life: Practical-Prophetic Ecclesiology* (Cambridge: Cambridge University Press, 2000), 25–51.

12. Dietrich Bonhoeffer, *Sanctorum Communio: A Theological Study of the Sociology of the Church*, trans. Reinhard Krauss and Nancy Lukens (Minneapolis: Fortress, 1998), 125.

Understanding what in the world the church is, is not an academic exercise but a critically practical theological matter for all Christians.

"THE UNINTENDED REFORMATION"

It is not possible for us to understand the church(es) we live in, either theologically or sociologically, without going back five hundred years to what is commonly called the Protestant Reformation but what might more accurately be called the Western church schism. Probing that history is not an exercise in antiquarian interest or an attempt to draw lessons from the past. It is simply to recognize that the church we experience now is a consequence of what happened then. We cannot know where we are unless we know where we were and how we got from there to here; the Reformation's living legacy shapes our apprehension of what *church* is. The Reformation and its continuing development provide the setting for contemporary apprehension of *church* in all its manifestations. As William Faulkner famously put it, "The past is never dead. It's not even past."[13]

In 1538, two decades after Martin Luther dramatically offered ninety-five theses on indulgences and true repentance, a young John Calvin was happily ensconced in Strasbourg, having been expelled from Geneva for refusing to abide by the city council's attempts to control certain sacramental and liturgical practices. With Calvin and his older colleague Guillaume Farel conveniently out of the way, Cardinal Jacopo Sadoleto, bishop of Carpentras in France, sent an open letter to the magistrates, council, and citizens of Geneva, imploring them to return to the Catholic Church. Several months later, from his exile in Strasbourg, Calvin responded to Sadoleto in an open letter of his own, defending Protestant reforms. Protestant seminarians sometimes read Calvin's reply to Sadoleto, but few have laid eyes on the cardinal's message.

Sadoleto's letter is an intelligent, often winsome document, pleading with Genevans "to return to concord with us, yield faithful homage to the Church, our mother, and worship God with us in one spirit."[14] In addition to discussing central theological issues knowledgeably and reasonably, he

---

13. The line is from Faulkner's 1951 play, "Requiem for a Nun." William Faulkner, *Requiem for a Nun* (New York: Vintage International, 2011).

14. Jacopo Sadoleto, "Sadoleto's Letter to the Genevans," in *A Reformation Debate: John Calvin and Jacopo Sadoleto*, ed. John C. Olin (New York: Fordham University Press, 1966), 42.

pointed to the harm caused by the split in the church. "How will this be borne?" he asked Genevans, "that they [the reformers] attempted to tear the spouse of Christ in pieces, that the garment of the Lord, which heathen soldiers were unwilling to divide, they attempted not only to divide, but to rend? For already, since these men began, how many sects have torn the Church? Sects not agreeing with them, and yet disagreeing with each other. . . ."[15] How many indeed! What might Sadoleto say if he could see the current profusion of thousands upon thousands of what we call denominations strewn across the world?

Calvin's reply dealt confidently and deftly with Sadoleto's historical and theological points, but the cardinal's critique of division in the church cut close to the bone. "But the most serious charge of all," wrote Calvin, "is that we have attempted to dismember the Spouse of Christ. Were that true, both you [Sadoleto] and the whole world might well regard us as past redemption." In the face of obvious church division, however, Calvin had to say more: "I admit that, on the revival of the gospel, great disputes arose where all was quietness before. But that is unjustly imputed to our side, who, in the whole course of their actions, desired nothing but that religion be revived and that the Churches, which discord had scattered and dispersed, might be gathered together into true unity."[16]

Calvin, Luther, and other early reformers certainly desired that dispersed churches be gathered together in unity, but it was not to be. The scattering and dispersal of the churches included the great rift between the German and Swiss reformations and disarray within the Swiss reformation itself. Calvin worked to repair the breach between Lutheran and Zwinglian understandings of the Lord's Supper (although he much preferred Luther to Zwingli), writing his *Short Treatise on the Lord's Supper*[17] as a contribution to resolving the eucharistic controversy. Despite efforts on both sides, however, the rift became a chasm as Lutheran and Reformed antagonisms hardened. Calvin also labored to heal the wounds of controversy among the Swiss churches, resulting in the *Consensus Tigurinus* that produced (uneasy) concord among the Swiss churches.

As time passed, Calvin became more and more disturbed by the continuing fragmentation of the church. Fourteen years after his reply to Sa-

---

15. Sadoleto, "Sadoleto's Letter to the Genevans," 40.

16. John Calvin, "Reply to Sadolet," in *Calvin: Theological Treatises*, ed. J. K. S. Reid (Philadelphia: Westminster, 1954), 255.

17. John Calvin, "Short Treatise on the Lord's Supper," in Reid, *Calvin*, 142–66.

doleto, Calvin wrote a letter to Archbishop of Canterbury Thomas Cranmer, in which he now echoed Sadoleto's charge against the reformation. "This other thing also is to be ranked among the chief evils of our time," he agonized, "that the Churches are so divided, that human fellowship is scarcely now in any repute among us. . . . Thus it is that the members of the Church being severed, the body lies bleeding."[18] Calvin's distress went beyond regret, for it led him to greet with enthusiasm Cranmer's proposal for a general council of all the reformation churches in order to bring unity out of separation. A few years later his vision broadened as he proposed a universal council of the church to put an end to all the divisions in Christendom. Calvin envisioned a council that would include representatives from the whole church, including the Catholic bishops as well as representatives of the reformation churches. He was even open to the possibility that the pope would preside (but not rule!).[19]

Half a millennium later blood still flows from the dismembered body of Christ. What is even more remarkable than the dizzying profusion of churches before our eyes is our easy acceptance of it all. We see thousands of separated churches scattered across the landscape of every country on the globe and take it in with a shrug as simply "the way things are." Partitions between Catholic and Orthodox and Protestant and Pentecostal have been supplemented by divisions within these traditions and, among Protestants and Pentecostals, the repeated dismemberment of their denominations. It is obvious enough that ecclesial fragmentation is "the way things are." But what is less obvious, because we no longer acknowledge it, is our comfortable acceptance of a reality that flies in the face of Jesus's prayer for us and ignores Paul's constant counsel to us. In the searing words of Ephraim Radner:

> Consider that the debilitation of the Body of Christ, the encroaching paralysis of its senses, is hardly a reality that its members greet with comprehension. . . . One might perhaps have thought a struggle would ensue against the torpor, a hard grasping after the remains of God's presence, a panting after the fragrance left by his passing. . . . But even the Church's sense of smell has been confounded. . . . Indeed, the most manifest mark

18. John Calvin, "Letter to Cranmer" (1552), in *Selected Works of John Calvin: Tracts and Letters*, ed. Henry Beveridge and Jules Bonnet (Carlisle, PA: Banner of Truth Trust, 2009), 5:347–48.

19. John Calvin, "Letter to the Reformed Churches of France" (1560), in Beveridge and Bonnet, *Tracts and Letters*, 7:158–61.

of the divided Church appears to be its own insensibility to the symptoms of its condition. No stench reaches its nostrils; no shame cracks its heart.[20]

The ecclesial pluralism that seems so natural now, so comfortable for the churches, fails to recognize fragmentation's effect on the churches themselves. Church fragmentation is not simply benign diversity, allowing expressions of rich variety in faithful ecclesial life. Calvin's calls for unity did not mean that German Lutheran churches should become Swiss Reformed churches, or that German and Swiss churches should merge into one European Protestant Church. The ecclesial problem was that local churches had become separated churches, and separated churches had become antagonistic churches. Today, detached churches have become strangers to one another, settling into patterns of benign neglect. But whether by hard alienation or soft indifference, "human fellowship is scarcely now in any repute among us."

The effect of ecclesial division is not restricted to its impact on the churches themselves. Brad Gregory notes that Reformation-engendered ecclesial pluralism leads an increasing number of people to conclude that "no religious claims are true" or that "it cannot be known which among them might be." This, in turn, "reinforces the relativizing impression that *all* religion can only be a matter of individual, subjective, and irrational personal preference."[21] The "debilitation of the body of Christ" is not only an ecumenical lament; it is a description of the church's impaired capacity to bear convincing witness to the grace of the Lord Jesus Christ, the love of God, and the communion of the Holy Spirit. In an age of religious toleration and doctrinal latitude, each church is now reduced to bearing witness to itself, reinforcing the impression that it is all a matter of personal preference.

THE INTENDED DEFORMATION

The obvious yet accepted reality of the church's splintering into multiple traditions, world communions, and denominations is shadowed by a self-inflicted, festering wound at the heart of the church. From the outset of

20. Ephraim Radner, *The End of the Church: A Pneumatology of Christian Division in the West* (Grand Rapids: Eerdmans, 1998), 277.

21. Brad S. Gregory, *The Unintended Reformation* (Cambridge: Harvard University ᴾ ˀˀˢ 2012), 111.

the European churches' involvement in the exploration and colonization of Africa and the "New World," racial classification and gradation, separation and exploitation of indigenous populations, and varieties of enslavement were woven into the theological and moral lives of the churches. The evangelization of subjugated peoples occurred within the framework of colonial rule that instituted multiple forms of "apartness" within the church itself. English, Dutch, Portuguese, and Spanish colonial policies enfolded willing churches that became fully complicit in European dealings with "heathen peoples." Willie James Jennings has pointed out that Christian "foreign missions" developed "as though Christianity, wherever it went in the modern colonies, inverted its sense of hospitality. It claimed to be the host, the owner of the spaces it entered, and demanded that native peoples enter its cultural logics, its ways of being in the world, and its conceptualities."[22]

Ecclesial racialism is not confined to an unfortunate past, now overcome by enlightened moral sensibilities; Christianity's "diseased social imagination" endures as a chronic deformity of the church. In North America, racially constituted denominations and congregations are dreary testimony to the persistence of racialism's legacy. Even Pentecostalism, born in a vision of the Holy Spirit's outpouring on all flesh, rapidly devolved into patterns of exclusion resulting in separate black and white denominations and congregations. Historic Black Protestant churches, born of their exclusion from white churches, have developed patterns of faith and faithfulness that continue to be overlooked by majority-white churches. Within majority churches, Native Americans are relegated to unnoticed congregations on neglected reservations, African Americans are marginalized, Hispanics are neglected, and Asian and "newer immigrant" groups are expected to adopt the theological and ecclesial orientations of their "hosts." Theologically and ecclesially, "whiteness" continues to be the norm by which other "ethnic" theologies are measured. In majority-white churches, as in society generally, white perspectives and values dominate ecclesial culture.

The *Confession of 1967* of the Presbyterian Church (USA) is built upon the theme of reconciliation in Christ and the church's ministry of reconciliation. Included in its treatment of problems and crises that were considered "particularly urgent" is the need to break down "every form of discrimination based on racial or ethnic difference, real or imaginary." The Confession declared to its denomination, perhaps boldly for its time,

---

22. Willie James Jennings, *The Christian Imagination: Theology and the Origins of Race* (New Haven: Yale University Press, 2010), 8.

"Congregations, individuals, or groups of Christians who exclude, dominate, or patronize others, however subtly, resist the Spirit of God and bring
contempt on the faith which they profess."[23] Fifty years later, exclusion,
domination, and patronizing continue within churches whose social pronouncements regularly issue "prophetic" calls for society to bring them to
an end. Meanwhile, exercises of implicit power and the perseverance of
idealistic self-accounts combine to deceive the church about its ongoing
complicity in racialism's "the way things are."

At the outset, three issues need to be addressed. The first is that the
reality of ecclesial fragmentation renders problematic any talk about *the*
church, as if we all know what we mean and all mean the same thing when
we utter the word. At best, talk about the church is bound to be an abstraction, an almost Platonic ideal lost in the shadows cast by multiple steeples.
Second, comfortable reliance on various notions of the "invisible church"
is problematic at best, and always misleading. Finally, and most impor-
tantly, we need to confront the reality that our easy acceptance of—no, our
satisfaction with—church separation results in a veiling of the gospel itself.

THE CHURCH?

The World Council of Churches Commission on Faith and Order has been
working for nearly a quarter century on "a common—or convergent statement on ecclesiology, intended to draw churches into closer communion."
The Church: Toward a Common Vision is a thoughtful attempt to move
toward a shared understanding of *church.* The attempt is challenging; the
document itself notes that it aims to address "the most difficult issue facing the churches in overcoming any remaining obstacles to their living
out of the Lord's gift of communion: our understanding of the nature of
the church itself."[24] The even more difficult issue is the study's implicit
assumption that there is a transcendent reality called *the Church* that can
be identified and described through the process of committed dialogue.

Faith and Order's work is a significant step along the way to deeper
understanding, mutual recognition, and increased communion among

23. Presbyterian Church (USA), *The Confession of 1967*, "Inclusive Language Version"
prepared by the Office of Theology and Worship (Louisville: Congregational Ministries
Publishing, 2002), 9.44.

24. Faith and Order Commission, *The Church: Toward a Common Vision*, Faith and Order
Series 214 (Geneva: WCC Publications, 2013), 1.

the churches. Yet a common understanding of *the Church*—even one restricted to WCC Faith and Order churches—remains doubtful. Veli-Matti Kärkkäinen's brief introduction to ecclesiology sets out seven major ecclesiological traditions supplemented by seven contextual ecclesiologies.[25] Each of these traditions and ecclesiologies presents a singular view of the church that differs from other views. Theological assertions purporting to be about *the* church invariably express distinctive convictions about particular churches.

While it might be possible to integrate disparate ecclesial perspectives conceptually, the result would be an abstraction that would not describe any actual church. Each tradition and ecclesiology is found at the headwaters of a broad, deep river of meaning that flows through distinctive landscapes of Christology and pneumatology, soteriology and missiology, ministry and eschatology. Because perceptions of the church derive from distinct ecclesial locations, talk about the church should neither privilege one perception, nor imagine that a synthesis of perceptions would result in a comprehensive vision of the church recognized by all churches.

Talk about the church as a metaphysical entity that is more or less evident in actual churches quickly becomes speculative and thus removed from the reality of actual churches. When Clement wrote from "the church of God which resides as a stranger at Rome" to "the church of God which is a stranger at Corinth," these churches of God were distinct Christian communities, one of them admonishing and advising the other.[26]

INVISIBLE CHURCH?

Are we left, then, with nothing more than a jumble of different, often incompatible understandings by the various churches? If we are, what does it mean to confess the one, holy, catholic, apostolic church of the foundational creed? In the face of the obvious proliferation of separated churches and the conflicting variety in perceptions of the church, a Protestant strategy has emerged that enables many Christians to speak of the real and present unity of the church. Attempts are made to rescue the

25. Veli-Matti Kärkkäinen, *An Introduction to Ecclesiology* (Downers Grove, IL: Inter-Varsity Press, 2002).

26. Clement of Rome, "The Epistle to the Corinthians," in *The Epistles of St. Clement of Rome and St. Ignatius of Antioch*, Ancient Christian Writers 1 (New York: Paulist, 1946).

church's essential unity by recourse to versions of the "invisible" church, a universal company of all who truly believe in Jesus Christ, a congregation of saints that rises above all the churches we experience. This authorizes the claim that Christians are all united in Christ, even amid obvious churchly divisions.

Distinctions between the visible and invisible church have been made since Augustine, although he did not use the terms. In the classical version of the distinction, the invisible church consists of the communion of saints throughout time and space while the visible church is perceived in the actual Christian communities evident at any given time. Calvin noted that Scripture speaks of the church in two ways, sometimes signifying all the living and dead who are in the presence of God and sometimes referring to living people who now profess the one true God. But since the elect who are in God's presence are known only to God, Calvin immediately turned his attention to the only church that is humanly knowable, the visible church. "Just as we must believe, therefore, that the former church, invisible to us, is visible to the eyes of God alone," wrote Calvin, "so we are commanded to revere and keep communion with the latter, which is called 'church' in respect to men."[27]

Calvin's distinction between the invisible and visible church deals with more than time and space, however, because, unlike the invisible church, the visible church is a *corpus permixtum*, a body in which not all who profess Christ are in communion with Christ. Even so, Calvin insisted that we are called to keep communion with this visibly mixed body since we are unable to know what God alone knows—who is elect in Christ and who is not. Because of the obvious limitation of human knowledge and judgment, Calvin notes that God has given us a "certain charitable judgment whereby we recognize as members of the church those who . . . profess the same God and Christ with us,"[28] rather than imagining that we can judge between true and false professions. Calvin's understanding, consistent with the stream of Christian thought from Augustine on, is abandoned by current popularized versions that reverse the classical focus. The reversal can be detected in two nineteenth-century Reformed theologians—Friedrich Schleiermacher (1768–1834) and Abraham Kuyper (1837–1920)—who are representative, though not always recognized, influences on popular ecclesiology.

27. Calvin, *Institutes*, 4.1.7, 1022.
28. Calvin, *Institutes*, 4.1.8, 1022–1023.

When addressing its "cultured despisers," Schleiermacher identified the church as "the congregation of the pious," ascribing to it qualities of communion, harmony, unity, and love. Since this description did not match any church that a cultured despiser could see, one might think that Schleiermacher was describing what the church ought to be. But Schleiermacher's objective was to turn attention away from the church that can be seen toward a deeper reality: "I assure you, however, I have not spoken of what should be," he wrote, "but of what is. . . . The true church has, in fact, always been thus, and still is, and if you cannot see it, the blame is your own, and lies in a tolerably palpable misunderstanding."[29] For Schleiermacher, the congregation of the pious that cannot be seen is the true church, while the church that can be seen is merely an "institution for pupils in religion," those who have not yet become part of the sanctified community.

Schleiermacher's conceptual categories in his monumental *The Christian Faith* are more fully developed, but his understanding of the church remains the same. "The body, then, which in ordinary usage is known as the invisible Church is for the most part not invisible," he claims, "and what is known as the visible is for the most part not Church."[30] Whereas Calvin, having made the invisible/visible church distinction, proceeds to discuss the only one of the two that is accessible to human judgment, Schleiermacher makes the distinction in order to direct attention away from shabby all-too-visible churches to the true, pure, sanctified inner fellowship of Christians.

Dutch Reformed theologian Abraham Kuyper also understood the true church as the spiritual community of believers. But in his ecclesiology the actual churches are not even training grounds for the not-yet-sanctified. The institutional churches are merely human organizations called to do a job, which any given church may do well or poorly. Thus, in Kuyper's view, the true church is the invisible spiritual community of believers, while the visible church is reduced to a blend of humanly constructed ecclesiastical institutions and the actions of true Christians in society. Although he wrote eloquently about the unity of the church, he understood unity as a quality of the true, spiritual, invisible church, not of the visible churches, which are only and always disposable organizations. For Kuyper, as for Schlei-

---

29. Friedrich Schleiermacher, *On Religion: Speeches to Its Cultured Despisers* (New York: Harper & Brothers, 1958), 156–57.

30. Friedrich Schleiermacher, *The Christian Faith* (Edinburgh: T&T Clark, 1928), 677–78.

ermacher, the church that can be seen is not the real church, and only the church that is not observable is the true church.[31]

The enduring legacy of the line of thought represented by Schleiermacher and Kuyper is a popularized version of the invisible/visible church dyad that is prevalent among ministers and members alike, in which the invisible church is the true church, the body of Christ, while the visible churches are flawed human constructions, genuine churches only to the extent that they conform faith and life to the invisible church. The predictable result is deprecation of all institutional embodiments of the visible church, combined with their dispensability, often resulting in justification for easy exit from denominations and the multiplication of separated churches. Effortless confidence in the intangible unity of the invisible church opens the revolving door to endlessly repeated church ruptures, separations, splits, and schisms. The invisible church is presented as the real thing whose spiritual unity remains untouched by any and every division.

Popular confidence in the essential priority of the invisible, undivided church renders Cardinal Sadoleto's critique of church division and proliferating sects inconsequential, for what is most "real" is undivided. Calvin need not have been distressed, for the body that matters does not lie bleeding. Current splits in Presbyterian, Lutheran, Episcopalian, and Baptist denominations, already separated from one another, do not divide the real church, but only readjust human structures. The popular appropriation of Schleiermacher, Kuyper, and others departs from recognizing visible churches—in all their ambiguity—as God's chosen witnesses in the world. Settling instead for an unseen, intangible unity, diminishing distress at churches' visible disunity, expedites schism and encourages multiple forms of ecclesial proliferation.

THE CREDIBILITY OF THE GOSPEL

When we look at the faith and life of the churches, what we see are multiple ecclesiastical and racial divisions among them. We hear from them theologies of the church that are actually projections from particular ecclesial locations. We also encounter pop versions of the invisible church that are sedatives masking the pain of ecclesial dissection. None of this comes as

---

31. See Abraham van de Beek, "The Disunity of the Reformed Churches," in *The Church in Reformed Perspective* (Geneva: Centre International Réformé, 2002), 120–24.

news to us and, by itself, is not especially interesting. The division of *church* into distinct ecclesial communities of differing convictions and separated races is all we have ever known and, to be honest, all we ever expect to know.

What may come as news, however, and hold some interest is the stark reality that the profusion of detached and dispersed churches, and the persistence of racial, ethnic, and economic gradations among and within them, veils the very gospel that churches purport to proclaim. The credibility of the gospel—the good news meant to be proclaimed to a world in desperate need—is called into public question by the cacophony of incongruent articulations of what each ecclesial voice claims is Christian truth, and contrasting expressions of what each claims about the faithfulness of its own life. The credibility of the gospel is also called into public question by the calculated homogeneity of congregations and denominations that purport to represent the unity in diversity that God intends for all of creation. The gospel's proclamation that God was in Christ reconciling the world to himself, entrusting the church with the ministry of reconciliation, sounds implausible to many when voiced by unreconciled, socially segmented Christian churches.

Christianity has never been monolithic, of course; it has been richly diverse from the beginning. Yet, from the beginning, Christian diversity has been found within a common confession of the grace of the Lord Jesus Christ, the love of God, and the communion of the Holy Spirit. Christian faith and life have a theological and moral center; Christian diversity enriches that core through multiple, varied perspectives. What Alasdair MacIntyre says about traditions in general has always applied to Christian tradition: "A living tradition then is an historically extended, socially embodied argument, and an argument precisely in part about the goods which constitute that tradition."[32] However, the credibility of the gospel is called into question when the argument within a unified Christian tradition hardens into opposing institutional factions, each denying or qualifying the essential truth and faithfulness of the others.

It was not long ago that Protestant denominations agreed only on their condemnation of Catholicism, while continuing to assert their theological, sacramental, and ecclesiastical differences from one another. Accompanying theological difference and disagreement, perhaps resulting from them, are pervasive moral differences and disagreements. Absent coherent faith,

---

32. Alasdair MacIntyre, *After Virtue: A Study in Moral Theory*, 2nd ed. (Notre Dame: University of Notre Dame Press, 1984), 222.

it is not surprising that coherent morality is lacking as well. The effects of centuries-long ecclesial hyper-pluralism is becoming increasingly evident as more people determine that no religious claims are persuasive. Competing theological claims appear to be nothing more than intramural games with no real-life relevance. Contending moral values do not convince but merely sanction the primacy of personal choice.

Overt denominational triumphalism is now a receding memory for most churches in North America, having been replaced by mutual forbearance and polite relationships. Admittedly, this new openness is partially comprised of bourgeois Western tolerance, postmodern uncertainty, and confessional minimalism, but it also represents genuine recognition of each other as authentic expressions of Christian faith and life. This newfound amiability has an underside, however. Mutual civility leads the various Protestant churches not only to recognize the ecclesial integrity of other churches, but also to understand others as well as themselves as ecclesially self-sufficient. Because each understands itself as an expression of the one, holy, catholic, apostolic church, each believes it has everything needed to be Christ's faithful church. The result is the assumption that each has no essential need of the others.

Unwillingness to give offense by asserting flaws in other churches is accompanied by unwillingness to acknowledge the possibility of essential deficiency in our own churches. Since we believe we possess everything we need to be Christ's faithful church, we also believe that any recognition of inadequacy in ourselves can be dealt with by internal renovation. And if we easily acknowledge that the other churches also possess everything needed to be Christ's faithful church, we need not comprehend the disgrace of our continuing division. The implicit conviction of self-sufficiency is so fundamental to denominational self-understanding that denominations explicitly perpetuate their own institutional autonomy while voicing mild, customary regret about the reality of continuing church division.

Interdenominational civility and ecumenical indifference have created a problem for denominations, however. When separated churches were more doctrinally coherent and organizationally distinctive, denominational loyalty was easier to maintain. Presbyterians, for instance, spoke about their faith using shared vocabulary shaped by a literature of psalmody, hymns, and prayers. They tended to be loyal Presbyterians, studying Presbyterian materials, supporting Presbyterian mission, and breeding more Presbyterians. Across the ecclesial spectrum, denominationally differentiated theology, polity, and mission promoted denominational cohesion and continuity. But as denominational distinctives blurred in a haze of mutual forbearance, denominational loyalty was replaced by an increase in denominational switching and "church shopping."

It is a cruel irony that the welcome cessation of interdenominational hostilities has not eliminated religious conflict but merely displaced it. The old assertions of denominational superiority have been exchanged for competing claims of faithfulness within denominations. Intradenominational hostilities intensify as major ruptures occur within denominations. How, then, in the face of switching and church shopping by ministers, members, and congregations, are denominations and their congregations to maintain and attract members?

MARKET FORCES

The term "church shopping" is telling, for America is a nation of shoppers. The advance of consumer capitalism has shaped a society driven by what Daniel Bell calls "the economy of desire."[33] North American society functions on the model of a sprawling shopping mall. The Mall of America is not just a huge complex in suburban Minneapolis; it is America itself. Large department stores and internet emporiums anchor a maze of specialty stores scattered randomly throughout the mall and across the web, catering to diverse tastes while offering ever-new possibilities and encouraging impulse purchases. Churches are confined to small religious boutiques located in one wing of America's mall, competing with one another for a dwindling market share of a declining demographic. As people surf through society's marketplace, they are free to choose whether to enter any of the religious shops and what, if anything, they will buy.

In a limited sense, this is an old story for the church. American religious life has long been characterized by personal freedom of choice. What is new, at least in degree, is the churches' explicit embrace of consumer capitalism, both denominationally and congregationally. Daniel Bell notes that "capitalism's global extension hinges on its successful capture of the constitutive human power that is desire. In other words, capitalism is not merely an economic order but also a discipline of desire."[34] The disciplining of

33. Daniel Bell, *The Economy of Desire: Christianity and Capitalism in a Postmodern World* (Grand Rapids: Baker Academic, 2012).

34. Bell, *The Economy of Desire*, 38.

desire begins with the creation of desire. And desire is created by investing products with meaning, promising fulfilling experiences that are destined to remain unfulfilled, thus creating space for more promise and endlessly renewed desire. In the words of Steve Jobs, "People don't know what they want until you show it to them."[35] Showing it to them, and making them want it, is the business of marketing and advertising.

Positioned within the culture as voluntary associations, dependent upon choices made by individuals, churches are unable to resist becoming consumer commodities in a marketplace society. Denominations and congregations spend time and energy developing institutional "branding" and marketing strategies, all with the help of professional consultants. Capital campaigns and media promotions highlight churches' efforts to sell themselves as providers of religious goods and services. Meanwhile, the gospel recedes into the ecclesial background as a taken-for-granted assumption, while the gospel's mission in the world is reduced to episodic acts of compassion and service. Marketing strategies have no place for a God who judges us, and so we are left with a god who blesses our positive judgments of ourselves and even validates our harsh judgments of those who violate our values.

Denominational marketing ranges from the United Methodist soft-sell—"open doors, open hearts, open minds"—to the United Church of Christ's hardline contrasting of its own inclusive welcome to the implied intolerance of other churches: "Jesus didn't turn people away. Neither do we." Other marketing efforts include the Evangelical Lutheran Church's direct if vague appeal to consumers—"there is a place for you here"—and the Presbyterian Church (USA)'s puzzling and mercifully forgotten "awareness campaign"—"Here and Now!" But note: whether skillfully or clumsily, denominations try to sell themselves, their institutional selves, by promoting brand awareness and promising fulfillment of personal needs differently from and better than other churches.

Competitive marketing is also evident at the level of congregations. Local churches present themselves as "a thinking, feeling, healing community of faith," as "many journeys united in Christ," or as congregations "going the distance." Consumer choice is highlighted by a variety of worship options. (My favorite church sign trumpets a 2:00 afternoon service by proclaiming, "At last you can sleep in on Sunday!") New church plants emphasize their difference from staid traditional churches by naming themselves "Hot Metal Bridge," "Revolution," or "Destiny," and emphasizing that they

35. Walter Isaacson, *Steve Jobs* (New York: Simon & Schuster, 2011), 143.

are "a new way of doing church." Market-tested names and "new all new" religious goods and services parallel standard American advertising strategies, differing only by their lack of subtlety and innovation.

In a stunning reversal of Paul, who said, "What we proclaim is not ourselves, but Jesus Christ as Lord" (2 Cor 4:5), the churches proclaim themselves, their institutional selves, without a hint of discomfort or embarrassment. Church branding, institutional slogans, marketing strategies, and ad campaigns seem quite normal, unquestioned means of appealing to consumer preference by distinguishing one church from the rest of the pack. Less obvious is that, as churches employ the marketing methodologies of consumer capitalism, they position themselves as commodities to be selected and consumed in the same way that we select and consume everything from laundry detergent and smart phones to movie tickets and vacation packages. And as commodities, the churches become susceptible to characteristic consumer capriciousness and fickleness: today's "Hot Metal Bridge" may become yesterday's BlackBerry.

Beneath the commodification of church life lie deep structural consequences for Christian faith itself. Just as shopping malls and web retailers offer an array of discrete, unrelated products in multiple departments, so consumer-driven church life fragments the cohesive whole of the Christian tradition into a mélange of free-floating elements disconnected from their intrinsic relationship to each other. Beliefs, rituals, and practices all appear as collections of distinct items available for consumer choice. Belief in God's love has no necessary relationship to the Word made flesh; Baptism is isolated from Eucharist; convictions about war, capital punishment, euthanasia, and abortion can be held independently of one another. Benign diversity in Christian faith and life gives way to the incoherence of impulse purchases.

Religious impulse purchases are not only akin to material consumerism; they may become aligned with its market culture. "Religious beliefs are in danger of being abstracted from the complex cultures, institutions, and relationships that enable them to inform daily life," says Vincent Miller in *Consuming Religion*. "As a result, they are in danger of being reduced to abstracted, virtual sentiments that function solely to give flavor to the already established forms of everyday life or to provide compensations for its shortcomings."[36] Christian faith and life become essentially shaped by other forces. The problem goes even deeper. As purveyors of religious

---

36. Vincent J. Miller, *Consuming Religion: Christian Faith and Practice in a Consumer Culture* (New York: Continuum, 2008), 105–6.

goods and services in a consumer-driven market economy, churches are susceptible to the short leaps from the commodification of the church to the commodification of faith to the commodification of God. The progression from choosing beliefs, to choosing a church, to choosing a god, leads directly to "I determine what God is."[37] The ecclesial economy of desire beckons us toward the god of our desiring.

WHAT (IN THE WORLD) IS THE CHURCH?

Ecclesiology is talk about the church as it is. This means talking theologically about the actual church. It is possible to talk about church in purely theological terms, and this is often what ecclesiology amounts to, but this describes only a vision. Visions are lovely and even inspirational. They may stimulate greater efforts to make reality correspond to what we want the church to be. But when the results still fall short, the lingering vision will trigger discouragement and even provoke cynicism about the church. It is also possible to talk about the church in purely empirical terms, and this is usually what sociology amounts to, but this describes only an analytical classification. While analytical categories are rarely lovely, they may encourage innovative church strategies and tactics. Yet even when these efforts produce enduring success—and they fall short more often than they achieve their aim—the result may be a mere commodity that must constantly respond to changing market forces.

None of this is meant to disparage either theological or sociological talk about the church. It is simply to say that responsible ecclesiology does not deal in one without the other. The apostle Paul describes the church as having "treasure in clay jars" (2 Cor 4:7). To imagine the treasure apart from the clay jar is to conceive of a disembodied gospel; to imagine the clay jar without its treasure is to conceive of a generic religious institution. The treasure inside the clay jar is what makes the jar valuable, however, and so ecclesiology must first look at the treasure within the jar. Only then can the jar be understood and appreciated for itself.

---

37. Ingolf Dalferth, "I Determine What God Is!" *Theology Today* 57, no. 1 (April 2000): 5–23.

Chapter 2

WE BELIEVE?

Now I would remind you, brothers and sisters, of the good news that I proclaimed to you, which you in turn received, in which also you stand, thorough which also you are being saved, if you hold firmly to the message that I proclaimed to you—unless you have come to believe in vain. For I handed on to you as of first importance what I in turn had received. . . .

1 Corinthians 15:1–3

Are you a Christian?
    No, I'm not a Christian.
What do you believe, then?
    Believe about what?
The things that religious people think are important.
Whether there is a God.
How do you explain evil? What happens when we die? Why are we here?
How ought we to live our lives?

P. D. James, *The Children of Men*

All-too-obvious ecclesial fragmentation and the church's self-selected guise as assortments of product placement in America's cultural emporium are not the whole story. The treasure is in clay jars, but it is not buried. Present within the disarray of innumerable denominations is an indistinct yet detectible Christianity embodied in generally recognizable Christian churches. Church is not solely reducible to a jumble of rival religious institutions, and church is something more than a place where people find genuine community, opportunities for meaningful service, global connection, or a safe haven. Church may be all those things and more, but its life is not exhausted by its division, its self-absorption, its market orientation, or its community-building endeavors. At the core of the church's life, beneath every activity, is the church's shared faith.

It may seem audacious to speak of the church's shared faith. The life of the churches seems to be characterized not only by wide diversity of design and practice but also by interminable disputes about differences over the shape of Christian faith and morals. The great schism between the churches of the Greek East and the Latin West, the Reformation schism within the Western church, and the subsequent fragmentation of Protestantism were (and are) all characterized by theological differences both great and small. Disputes over sacraments, ministry, authority in the church, Scripture and tradition, sanctification, divine grace and human faith, a range of moral issues, and more are all played out theologically. Much of the ecumenical movement's energy has been dedicated to bilateral and multilateral dialogues among churches that attempt to reconcile doctrinal differences; simultaneously, doctrinal differences continue the process of ecclesial shattering.

The result of grand and petty disputes about Christian faith itself is a global profusion of separated churches. Yet, despite their obvious differences, all these traditions, denominations, and congregations are identifiably Christian churches, variations on a recognizable theme. Ordinary conversation uses the single term "Christian church" to refer to a variety of denominations, expressing a certain commonality among Catholics and Pentecostals, Protestants and Orthodox. Beneath historic division, continuing separation, barely restrained competition, and outbreaks of hostility, there is an underlying connection that distinguishes Christian churches from religious communities of other faiths as well as from nonreligious organizations and institutions. The connection is established by more than historical contingency, sociological classification, or sentimental attachment. It is a link forged from certain core affirmations that identify Christian churches as Christian.

Christian commonality can be perceived by attending to the language used within churches to describe their apprehension of the presence of God. Even a thin sociological account points to the use of common vocabulary connoting basic elements of churches' faith and life: Father, Son of God, Holy Spirit, Christ, baptism, salvation, Lord, Holy Communion, cross, resurrection, and so on. Churches may use common vocabulary differently, intending distinct senses and assigning various values, but all of this occurs within a matrix of broadly shared language.

A more theological depiction of Christian commonality moves beyond shared vocabulary to look at the grammatical structure shaping how the words are used—how nouns and pronouns, active and passive verbs, adjectives and adverbs, prepositions and conjunctions combine to order and affect meaning: Jesus is Lord, the sovereignty of God, baptized into Christ, gifts of the Holy Spirit, one, holy, catholic, apostolic church, and more. Such grammatical coherence is less apparent among the churches than their common terminology, but the family resemblance is discernable nevertheless.

Beyond both vocabulary and grammar, an even more substantive description sets out the ways in which syntax orders the constituent elements of faith and life to produce a coherent whole: God was in Christ reconciling the world to himself; Christ has died, Christ is risen, Christ will come again; we believe in one God, the Father, the Almighty; for you are a people holy to the Lord your God. Variations are most noticeable at the level of syntax, yet even here differences can be discussed and debated because they employ mutually acknowledged formulations. Christian churches are identifiably Christian by their employment of a common vocabulary, similar grammar, and interrelated syntax to articulate shared faith and life.

Doctrinal differences among Christian churches are real, but they are played out within convictions that, however lightly held and loosely shared, identify communities of Christian faith. Churches that differ sharply over the nature of Christ's presence in the sacrament of the Lord's Supper (or Holy Communion, or Eucharist) share the conviction that (somehow), "as often as we eat this bread and drink the cup, we proclaim the Lord's death until he comes" (1 Cor 12:26). Churches that understand Genesis 1 quite differently agree that (by whatever means) God is Creator of heaven and earth. Churches holding different interpretations of spiritual gifts all believe that the Holy Spirit works (directly or implicitly) to empower the people of God. Beneath all-too-apparent difference, separation, and competition there is a degree of underlying concord, a recognizable tie binding communities of Christian faith together. The disparities are real, but they are encompassed within a matrix of commitments shared by Presbyterians in Kenya, Catholics in the Philippines, Orthodox in Russia, Pentecostals in Brazil, and millions of other Christians throughout the world.

Christian commonality can be overstated, of course, and it should never be taken for granted, but neither should it be disregarded. The web of shared

Christian belief may be fragile, at times stressed to the breaking point under the weight of theological, ethical, social, and cultural differences—within churches as well as among them—but it is nonetheless actual. Theological diversity may lapse into heterodoxy or heresy, but even these are understood as divergences from a common core. It is the actuality of identifiably Christian faith that makes it possible to speak, albeit with the greatest caution, of "the church" in the face of real and present diversity among the churches.

Purely sociological accounts of Christian commonality focus on the church as a social construction, characterized in part by its language and history. Yet when sociological accounts view the church solely as a social construction, they ignore the nature of churches' shared faith, characterized in part by shared language, continuous bonds, and common commitments. As Simone Weil observed, "sociology is very nearly right in its social explanation of religion. It only fails to explain one infinitely small thing; but this infinitely small thing is the grain of mustard seed, the buried pearl, the leaven, the salt. This infinitely small thing is God."[1] On the other hand, when purely theological accounts of Christian commonality focus solely on the church as a divine construction, they elide churches' linguistic differences and divisive history. In both restricted cases, what remains is a church that is unrecognizable, even to itself.

There is yet another sense in which it may be audacious to speak of the church's shared faith. The church, after all, is composed of people, and people hold to a wide spectrum of faith, ranging from fervent orthodoxy through customary assent, thoughtful doubt, selective belief, and cautious agnosticism, to practical atheism. Charles Taylor states that "in our world, a whole gamut of positions, from the most militant atheism to the most orthodox traditional theisms, passing through every possible position on the way, are represented and defended somewhere in our society."[2] And the same is true in our churches. Yet the presence of doubt, casual adherence, "cafeteria belief," resistance, and rebellion does not obviate the presence of recognizable Christian faith in the churches' confessions, liturgies, morality, and mission. Many will embrace all this gratefully, others will struggle with doubts that it is true, still others will resist it. But there remains an "it" to embrace, doubt, or resist.

---

1. Simone Weil, "A War of Religions," in *Selected Essays, 1934–1943* (London: Oxford University Press, 1962), 215.

2. Charles Taylor, *A Secular Age* (Cambridge: Belknap Press of Harvard University Press, 2007), 556.

THE CHURCH SPEAKS ITSELF

Some churches express Christian conviction in creeds and confessions of faith while others are explicitly non-creedal. Some confessional churches are closely bound to their doctrinal basis while the official confessional tradition of others has little impact on their faith and life. Overtly non-creedal churches are shaped by an implicit theological tradition that does not come to formal expression. Yet, whether acknowledged or not, the faith of all Christian churches has been broadly fashioned by a series of fourth- and fifth-century church councils that situated the trajectory of Christian faith. Emerging from controversies about Christ, the creeds of these councils articulate fundamentally irreversible understandings of who God is and how God is related to the world.

This is not to say that all churches consciously adhere to the formulations of Nicaea, Constantinople, Ephesus, and Chalcedon, much less those of subsequent ecumenical councils. It does not even mean that all churches are aware of these conciliar articulations. And it certainly does not mean that all individual Christians within churches—even the most orthodox among them—understand or adhere to Nicene faith. It does mean, however, that the basic vocabulary, grammar, and syntax of Christian faith was set out early in the church's life and that subsequent articulations, developments, controversies, and agreements continue to be played out on terms that were marked then. Colin Gunton, theologian and avid gardener, provided an apt metaphor for the dogmatic function of the church's formative creedal tradition:

> . . . dogma is that which delimits the garden of theology, providing a space in which theologians may play freely and cultivate such plants as are cultivable in the space which is so defined. . . . But the general point is that just as a garden is not a garden without some boundaries . . . so theology ceases to be Christian theology if it effectively ceases to remain true to its boundaries.[3]

"Nicene faith" sets the borders within which the church continues to shape its faith and life. The Nicene garden is not a small plot but an expansive one with varieties of theological plants. Even so, the garden's margins are often tested, sometimes contracted, at times enclosed by fences. Churches have occasionally wandered outside the garden, grown strange hybrids within

---

3. Colin Gunton, *Intellect and Action* (Edinburgh: T&T Clark, 2000), 1.

it, or allowed weeds to flourish. But through it all, churches have been broadly defined by foundational creedal affirmations, remaining identifiably Christian.

The Creed

In a culture and a church that pay scant attention to the past, it is not immediately apparent why anyone should reflect on the Nicene Creed. Novelist Gore Vidal's observation about American culture is also generally true of American church culture: "The past, for Americans, is a separate universe with its own quaint laws and irrelevant perceptions."[4] In an ecclesial culture that turns away from its own history, most Christians only encounter the creed, if at all, in worship. Even there, many experience it as burden rather than gift. Kathleen Norris expresses a common sentiment when she writes, "Of all the elements in a Christian worship service, the Creed, by compressing the wide range of faith and belief into a few words, can feel like a verbal strait jacket."[5] Perhaps this is because the creed is thought to be a theological check list, confronting Christians with a series of disembodied propositions to be memorized and recited, rather than an inclusive proclamation to be received and confessed.

Perhaps the creed can be rescued from its contemporary imprisonment in printed words by understanding its existential significance for the faith and life of earlier generations of Christians. The first great ecumenical council of the church met in AD 325 to resolve a controversy that threatened the peace, unity, and purity of the church. The great dispute, involving ordinary Christians as well as bishops and priests, focused on the very being of God—specifically, the unity of the Son of God with God the Father. The alternatives were stark. Is the Son of God, Jesus Christ, fully divine and commensurate with the Father? Or is the Son a created being, subordinate to the Father? Although the issue was theological, the debate was not abstract, for it went to the heart of Christian understanding of God, God's way in the world, and the shape of their own lives.

The controversy centered on the views of Arius, a priest in Alexandria, who was eager to advocate God's oneness in the face of the surrounding culture's pervasive polytheism. He was convinced that the unity of God

---

4. Gore Vidal, *The Golden Age* (New York: Vintage Books, 2000), 445.
5. Kathleen Norris, *Amazing Grace* (New York: Riverhead Books, 1998), 205.

could only be preserved by excluding distinctions from the divine nature. Thus, Arius held that the affirmation of God's oneness necessitated a lesser status for Christ and the Holy Spirit. While the Son and the Spirit were divinities, they were created, subordinate to the one and only God. "We know there is one God," said Arius and his associates; he is "the only un-begotten, only eternal, only without beginning, only true. . . ."[6] For the Arians, this strong affirmation of the one true God required a subordinate status for the Son: "He is neither eternal nor co-eternal nor co-unbegotten with the Father, nor does he have his being together with the Father."[7] The response from Arius's bishop, Alexander, was swift and strong: "What they assert [is] in utter contrariety to the Scriptures and wholly of their own devising. . . . Hence the Word is alien to, foreign to, and excluded from the essence of God; and the Father is invisible to the Son."[8]

The difference between the positions of Arius and Alexander came to be symbolized by the absence or presence of the little Greek letter *iota*. Is the Son of the same being (*homoousios*) as the Father or only of similar being (*homoiousios*) to the Father? Far from quibbling over an insignificant distinction, the question cut to the heart of Christian confidence in salvation and the character of Christian existence. Could Christians believe that the Son is "true God" and therefore trust that the salvation announced and accomplished in Jesus Christ is God's gracious will? Or is the Son something less than God, so that God's will remains an uncertain purpose behind, above, and beyond Jesus's words and deeds? Are men and women "in Christ" thereby reconciled to God? Or is there another step that must be taken to be reconciled to the still-hidden God who dwells behind Christ? Has God come to humankind in the person of Jesus Christ? Or has God remained aloof, only sending an emissary?

Nicaea insists that the unity of God—Father, Son, and Holy Spirit—is the essential guarantee that we can know God truly. If Jesus Christ is not "true God" as well as truly human, then he is merely a path toward a God who remains essentially unknowable. Similarly, if the Spirit is not the Holy Spirit of God, then our deepest spiritual experience is not an encounter with the one true God but only an approach to the God who remains essentially distant. The Nicene Creed, now as then, affirms that the church's

6. "The Confession of the Arians Addressed to Alexander of Alexandria," in *Christology of the Later Fathers*, ed. Edward R. Hardy (Philadelphia: Westminster, 1954), 332.

7. "The Confession of the Arians Addressed to Alexander of Alexandria," 333.

8. "Encyclical Letter of Alexander of Alexandria and His Clergy," in *A New Eusebius*, ed. J. Stevenson (London: SPCK, 1965), 343.

understanding of who God is depends on its understanding of who Jesus Christ is and who the Holy Spirit is.

Understanding who God is, knowing God the Father, Son, and Holy Spirit, is not merely a matter of the church getting its orthodox theology straight. The deeply theological matter decided by the council is also a deeply personal matter for the whole church. The existential significance of Nicaea for each believer and its significance for the church's ongoing faith and life is made clear in the creed's "second article" concerning the Lord Jesus Christ. First comes a series of theological affirmations that confesses the full divinity of the Son of God:

> We believe in one Lord, Jesus Christ,
> > the only Son of God,
> > eternally begotten of the Father,
> > God from God, Light from Light,
> > true God from true God,
> > begotten, not made,
> > of one Being with the Father;
> > through him all things were made.

Then comes a narrative of the life of Jesus Christ, the Son of God:

> **For us and for our salvation**
> > he came down from heaven,
> > was incarnate of the Holy Spirit and the Virgin Mary
> > and became truly human.
> > **For our sake** he was crucified under Pontius Pilate;
> > he suffered death and was buried.
> > On the third day he rose again
> > in accordance with the Scriptures;
> > he ascended into heaven
> > and is seated at the right hand of the Father.
> > He will come again in glory to judge the living and the dead,
> > and his kingdom will have no end.

The two parts of belief in Christ are linked by the declaration that it is all for us and for our salvation. It is for us that one Lord Jesus Christ is "of one Being with the Father." The creed reinforces this good news by emphasizing that suffering, crucifixion, resurrection, and ascension were all for our sake. The Nicene Creed assures ordinary believers that their salvation centers on the reality that true God from true God became truly human, and that it is all for our sake, for us and for our salvation. A Jesus Christ less than God or less than human would not have accomplished our salvation, would not have been for us.

The controversy that led to Nicaea endures within the life of contemporary churches. Although creedal language continues to characterize official theological and liturgical language, it has become fashionable in some circles within the church to dismiss Nicene faith as a mere opinion that became established as dogma by the winners of a human debate. A religious implication of the idea that "history is written by the victors" is the notion that the church must overcome oppressive orthodoxy by recovering the suppressed voices of defeated minorities. Elaine Pagels, for instance, contends that Gnostic Gospels were suppressed and forcibly eliminated by an ecclesiastical apparatus that would not tolerate the idea that people could find God by themselves. She also asserts that the recently discovered, so-called "Gospel of Judas" contradicts everything we have known about Christianity, presenting us with a version of history and beliefs that is more in tune with modern struggles than are the doctrines imposed at Nicaea.[9]

The notion that a narrow, ecclesiastically compelled orthodoxy suppressed Christian diversity in the early church could be encouraged by a misreading of Vincent of Lérins's famous fourth-century rule, "all possible care must be taken, that we hold the faith which has been believed everywhere, always, by all [ubique, semper, et ab omnibus]."[10] If taken literally, the rule is useless, for no element of Christian faith has ever been believed everywhere, always, or by all. Vincent's purpose in writing was to refute "the profane novelties of all heresies," which were obviously believed somewhere, sometimes, by some. Nevertheless, the modern suspicion may linger that the rule was intended to impose the conception of a fixed body of dogma that could then be used to suppress any departure from rigid ecclesiastical norms.

Vincent's aim was not to compel or promote unanimity, but to explore appropriate means of conserving the foundational truth of Christian faith. He did not propose that foundational truth is frozen in time, for he also affirmed that there is an appropriate development of doctrine in the church.

9. See, among others, Elaine Pagels, *The Gnostic Gospels* (New York: Vintage Books, 1979), and Elaine Pagels and Karel L. King, *Reading Judas: The Gospel of Judas and the Shape of Christianity* (New York: Penguin, 2007).

10. Vincent of Lérins, "A Commonitory," II [7], trans. C. A. Heurtley, *Nicene and Post-Nicene Fathers*, second series, vol. XI (Grand Rapids: Eerdmans, 1964), 132.

He acknowledged that "some will say perhaps, Shall there, then, be no progress in Christ's Church?" He responded by declaring that there must be "all possible progress. . . . Yet on condition that it be real progress, not alteration of the faith. For progress requires that the subject be enlarged in itself."[11] Vincent compared theological progress to the growth of the human body that ages, grows, and matures, yet remains the same person. "In like manner," says Vincent, "it behooves Christian doctrine . . . to be consolidated by years, enlarged by time, refined by age, and yet, withal, to continue uncorrupt and unadulterated . . . admitting no waste of its distinctive property, no variation in its limits."[12] For Vincent, doctrinal development in the church is growth in deepened faith and life, not novelty that rejects the church's faith and life.

"*We* believe," begins the Nicene Creed: we believe in one God . . . we believe in the Father, the Almighty . . . we believe in one Lord Jesus Christ, true God from true God . . . we believe in the Holy Spirit, the Lord, the giver of life. The Nicene Creed, completed in AD 381 at the council of Constantinople, set out the basic shape of shared belief and trust in the one God—Father, Son, and Holy Spirit. The creed is not a systematic theology, covering all the bases of Christian faith and life. It does not even define basic elements such as salvation, baptism, and the life of the world to come. Perhaps surprisingly, it does not mention Eucharist, nor does it have anything to say about the church's mission. The creed is not a *summa theologiae.* Its character and continuing significance lie in its foundational confession of who God truly is, its assurance that the one God is *for us*, its proclamation that God has revealed himself to us in Jesus Christ, and its guarantee that God continues to move among us as his Holy Spirit.

The Rule of Faith

The history of the Nicene Creed has often been told as if the primary business of the early church was promulgating doctrine, with bishops sorting out true faith from heresy by imposing universal requirements of truth for the ages. Creedal history has also been represented as the fusion of imperial and ecclesiastical politics to suppress diversity by establishing Constantinian uniformity in church and empire. Both descriptions grow from the

11. Vincent, XXIII [54], 147–48.
12. Vincent, XXIII [56], 148.

mistaken notion that the creed was "composed" in AD 325, emerging full blown from the deliberations of the church's bishops. The Nicene Creed was not an innovation, created *ex nihilo*, for it was deeply rooted in the church's baptismal life. Throughout the years of controversy leading up to the Council of Nicaea, theological positions were expressed by referring to local creed-like summaries of beliefs that shaped the faith of Christians. Underlying these references to local church teaching was the manner of preparing persons for baptism and incorporation into the church.

In the early centuries of the church's life, new converts were admitted to the community as *catechumens*—"hearers of the word"—for an extended period of instruction in the faith and life of the church prior to their baptism. During this time, catechumens participated in the first part of Lord's Day worship—prayers, hymns, psalms, scripture, and preaching—but left before the Eucharist. Their extended period of initiation included hearing Scripture, participating in community living marked by prayer and praise, and committing to the shape of the church's faith. The climax of this rich catechesis came at dawn on the Sunday morning of Easter. Following an all-night vigil, the catechumens descended into a large baptismal pool where they renounced Satan and all his works, confessed the faith of the church, and were baptized. Their confession of faith was structured by the commission of the risen Lord: "Go therefore and make disciples of all nations, baptizing them in the name of the Father and of the Son and of the Holy Spirit, and teaching them to obey everything that I have commanded you" (Matt 28:19–20). The great commission did more than institute baptism, however; it also gave baptism its substance. Baptizing "*into* the name of the Father and of the Son and of the Holy Spirit" gives incorporation into Christ and the church a Trinitarian structure that sets forth who God is and how God acts in the life of the world, the church, and each believer. The name of the triune God is not a mere formula but an expression of the essence of Christian faith.

The substance of the Nicene Creed emerged from these summaries of Christian faith that were taught to new believers by their local bishops and confessed at baptism. Because the summaries were specific to each bishop's diocese, their articulation varied from place to place. Yet they were not substantively divergent, for all were instances of what came to be called the *regula fidei*—the rule of faith—that provided the church with a norm of Christian faith and practice. In the second century, Irenaeus, bishop of Lyon in Gaul, set forth an already traditional summary of Christian faith:

The Church, indeed though disseminated throughout the world, even to the ends of the earth, received from the apostles and their disciples the faith in one God the Father Almighty, the Creator of heaven and earth and the seas and all things that are in them; and in one Jesus Christ, the Son of God, who was enfleshed for our salvation; and in the Holy Spirit, who through the prophets preached the Economies, the coming, the birth from a Virgin, the passion, the resurrection from the dead, and the bodily ascension into heaven of the beloved Son, Christ Jesus our Lord, and His coming from heaven in the glory of the Father to recapitulate all things, and to raise up all flesh of the whole human race . . . and that He would exercise just judgment toward all.[13]

Irenaeus concluded his rule of faith with the assertion that "the Church . . . though disseminated through the whole world, carefully guards this preaching and this faith which she has received, as if she dwelt in one house. She likewise believes these things as if she had but one soul and one and the same heart; she preaches, teaches, and hands them down harmoniously, as if she possessed but one mouth."[14] We can recognize in Irenaeus's images an idealized portrait of the church's unanimity, not unlike Vincent of Lérins, but this should not diminish our awareness of the church's substantial agreement about the shape of its faith. The *regula fidei*—its expression in catechesis and its summaries in baptismal confessions of faith—provided a basic digest of the Christian story and the focal point of Christian identity.

While expressions of the rule of faith, the catechetical teaching of the bishops, and the baptismal confessions were not fixed, they all summarized the same scriptural story in the familiar three-part structure with clauses about God the Father, the Son of God, and the Holy Spirit. Over a century before the Council of Nicaea, Tertullian, writing in Latin from North Africa, provided a rendition of the *regula fidei* that demonstrates the strong family resemblances among the versions of Irenaeus and other bishops throughout the Roman Empire.[15] Tertullian followed his rendition of the *regula fidei* with the counsel that, "provided the essence of the rule is not disturbed, you may seek and discuss as much as you like. You may

---

13. Irenaeus, *Against the Heresies*, 1.10.1 (quoted from *St. Irenaeus of Lyons*, Ancient Christian Writers 55, ed. Walter Burghardt [New York: Newman Press, 1992]), 48–49.

14. Irenaeus, *Against the Heresies*, 49.

15. Tertullian, "Prescriptions Against Heretics," 13, in *Early Latin Theology*, ed. S. L. Greenslade (Philadelphia: Westminster, 1956), 39.

give full reign to your itching curiosity where any point seems unsettled and ambiguous or dark and obscure."[16]

Irenaeus and Tertullian demonstrate both the rule of faith's clear ante-cedence to the Nicene Creed and the need for the creed. The summary of the faith in the *regula fidei* provided the building blocks of the creed, yet it surely left some things unsettled and ambiguous, even dark and obscure. Chief among the ambiguities that needed clarification was the relationship of the three actions of the one God—Father, Son, and Holy Spirit. While the creed set a trajectory for what makes faith Christian, it also left some things unsettled and ambiguous. The ongoing theological life of the church does not only confess the creed but also lives out creedal trajectories as it continues to think the faith, plumbing the riches of its theological in-heritance while searching for ways to express lived faith in new times and places.

THE CHURCH INTERPRETS ITSELF

The Nicene legacy—including the Apostles' Creed, which was developed from an early Roman baptismal confession of faith—gives the church a distinctive vocabulary, grammar, and syntax. Christians generally utilize these "rules of speech" as unconsciously as they use the rules of English, Spanish, Korean, or any native tongue. Nicene rules infuse liturgy, hym-nody, and prayer week after week (except when they don't), shaping and strengthening Christian consciousness (firmly or loosely). In any case, the creed continues to serve the church catholic by voicing Christian faith's fundamental identity. In confessing the truth about God and God's way in the world we say who we are as the people of God, the body of Christ, the communion of the Holy Spirit. The creed once inoculated believers against heresy and apostasy—and may do so again—but the more basic issue of the creed was and is Christian identity. Who is God? Who are we? Does God care about us? How does God act in our lives? How, in God's grace, shall we live together? The creed, like the older rule of faith in which it is grounded, tells the story of God and ourselves, the story of redemption and new life.

The creed is not a straightjacket, for, while it continues to function as the church's rule of faith, it does not constitute a doctrinal inventory. Like

16. Tertullian, "Prescriptions Against Heretics," 14, 40.

Tertullian's *regula fidei* it leaves the church free to "seek and discuss as much as it likes," even to "give full reign to its itching curiosity" as long as the essence of the faith is not cast aside. Luke Timothy Johnson makes the point that "the creed, far from being a restriction on Christian thinking, actually liberates the Christian mind. The simple and thrifty creed defines a few essential points and opens reasoning faith to many others. In this way it proves a model of establishing boundaries that are not barriers."[17] The church's Nicene rule of faith provides defining identity to a diversity of churches as well as to diversity within particular churches.

Nevertheless, it is apparent to any observer of actual churches that there is a gap between the form of Christian identity and the casual way that identity is held, not only by individuals but by the churches themselves. In actual congregations, what is believed or not believed may bear only surface resemblance to the Nicene core. In actual denominations, the Nicene Creed and subsequent confessional standards may play a minor role in shaping policies and programs. "Religion is a curious appetite," John Updike writes, "and as with the appetite for food a great variety of substances will satisfy it, including some pretty bizarre dishes if the appetite is strong enough."[18]

Churches are home to many persons who misunderstand or doubt or reject some elements of core Christian identity. It is neither surprising nor novel when some church members, pastors, and professors discard central components of Christian faith. It may be somewhat surprising, however, when denominations and their congregations continue to express official corporate faith in the vocabulary, grammar, and syntax of the originating creed while consigning core Christian identity to the periphery of their thinking, praying, and living.

Some may wonder, then, why creedal language and the rule of faith are held out as core identifiers of the church's faith. Isn't Scripture the common core? The Reformation motto *sola scriptura* presumes that "the rule of faith and life"[19] is Scripture itself, the authority by which all creeds and confessions are themselves judged. Yet, while most if not all Christian churches agree that Scripture is "the norm that norms all norms," the same churches continue to disagree among and within themselves about scrip-

17. Luke Timothy Johnson, *The Creed: What Christians Believe and Why It Matters* (New York: Doubleday, 2003), 320–21.

18. John Updike, *In the Beauty of the Lilies* (New York: Knopf, 1996), 436.

19. "The Westminster Confession of Faith," 6.002, *The Book of Confessions* (Louisville: Office of the General Assembly), 150.

tural interpretation. The agreed-upon norm—Scripture—soon becomes the locus of disagreement!

It is telling that the need for Nicaea and the subsequent ecumenical councils grew from conflicting interpretations of key passages in the Gospels. Because Scripture was understood differently, the early church sought to provide a lens through which Scripture could be read and understood. A similar understanding of the need for a guide to scriptural interpretation comes from the *sola scriptura* Reformation itself. John Calvin, whose devotion to the supreme authority of Scripture is beyond reproach, understood the purpose of his monumental *Institutes of the Christian Religion* to be "to prepare and instruct candidates in sacred theology for the reading of the divine Word, in order that they may be able both to have easy access to it and to advance in it without stumbling."[20] Creeds and confessions have a twofold relationship to Scripture: on the one hand, they summarize the scriptural witness to aspects of God's way in the world; on the other hand, they provide the frame within which Scripture can be seen, read, interpreted, and lived.

Creedal language can become merely customary, words spoken indiscriminately so that while the form remains, its substance is reduced to a shadow. Although the Christianity of Christian churches can devolve into a mere sociological identifier with more cultural than theological content, this indicates the pressing need for the creed, not its insignificance. "The church today desperately needs a clear and communal sense of identity," says Luke Timothy Johnson: "What does it mean to be Christian?"[21] The desperate need for a clear and communal sense of shared faith—and the desperate need to experience at the deepest level what it means to be Christian—may become more apparent when we recognize that Christian identity entails saying "No" to some things as well as "Yes" to others. Genuine confession of faith is always both affirmations and corresponding denials. "If the Yes does not in some way contain the No," says Karl Barth, "it will not be the Yes of a confession. . . . If we have not the confidence to say *damnamus* [what we refuse], then we might as well omit the *credimus* [what we believe]."[22] The identity of a community as Christian entails re-

---

20. John Calvin, "To the Reader," *Institutes of the Christian Religion*, trans. Ford Lewis Battles (Philadelphia: Westminster, 1960), 4.

21. Johnson, *The Creed*, 297.

22. Karl Barth, *Church Dogmatics* I/2 (Edinburgh: T&T Clark, 1956), 631, 630.

nunciation of what is not from God as well as affirmation of God and God's new Way.

Sometimes the "No" is explicit, as in the "Theological Declaration of Barmen" from 1930s Germany. Each of the Declaration's six "evangelical truths" is followed by, "We reject the false doctrine. . . ."[23] More often the "No" is implicit, as with the Nicene and Apostles' Creeds. But always, in the community's struggle to define itself in fidelity to the grace of the Lord Jesus Christ, the love of God, and the communion of the Holy Spirit, it is called to say "Yes" to God's way in the world, and "No" to the ways of the world apart from God. Barmen says "Yes" to something that the church too often forgets:

> The Church's commission, upon which its freedom is founded, consists in delivering the message of the free grace of God to all people in Christ's stead, and therefore in the ministry of his own Word and work through sermon and sacrament.

We may hear those words and nod casually, "Of course." Until we are confronted with Barmen's accompanying "No":

> We reject the false doctrine, as though the Church in human arrogance could place the Word and work of the Lord in the service of any arbitrarily chosen desires, purposes, and plans.[24]

An institutionalized church—institutionalized denominations and their institutionalized congregations—is always in danger of placing the gospel in the service of its own desires, purposes, and plans. Rhetoric about the primacy of the church's mission can become a justification for pushing the Word and work of Christ aside in a rush to promote institutional purposes and achieve organizational aims. Welcoming, hospitable worship may submerge Word and sacrament beneath a congregation's desire to become an attractive option in the church marketplace. Attention to the *damnamus* can awaken churches to the reality that they cannot say "Yes" to everything, and that if they say "Yes" to their Lord it will mean saying "No" to the dream wishes of their chosen desires, purposes, and plans.

---

23. "Theological Declaration of Barmen," 8.10–8.28, in *The Book of Confessions* (Louisville: Office of the General Assembly), 249–50.

24. "Theological Declaration of Barmen," 8.26.

The Nicene rule of faith calls Christian communities to confess the faith of the church as their faith. Saying "Yes" to the central affirmations of Christian faith is more than reciting comfortable liturgical orthodoxy; it is also saying "No" to comfortable cultural religiosity. Both the "Yes" and the "No" are present from the very outset. When the creed begins by confessing faith in one God, it is usually assumed that everyone knows what is meant whenever the word *God* is uttered. Even in the church, preaching and teaching operate in the naïve belief that talk about God is intended and heard in the same way by all. However, both sociologists and theologians tell us what we should know already: *God* is a word that can be filled with some pretty bizarre meanings.

As a young priest, New Testament scholar N. T. Wright served as chaplain at Worcester College, Oxford. His welcoming visits to first year students were often punctuated by their remark, "You won't be seeing much of me; you see, I don't believe in God." Wright developed a standard response: "Oh, that's interesting; which god is it you don't believe in?" The students were surprised because they regarded the word *god* as having self-evident meaning. Often, after students stumbled through a few characteristics of the god they didn't believe in, Wright would comment, "Well, I'm not surprised you don't believe in that god. I don't believe in that god either."[25]

Ludwig Feuerbach understood religious references to god as disclosing that "theology is anthropology." He asserted that humans create god, for "man's God is nothing other than the deified essence of man."[26] Feuerbach was half right, for much of popular religiosity is just that—projection of human desires onto "god." The god of human projection is often expressed negatively as, "I can't believe in a god who would . . . ," thus requiring that the divine conform to human standards. Baylor University's 2008 Survey of Religion summarized the four gods Americans do believe in—the Authoritative God, the Benevolent God, the Critical God, and the Distant God.[27] The National Study of Youth and Religion characterizes the beliefs

---

25. N. T. Wright, "The Biblical Formation of a Doctrine of God," in *Who Do You Say That I Am? Christology and the Church*, ed. Donald Armstrong (Grand Rapids: Eerdmans, 1999), 50.

26. Ludwig Feuerbach, *Lectures on the Essence of Religion*, trans. Ralph Manheim (New York: Harper & Row, 1967), 17.

27. Rodney Stark, *What Americans Really Believe: New Findings from the Baylor Surveys of Religion* (Waco, TX: Baylor University Press, 2008).

of American youth (and the churches that teach them) as "therapeutic moralistic deism."[28]

Popular culture both reflects and shapes understanding of God in the church. Movies and television portray god as a humorous meddler or a helpful intervener. In sequential versions of "the power of positive thinking" and the "health and wealth gospel," god is represented as the fulfiller of every wish. Social historian Charles Lippy traces a generic American religiosity that sees god as a divine power directly accessible to ordinary people, tapping a reservoir of latent power within the self.[29] None of this is new or unusual. Calvin characterized human nature as "a perpetual factory of idols,"[30] for the constant human temptation is the effortless creation of god in our image.

Barth recognized the power of Feuerbach's critique. Our knowledge of God, he wrote, "could so easily be an empty movement of thought— that is to say, if, in the movement which [we] regard as the knowledge of God, [we] are really alone and not occupied with God at all but only with [ourselves], absolutizing [our] own nature and being, projecting it into the infinite, setting up a reflection of [our] own glory. Carried through in this way, the movement of thought is empty because it is without object. It is a mere game. . . . We are not dealing with God, but at bottom with ourselves."[31] The church's rule of faith guards against an "empty movement of thought" by pointing to Scripture's naming and narrating of God as the Father, the Almighty, maker of all that is, seen and unseen. The rule of faith refuses a generic deity that is a mere presupposition behind a Jesus who is, in turn, the tragic hero or moral exemplar of pop historicism. Instead it confesses the Son of God who became truly human for us and our salvation. The rule of faith knows nothing of a generic "spirit" that bypasses the embarrassment of Christological particularity, narrating instead the Holy Spirit who is the Lord, the Giver of life. All of this says "No" to the monistic deity of bourgeois Protestantism by proclaiming the Holy Trinity.

The task of expressing the appropriate center of Christian faith and faithfulness—and their appropriate boundaries—was not exhausted seventeen centuries ago, nor has it been present in some subsequent generations while

---

28. Kenda Creasy Dean, *Almost Christian: What the Faith of Our Teenagers Is Telling the American Church* (Oxford and New York: Oxford University Press, 2010).

29. Charles H. Lippy, *Being Religious, American Style: A History of Popular Religiosity in the United States* (Westport, CT: Praeger, 1994).

30. Calvin, *Institutes* 1.11.8, 108.

31. Karl Barth, *Church Dogmatics* II/1: *The Doctrine of God*, trans. T. H. L. Parker et al. (Edinburgh: T&T Clark, 1957), §26, 71.

absent from others, nor is it limited only to some churches. It is an ever-present and continuous process that draws from the church's past as it presses toward hope in the future that God is bringing to be. "Memory and hope, story and promise, occur inseparably in the apostolic tradition," says Christopher Morse. "To keep the memory from blocking the hope (the temptation of conservatives), and to keep the hope from severing itself from the memory (the temptation of liberals) is the task of all dogmatics that seeks to be attentive to apostolic tradition."[32] Christian tradition, faithful to the Nicene trajectory, is the memory and the hope of the church as it strives to live out a clear and communal identity that is capable of proclaiming the gospel, nurturing the faithful, worshiping in spirit and in truth, fostering justice in church and society, and displaying to the world the coming reign of God.

Interpretation of the creedal rule of faith has become an urgent task in our time and place. In a diverse, highly segmented society, patterns of belief are no longer shaped by customary articulations or associations. Convictions and actions have become matters of individual choice and private decision. There are no paths that people must follow or authorities to which they are accountable—whether families, or advisers, or specialists, or systems, or institutions. Instead, individuals assume that *they* are the authority deciding which of multiple possibilities to choose. What is true of our culture is also true within the church. The contemporary church is not a community of shared certainty in commonly acknowledged truths. The church has never been a uniform community of unanimous views, of course. Even a casual reading of the New Testament letters is sufficient to confirm that the church has been characterized by diversity from the beginning. Yet the New Testament letters assume that, within the matrix of rich human diversities, unity in the faith is a central intention of Christian community. That assumption does not go unquestioned among us.

In a pluralistic church, interpretation of the creedal rule of faith is an essential task. The intention of interpretation is not to impose dogmatic formulations or compel assent to an institutional orthodoxy. Instead, common attention to the rule of faith engages Christians in a shared exploration of the truth about God and ourselves—truth that can liberate us from idolatry and self-deception, truth that can set us free to love God and neighbors. The Nicene Creed itself is especially suitable for shared inquiry precisely because it has been the nearly universal expression of Christian faith for almost seventeen hundred years. Orthodox Churches of the East, the Cath-

---

32. Christopher Morse, *Not Every Spirit* (New York: Trinity Press International, 1992), 48.

olic Church and Protestant churches of the West, and younger churches of the South have joined their voices to confess together the apostolic faith. This primacy of time and space gives to the Nicene Creed a claim on our attention. Through the creed, we are called by our forebears in the faith to join them in a common search for shared faith and faithfulness.

Several years ago, the Lilly Endowment funded the most comprehensive survey ever conducted of American congregations and their pastoral leaders. The survey revealed—perhaps counterintuitively—that most pastors find their vocation to be genuinely satisfying. But the survey dug deeper, asking pastors to identify the aspects of their vocation that were most and least satisfying. The least satisfying, voiced by a large majority, was "difficulty reaching people with the gospel today." Does the difficulty lie in pastors' capacity to proclaim the gospel? Or are the difficulties posed by American culture? Or is it a matter of uncertainty and confusion about the shape of the gospel itself? Probably all of the above, but it is likely that the basic problem is the absence of clarity about the gospel itself. The deep tradition of the church—expressed in the church's rule of faith—has an answer that is not simply a treasure to be preserved but a proclamation to be made in a culture that does not know what God has done *for our sake, for us and for our salvation.*

EMBODIED FAITH

The church's faith is not confined to an immaterial rule of faith. The faith of the church is lived faith, embodied in the lives of the faithful. But how do the faithful come to faith? The church's treasure must come to expression, for "how are they to call on one in whom they have not believed? And how are they to believe in one of whom they have never heard?" (Rom 10:14). The faith of the church must be proclaimed, and the proclamation of the gospel can, should, and does take place in a variety of ways, some clearer than others. Traditionally, Word and sacrament are understood to be the principal means of proclamation, from which other forms of proclamation—both in words and deeds—proceed. The good news must be spoken and enacted in the church. The ways that Word and sacrament are central witness to the gospel are not always evident, however, so it is to the church of the Word and sacrament that we now turn.

Chapter 3

CHURCH OF THE WORD AND SACRAMENT

The cup of blessing that we bless, is it not communion in the blood of Christ? The bread that we break, is it not communion in the body of Christ? Because there is one bread, we who are many are one body, for we all partake of the one bread.

1 Corinthians 10:16–17

The only thing that marked the days was the liturgy, which passed in and out of ordinary time, through Lent and Easter and Advent and Christmas. It was perhaps for this reason that she became a daily communicant during this period, though she had been rather casual about going to mass in the first years after her conversion. Back then, with the memory of the great transformation alive within her, the terrestrial obligations of the faith seemed less pressing. But spending each day going over the things she'd written as a lost girl made her feel lost again, and so she started attending St. Agnes each morning, to remind herself of the force of her faith.

Christopher Beha,
What Happened to Sophie Wilder

The Swiss Reformation's approach to the nature and purpose of the church began, not with the church itself, but with Christ. In the words of the Ten Theses of Berne (1528), "The holy Christian Church, whose only head is Christ, is born of the Word of God, and abides in the same, and listens not to the voice of a stranger."[1] Church begins with the Word of God, Jesus Christ, made known to us in the word of God, Scripture. As the creation of the Word, the church does not generate itself nor does the church belong to itself. John Calvin's discourse on the Christian life includes a lovely passage that speaks to the Christian community and to individual Christians within it: "We are not our own: let not our reason nor our will, therefore, sway our plans and deeds. We are not our own: let us therefore not set it as our goal to seek what is expedient for us according to the flesh. . . . Conversely, we are God's: let us therefore live for him and die for him. We are God's: let his wisdom and will therefore rule all our actions."[2]

The declaration that the church is born of the Word alone and does not listen to alien voices is more than a self-evident bromide, for the Word of God sounds in the midst of many other voices—cultural, societal, political, and religious—and the church hears them all too well. So the church must always be called back to its true self. Centuries after Berne, the Theological Declaration of Barmen sought to recall the church to the evangelical truth that "as the Church of pardoned sinners, it has to testify in the midst of a sinful world, with its faith as with its obedience, with its message as with its order, that it is solely [Christ's] property, and that it wants to live solely from his comfort and from his direction." Barmen went on to "reject the false doctrine, as though the church were permitted to abandon the form of its message and order to its own pleasure or to changes in prevailing ideological and political convictions."[3]

Congregations are not their own; they belong to God. Denominations are not their own; they belong to God. World communions are not their own; they belong to God. The early church understood itself and its actions as *kyriakos*—"belonging to the Lord"—from which we get the German *kirche*, the Scottish *kirk*, and the English *church.* No form of church is free to shape its life according to its own aspirations or the perceived desires of its members, as if churches were mere democracies or market-driven dispensers of religious goods and services. While few congregations, denominations, or world communions would deny that they belong to the Lord and not to themselves, churchly capacity for self-deception is a real and ever-present danger. The siren calls of strangers are as subtle and al-

---

1. "The Ten Conclusions of Berne," in *Creeds of the Churches*, ed. John H. Leith, 3rd ed. (Louisville: John Knox, 1982), 129.

2. Calvin, *Institutes*, 3.7.1, 690.

3. "Theological Declaration of Barmen," in *The Book of Confessions*, 8.17–18, 283.

luring as the voice of the serpent in the Garden, and churches regularly accede. How, then, are churches to recognize their own self-assertion and gauge fidelity to their God-given reality as dependent creatures?

A CHURCH OF THE WORD AND SACRAMENT

It is a fundamental principle of classic Reformed ecclesiology that the gathered congregation is the basic form of church but not a sufficient form of church. The gathered congregation *is* the one, holy, catholic, apostolic church but not of itself alone—as if it were a solitary, self-sufficient ecclesia. The gathered congregation *is* the one, holy, catholic, apostolic church *only* in its essential communion with the Lord and therefore in its communion with other gathered congregations. The conviction that the congregation is the basic yet insufficient form of church is deceptively direct, however. In practice, regardless of ecclesiastical polity, the delicate balance is often lost by placing excessive weight either on the congregation or on broader ecclesial structures of the church.

The congregation is most truly itself when it is gathered around word, water, bread and wine in worship of the one God whose active Word is spoken: "I will be your God and you shall be my people" (Lev 26:12). Calvin provides a helpful point of entry into this understanding. As a second-generation reformer, he understood his primary task as shaping a Christian community that would be capable of conserving re-formed faith and nurturing re-formed faithfulness. Thus, the church was central in Calvin's writing and pastoral labors in Geneva. In our time of ecclesial disarray, renewed attention to Calvin's reform of the shape of the church may be suggestive.

If the church is born of the Word of God, how can we recognize this creature of the Word when we see it? Calvin shared the Reformation belief that "the church comes forth and becomes visible to our eyes" through the presence of Word and sacraments: "Wherever we see the Word of God purely preached and heard, and the sacraments administered according to Christ's institution, there, it is not to be doubted, a church of God exists."[4] The Word of God rightly proclaimed and heard . . . baptism and the Lord's Supper celebrated in fidelity to Christ . . . *these* are the clear indicators of the one, holy, catholic, apostolic church. In Calvin's view, wherever we

4. Calvin, *Institutes*, 4.1.9, 1023.

see faithful proclamation and sacramental life we see the church. Proc-lamation—preaching and teaching—and sacramental life—baptism and Eucharist—are not all that we see, of course. Yet Word and sacraments are the essential foundation of the church because they ground the church's faith and its life without restricting them.

Sixteenth-century reformers who recognized the centrality of Word and sacrament built upon this foundation in various ways. John Knox's Scots Confession (1560) added a third mark, "ecclesiastical discipline uprightly ministered, as God's Word prescribes, whereby vice is repressed and virtue nourished."[5] Martin Luther elaborated on Word and sacraments by enu-merating additional marks by which "the holy Christian people are recog-nized: . . . the office of the keys [discipline], offices of ministry, prayer, and cross-bearing."[6] The broad category of discipline—in more contemporary terms a combination of church order and pastoral care—does not stand on its own, however, but is designed to give Word and sacrament space to breathe freely in the life of the church. Similarly, ordered ministry is central because it ensures the integrity of Word and sacrament. For both Luther and Knox, proclamation and sacraments are not static categories, but life-giving "means of grace" that engender growth in faithfulness throughout the church's life.

These markers were not the only things that sixteenth-century churches did, and they are certainly not the sole activities of contemporary churches. Churches engage in many other forms of ministry and mission—from youth groups and church suppers to prison ministries and shelter for the homeless, from support groups and discipleship training to refugee reset-tlement and efforts to end sex trafficking. Yet the broadly shared Refor-mation view is that God's spoken and enacted Word must be at the heart of it all, animating and shaping everything else. So central are these two marks, Calvin continued, that we must embrace any church that has them, "even if it otherwise swarms with many faults."[7]

The Reformation's two marks of the church are not abstract theologi-cal concepts; their purpose is to focus attention on the core of lived faith. They point to congregations, not academies; to assemblies of people, not libraries; to worship, not books. They are misused if employed to pro-

---

5. "The Scots Confession," in *The Book of Confessions*, 3.18, 19–20.

6. Luther, "On the Councils and the Church," in *Martin Luther's Theological Writings*, ed. Timothy F. Lull, 2nd ed. (Minneapolis: Fortress, 2005), 366–76.

7. Calvin, *Institutes*, 4.1.12, 1025.

nounce some churches true and others false, for their purpose is ecclesial *self*-interrogation. Word and sacrament place the gospel of Jesus Christ at the heart of ecclesial life. By preaching and teaching and living the Word, and by faithfully communicating Christ through baptism and the Lord's Supper, the church can know itself as *kyriakos*.

Two features of Calvin's formulation should be emphasized, one explicit and the other implicit. First, Calvin adds the two little words "and heard" to the preaching of the Word. A faithful congregation is where the proclaimed Word is heard, not in a merely auditory manner of course, but rather received, believed, and lived. Proclamation, whether in sermon, teaching, or other forms of witness, is not the private property of pastors or the interior province of individuals but the terrain of the whole church. Similarly, Eucharist and baptism are not acts of individual piety or family observance. They are "administered"—carried out, conducted, celebrated—within and by the whole assembly in accordance with Christ. Word and sacrament are not mere sacerdotal functions or individual experiences but characteristics of the whole people of God who are called to faithful living under the Word, resisting the siren voices of strangers.

Second, Calvin was certain that proclaiming the present Word of God in Christ, and being united with Christ through baptism and the Lord's Supper, formed committed disciples in a community that was equipped for faithful living in the world. "Our faith receives from baptism the advantage of its sure testimony to us that we are not only engrafted into the death and life of Christ," Calvin wrote, "but so united to Christ himself that we become sharers in all his blessings."[8] Similarly, the "special fruit" of the Lord's Supper is "the wonderful exchange which, out of his measureless benevolence, he has made with us; that, becoming Son of man with us, he has made us sons of God with him. . . ."[9] It is in baptism and Eucharist that the people of God are drawn to Christ's death and resurrection, to the Lord's continuing presence among them, and so to union with Christ.

Word and sacraments provide churches with foundational identifiers of ecclesial faithfulness. The question to be asked of any congregation or denomination is whether Word and sacraments are found at the heart of its common life. When we look at *our* Christian community, do we see—at the center of its life—spoken and enacted proclamation of the gospel? Although congregations and denominations engage in a wide variety of

8. Calvin, *Institutes*, 4.15.6, 1307.
9. Calvin, *Institutes*, 4.17.2, 1362.

activities and mission that grow from preaching, teaching, and celebrating the sacraments, these multiple programs, services, and mission initiatives must not bury Word and sacrament or push them to the periphery of church life. The whole range of church life must remain subject to authentication by Word and sacrament, the embodiment of the gospel in the life of Christ's women and men.

Word and sacrament *together* are the heart of the church's true and faithful life. Neglect of one leads inexorably to deformation of the other, for when either Word or sacrament exists alone it soon becomes a parody of itself. Reformed Christians may be aware of how baptism and especially Eucharist can become objects of eccentric piety when sacraments are exalted and preaching is minimized. But they may be less aware of how easily preaching and teaching can deteriorate into idiosyncratic monologues, institutional marketing, human potential promotion, or bourgeois conformity when preaching is magnified while baptism and Eucharist are marginalized. Sacramentally minimalist churches may also be less aware of how baptism can devolve into a sentimental celebration of an infant rather than union with Christ in his crucifixion and resurrection and how the Lord's Supper can mutate into a chummy celebration of congregational togetherness rather than union with Christ in suffering and hope.

THE REAL PRESENCE OF CHRIST

Reformation disagreement about the nature of Christ's presence in the sacrament of Holy Communion divided Protestants and Catholics, Lutheran and Reformed, Anglican and Independent. Disputes centered on the relationship of Christ to eucharistic bread and wine: Transubstantiation? Consubstantiation? Spiritual presence? Symbolic presence? Remembered presence? These differences, coupled with questions about who is authorized to preside, continue to divide churches. Eucharistic controversies have so dominated ecclesial discussion of real presence that Christ's presence in baptism and proclamation has been less clearly understood and expressed. Faithful proclamation of the Word of God and faithful celebration of baptism as well as Eucharist disclose the real presence of Christ in the church.

Augustine noted that apart from the word, "the water is neither more nor less than water." However, "The word [the gospel] is added to the element and there results the Sacrament, as if itself also a kind of visible word."[10] Sacraments are visible word, while proclamation is audible word. Just as water without the word is simply water, so in proclamation "the passing sound is one thing, the abiding efficacy another."[11] That is why Calvin takes it as "a settled principle that the sacraments have the same office as the Word of God: to offer and set forth Christ to us, and in him the treasures of heavenly grace."[12] Both proclamation and sacraments set forth the grace of the Lord Jesus Christ, the gracious presence of the living Lord, so that the church that is born of the Word of God "abides in the same."

Calvin was confident that Word and sacrament are effective: they give to us precisely what they portray. Preaching God's word imparts Christ himself to us, maintaining Christ's living presence among us: "Indeed, the word of God is living and active" (Heb 4:12); "Let the word of Christ dwell in you richly" (Col 3:16). Baptism re-presents the person and work of Christ, making visible among us Christ's very presence: "We were buried therefore with him by baptism into [his] death, so that as Christ was raised from the dead by the glory of the Father, we too might walk in newness of life" (Rom 6:4). Eucharist conveys Christ's living presence: "The cup of blessing which we bless, is it not a communion in the blood of Christ? The bread which we break, is it not a communion in the body of Christ?" (1 Cor 10:16). The church, born of the Word made flesh, abides in union with the crucified and risen Christ through proclamation and sacraments, for they are more than liturgical activities and more than mere memory of a long ago and far away Jesus; they are the principal means by which the church comes to life as the body of Christ.

Or are they? We have all listened to sermons that conceal more of the gospel than they reveal, witnessed baptisms that celebrate family rather than the grace of God, and endured services of Holy Communion that glumly reference a sad death instead of hope in new creation. Scriptural and sacramental theology sometimes sink under the weight of churchly reality.

PROCLAIMING THE WORD OF GOD

The sixteenth-century Second Helvetic Confession makes the bold claim that "the Preaching of the Word of God Is the Word of God."[13] Experience

---

10. Augustine, "Tractates on the Gospel of John," 80.3. www.newadvent.org/fathers/1701080.htm.

11. Augustine, "Tractates on the Gospel of John," 80.3.

12. Calvin, *Institutes*, 4.14.17, 1292.

13. "The Second Helvetic Confession," in *The Book of Confessions*, 5.004, 77.

may suggest that the claim is more foolish than bold, for all of us have heard (and some of us have preached) sermons that have a tenuous relationship to God's Word. Protestant pride in the primacy of preaching runs up against the reality of sermonic exercises that reveal much about the preacher and little about God. A prominent Catholic observer expresses a reality that any Protestant can recognize:

> Today, many Christians, myself included, experience a quiet uneasiness about attending divine services in a strange church; they are appalled at the thought of the half-understood theories, the amazing and tasteless personal opinions of this or that priest they will have to endure during the homily—to say nothing of the personal liturgical inventions to which they will be subjected. No one goes to church to hear someone else's personal opinions. I am simply not interested in what fantasies this or that individual priest may have spun for himself regarding questions of Christian faith. . . . When I go to church, it is not to find there my own or anyone else's innovations.[14]

Grand theological claims for preaching appear irresponsible, for most Christians have heard enough dreadful sermons to doubt that God's voice resounds in preachers' mouths. Yet the claims for preaching do not depend on the wisdom or skill of those who speak but on their fidelity to the scriptural witness. The Second Helvetic Confession's assertion that preaching is the Word of God is qualified by the specification that it is preaching *of* the Word of God that *is* the Word of God. But what marks preaching of the Word of God as distinct from preachers' "amazing and tasteless personal opinions"? Karl Barth's discussion of "The Word of God as Preached" notes the aporia: "proclamation must become proclamation; from being an act which claims to be and should be proclamation it must become an act which is proclamation."[15] If not all proclamation is proclamation in the proper sense, how can we know when churchly words become proclamation?

Preaching need not be confined to lectionaries and exposition of a text, and teaching need not be limited to Bible study. But proclamation

---

14. Joseph Ratzinger, *Principles of Catholic Theology: Building Stones for a Fundamental Theology* (San Francisco: Ignatius Press, 1987), 283.

15. Karl Barth, *Church Dogmatics* I/1: *The Doctrine of the Word of God*, trans. G.T. Thompson (Edinburgh: T&T Clark, 1936), 98.

in preaching and teaching—both formal and informal—must be faithful to Scripture's narrative arc of "God with us" in creation and covenant, judgment and redemption, incarnation and consummation. Fidelity to the scriptural witness expresses the church's certainty that God has made himself known through Israel and in Jesus Christ, the church's confidence that God's self-revelation finds authentic and reliable witness in the Old and New Testaments, and the church's faith that the Holy Spirit is active in both the speaking of the preacher and the hearing of the congregation. To say that preaching *of* the Word of God *is* the Word of God is not a grandiose claim for church proclamation, but a confident declaration about the continuing presence of God, Father, Son, and Holy Spirit, with his people.

Edward Farley notes that the focus of early Christian preaching "is not the content of passages of Scripture. It is the gospel, the event of Christ through which we are saved. To think that what is preached is the Bible and the content of its passages is a quite different way of thinking about preaching."[16] Farley is not calling for preachers to abandon attention to Scripture but warning against confining attention to disconnected passages of Scripture. "To see a letter of Paul, a Gospel, or a prophetic tract as an aggregate of discrete units is surely to miss the writing as an argument, a polemic, a set of imageries, a theological perspective, a narrative," says Farley. "The very thing that gives the writing its power is its unity, its total concrete vision, its total movement."[17] What is true about passages within a particular biblical writing is also true about biblical writings within the whole of Scripture. To see the Bible as an aggregate of unconnected "books" is surely to miss knowing Scripture, in all its variety, as a coherent witness to the one God who creates, sustains, reconciles, and redeems.

What it means to preach the gospel rather than preach a text may be illustrated by the method of the legendary directing and acting teacher, Constantin Stanislavski.[18] He insisted that an actor must not only learn her lines and actions but must also know everything about the character she plays, even becoming her character. She must also enter the drama's broad horizon of meaning that embraces and animates the role. Every spoken line, gesture, and movement of the actor should be related to the main idea of the play. Similarly, every proclamation—sermons, teaching, sacraments,

16. Edward Farley, *Practicing Gospel* (Louisville: Westminster John Knox, 2003), 74.

17. Farley, *Practicing Gospel*, 76.

18. I owe this illustration to Kevin Vanhoozer in *Faith Speaking Understanding* (Louisville: Westminster John Knox, 2014), 118–19. However, I put Stanislavski's "method" to a somewhat different use.

ministry, mission—should be related to the main thrust of Scripture, to the gospel. Sermons that focus narrowly on a scriptural snippet in isolation from the whole are susceptible to becoming mere object lessons, moralisms, therapeutic exercises, or self-help tips rather than news that is good about God's way in the world.

Proclamation in and by the church does not begin with the Bible but with Jesus Christ, who *is* the Word of God present now in the church.

> In the beginning was the Word,
> and the Word was with God
> and the Word was God. . . .
> And the Word became flesh, and dwelt among us,
> full of grace and truth;
> we beheld his glory,
> glory as of the only Son from the Father. (John 1:1–2, 14, RSV)

Centuries ago, Calvin expressed his puzzlement about Jerome's Latin translation of John's prologue: "I wonder what induced the Latins to render ὁ λόγος as *Verbum* [the Word], for that would rather have been the translation of τὸ ῥῆμα [the word]. But granting that they had some plausible reason, still it cannot be denied that *Sermo* [Speech, Speaking, Discourse] would have been far more appropriate."[19] Although Calvin was well aware of philosophical uses of *logos*, he believed *sermo* to be truer to John's intention: "As to the evangelist calling the Son of God *the Speech*, the simple reason appears to me to be, first, because he is the lively image of His purpose; so it is not inappropriate to . . . say that He reveals Himself to us by His *Speech*."[20] What John's Gospel presents is less the enfleshment of a "noun" than the incarnation of God's active, verbal presence.

It is Jerome's translation, however, not Calvin's, that has influenced English translations. In turn, the consistent use of "Word" to translate *logos* has encouraged interpretations that imagine a philosophical "Logos Christology" behind the prologue to John's Gospel. All too often, then, philosophical *logos* is used to define "John's Christ." Alternatively, following Calvin's insight, understanding John's use of *logos* to signify speech/speaking/discourse, points to Genesis 1 as the obvious setting for John 1.

---

19. John Calvin, *Commentary on the Gospel According to John*, trans. William Pringle (Grand Rapids: Eerdmans, 1956), 1:28.

20. Calvin, *Commentary on the Gospel According to John*, 1:26.

The relationship between the Greek *logos* of John 1 and the Hebrew דבר (*dabar*)—say/speak/command/promise—of Genesis 1 makes clear the dynamic rather than the static intent of John's prologue. Not an object, "word," but an action, "speaking," is at the heart of John's proclamation.

Genesis 1	John 1
In the beginning	In the beginning was the *Speaking*
God	the *Speaking* was God
created	were made through him
the heavens and the earth	all things
And God *said*,	the *Speaking* was with God,
"Let there be light	In him was life, the light of all people
God separated the light	The light shines in the darkness
from the darkness	
So God created humankind	And the *Speaking* became flesh
in his own image	
It was very good	grace upon grace

In Genesis 1, God's *speaking* is an active force that creates: "God said . . . and there was." Throughout the Old Testament God's speech is God's creative action in the world: "and the glory of the LORD shall be revealed, and all flesh shall see it together, for the mouth of the LORD has spoken" (Isa 40:5). The *dabar* of the Lord is God's dynamic discourse with Israel: "Hear the word of the LORD, O people of Israel." God's speech, God's communication, is the revelatory action of God, disclosing who God is and establishing God's relationship with his people. John's Gospel now declares that God's revelatory self-disclosure has become flesh. God now speaks in human terms, in a human life, "*and we have beheld his glory*" (John 1:14).

Preaching of the Word of God that *is* the Word of God, the preaching that becomes proclamation, is that which bears faithful witness to God's generative *Speech*. It is proclamation of the Lord's providential action throughout all of creation, of God's dynamic discourse with his people Israel, and of God's living presence in the incarnation, crucifixion, resurrection, and ascension of Jesus Christ. In short, it is proclamation of the gospel made known through the revelatory witness of the whole of Scripture. Moreover, as both Genesis and John display, proclamation of God's generative *Speech* accomplishes what it intends.

BAPTISM

In the not-too-distant past, baptism in North American churches was a customary rite, a routine act performed on babies as a matter of course. In recent years, however, baptism has been transformed into a chummy expression of congregational welcome. The pastor reads gracious words from Scripture and prays familiar prayers, well-known questions are asked and answered, and water moistens an infant head. Then the pastor carries the baby up and down the aisle, introducing the child to people who are arbitrarily identified as the child's "church family."

In typical baptism services, everything focuses on celebrating the incorporation of an infant (or teenager or adult) into the life of a congregation. While the words of Scripture and prayers may describe a broader, deeper reality, the action itself narrows the sacrament to only one aspect of its significance. The folksy demeanor of the pastor, introductions of family and friends, a hasty recital of brief readings and prayers, the minimal sight and sound of water, reminders of church programs, and the leisurely stroll through the congregation all combine to collapse meaning into the reception of a singular child into a particular congregation.

Baptism is the sacrament of reception into the *whole* community of believers, of course. But it is not only that. Baptism's capacity to unite us to God through Christ in the power of the Holy Spirit is only hinted at in most actual baptismal services. Unlike Eucharist, baptism lacks "words of institution" that frame its meaning. However, a mere sample of New Testament baptismal texts reveals rich baptismal images cascading over one another in a stream of living water that flows through discipleship (Matt 28:16–20), forgiveness of sins and the gift of the Holy Spirit (Acts 2:37–42), response to the good news and life in the community of faith (Acts 10:44–48), dying and rising with Christ and union with Christ (Rom 6:1–11), a new exodus from slavery to freedom in Christ (1 Cor. 10:1–4), union with sisters and brothers in Christ (1 Cor 12:12–13), distinctions no longer divisions (Gal 3:26–29), new circumcision (Col 2:11–15), new covenant, new community, new openness to the world (1 Pet 3:18–22), eschatological sign of the coming reign of God (Rev 22:17)!

In short, baptism is a sign of the fullness of God's gracious love and effectual calling that, in one moment, is poured over a single human being. The moment is not isolated, however, as a point in time that recedes into distant memory. Baptism is the sure promise of God's continuing faithfulness, Christ's continuing presence, and the inauguration of new life within

God's Way. The French Confession of 1559 puts it nicely: "In Baptism we are grafted into the body of Christ, washed and cleansed by his blood, and renewed in holiness of life by his Spirit. Although we are baptized only once, the benefit it signifies lasts through life and death, so that we have an enduring testimony that Jesus Christ will be our justification and sanctification forever."[21]

It is too small a thing that this ocean of meaning, deep and moving, should be reduced to a ritual of congregational welcome. It is true enough that baptism welcomes persons into the church, but it makes all the difference whether our sacramental action is polite introduction to a friendly gathering or union with Christ in his death and resurrection, incorporation into the very body of Christ, enfolding into a community of belief, trust, loyalty, and obedience. Theological care is necessary if baptism is to be rescued from churchly banality, but it is essential that it be accompanied by faithful baptismal practice that opens the church to the flood of significance that defines our very being as humans together in Christ.[22]

Baptism does even more than present the fullness of the gospel. Baptism is a means of grace, communicating and bringing about the very thing it signifies. Baptism does not only tell us about Christ, point to Christ, or signify Christ. In baptism, Christ is present with us as we are made one with him in a death like his and will become one with him in a resurrection like his. The question that is before the churches is how an unabridged, sacramental theology, expressed in rich, liturgical texts, can be incorporated in faithful, sacramental practice. Baptismal prayers echoing Martin Luther's "Flood Prayer" provide congregations with liturgical expressions of baptism's centrality in Christian faith and life. Like the Eucharist's Great Thanksgiving, thanksgiving over the water is both prayer and proclamation of the gospel.

Even if a congregation should recover the full sacramental significance of baptism, embedding its proclamation of the gospel in re-formed baptismal practice, a fateful problem remains. The sacrament of union with Christ and incorporation into the body of Christ is celebrated in separated, sometimes estranged, and even hostile denominations and their congregations, some of which refuse even to recognize baptisms that occur in other churches.

---

21. *The French Confession of 1559*, trans. Ellen Babinsky and Joseph D. Small (Louisville: Presbyterian Church (USA), 1998), XXXV, 16.

22. For an example of congregational re-formation of its baptismal practice, see Joseph D. Small, "Salt and Light," *Reformed Liturgy and Music* XV, no. 4 (Fall 1981).

The story of God-with-us that is enacted in baptism, and the story we tell about ourselves as God's people, is an incomplete story if it fails to acknowledge the reality and experience the pain of the church's division.

Baptism is the beginning of the gospel. Just as Jesus's own baptism marked his bonding with sinners, his disclosure as the Beloved Son, and the commencement of his proclamation of the kingdom of God, so our baptisms mark us as adopted children of God and call us to bear witness to God's way in the world. Central to that way is the barrier-breaking reality that "as many of [us] as were baptized into Christ have put on Christ. There is neither Jew nor Greek, there is neither slave nor free, there is neither male and female; for [we] are all one in Christ" (Gal 3:27–28). Yet there is an obvious sense in which we are *not* all one in Christ. Centuries of ecclesial racialism continue the division of American Christianity into racially constituted congregational enclaves. The story we tell about ourselves in baptism is, at best, an incomplete story, for it fails to recognize the deep wounds in the body of Christ. There *is* Jew and gentile, poor and rich, male and female, black and white. Baptism—the beginning of the gospel— should lead the church to hear its Lord announce once again that because the kingdom is at hand we must repent, turning away from acceptance of ecclesial and racial divisions as we gather at the font.

EUCHARIST

"It would be well," wrote Calvin, "to require that the Communion of the Holy Supper of the Lord be held every Sunday at least as a rule."[23] Calvin failed in his efforts to convince Reformed churches (then and now) to celebrate the Lord's Supper every Lord's Day, although this was the practice of the early church and remains the practice of many contemporary churches. For centuries, quarterly Communion was typical Protestant practice, although recent years have brought more frequent celebrations of the sacrament to some denominations. But while Eucharist is now a monthly rite in many congregations, the arbitrary designation of the first Sunday of the month as Communion Sunday indicates its institutional rather than ecclesial function.

---

23. John Calvin, "Articles Concerning the Organization of the Church and of Worship at Geneva," in *Calvin: Theological Treatises*, ed. J. K. S. Reid (Philadelphia: Westminster, 1954), 49.

Many Eucharist liturgies invite people to the table with the words, "Friends, this is the joyful feast of the people of God," but in too many churches the Lord's Supper remains a gloomy exercise in silent introspection. This should not be surprising, for church members have been schooled to think of the *Lord's* Supper exclusively in terms of the *last* supper. The liturgical prominence of the "words of institution" from 1 Corinthians 11:23–26 as warrant for the sacrament reinforces congregational perception that the purpose of its observance is remembering and in some sense replicating the experience of disciples on the last night of Jesus's life. If that is the sole model for the sacrament, it is little wonder that the corporate demeanor of too many churches is somber and introspective.

Paul's transmission of the Lord's Supper tradition in 1 Corinthians 11 is central because it is the earliest written expression of the church's wide and deep eucharistic discernment. The pattern of the tradition Paul received and handed on is familiar: Jesus *took* bread, *gave thanks,* and *broke it.* The Synoptic Supper tradition follows the pattern: Jesus *took* bread, *blessed/ gave thanks, broke* it, and *gave* it to them (Matt 26:26–29, Mark 14:22–25, Luke 22:14–23). This Lord's Supper tradition is not confined to the night when he was betrayed, however. The Gospel writers narrated the feeding of the thousands with the same eucharistic pattern: "*Taking* the five loaves and the two fish, he looked up to heaven, and *blessed* and *broke* the loaves, and *gave* them to his disciples to *set before* the people" (Mark 6:41; see also Matt 14:19, John 6:11). The form is also found in the risen Christ's meals with his disciples: "When he was at table with them, he *took* bread, *blessed* and *broke* it, and *gave* it to them. Then their eyes were opened and they recognized him" (Luke 24:30–31). And, in a clear echo of the feeding of the thousands, "Jesus said to them, 'Come and have breakfast.'. . . Jesus came and *took* the bread and *gave* it to them, and did the same with the fish" (John 21:12–13). All of these clearly eucharistic texts cohere with the scriptural accounts of Jesus eating and drinking with sinners, for the risen Christ eats and drinks with sinners still. Finally, the eucharistic trajectory leads to hope in the "heavenly banquet," for "blessed are those who are invited to the marriage supper of the Lamb (Rev 19:9).

In the first centuries of the church, the community gathered every Lord's Day, sometimes at risk to liberty or life, to share eucharistic bread and wine. The church did not gather every Thursday night, but every Sunday morning; the church did not come together in remembrance of the last supper, but in celebration of life with the resurrected, living Lord and hope in the day when all who "hunger and thirst for righteousness . . . will come from east and west, and from north and south, and sit at table in the kingdom of God" (Matt 5:6; Luke 13:29). Little wonder the early church celebrated the Lord's Supper every Lord's Day, for they were not mourning the tragic death of a hero or commemorating the premature death of an inspiring teacher. They were gathering in the presence of the risen, living Christ to be joined to him in his death and resurrection and to be fed by him, receiving nourishment for growth in the love of God and neighbors. From the eucharistic table the church was and is sent into a world in which thousands upon thousands of hungry people "have nothing to eat," a world where the risen Christ continues to say to his disciples, "You give them something to eat."[24]

Reduction of Eucharist to an infrequent memorial of Jesus's death is also a factor in the reduction of church to a voluntary assemblage of individual believers. Furthermore, it reduces Eucharist to an interior church rite that is disconnected from mission in the world. Calvin notes three benefits of the Lord's Supper: first, we receive Christ himself and participate in the blessings of his death and resurrection; second, we are led to recognize the continuing blessings of Christ and respond with lives of gratitude and praise; and third, we are aroused to holy living, for by receiving Christ our lives are conformed to Christ. Calvin goes on to note that even though conformity to Christ should be the reality in all parts of our life,

> it has a special application to charity [love], which is above all recommended to us in this sacrament; for which reason it [the Lord's Supper] is called the bond of charity. For as the bread, which is there sanctified for the common use of us all, is made of many grains so mixed together that one cannot be discerned from the other, so ought we to be united among ourselves in one indissoluble friendship. What is more: we all receive there the same body of Christ, in order that we may be made members of it.[25]

Eucharistic theology and liturgical texts envision baptized hearers of an individually preached word becoming, in the Lord's Supper, a community bound in the grace of the Lord Jesus Christ, the love of God, and the com-

---

24. Eucharist's implications for the mission of the church permeate the entire "bread cycle" in Mark 6:30–8:21.

25. John Calvin, "Short Treatise on the Lord's Supper," in *Calvin: Theological Treatises*, 151.

munion of the Holy Spirit. Theology and texts anticipate that as believers are united to Christ they will be united to one another in a communion that is the body of Christ and so is no longer closed in upon itself. In Eucharist, the community becomes open to the thousands, including the tax collectors and sinners. Biblically faithful eucharistic theology and theologically faithful eucharistic texts are necessary, but if the Lord's Supper is to nourish one, holy, catholic, and apostolic community, Communion must be embodied in eucharistic practice that enacts the fullness of the church's eucharistic theology and animates the church's rich Eucharistic texts.

The church lives in union with Christ, the living and present Savior and Lord of the church. We are not left with a distant God or a merely remembered Jesus. "As if we ought to think of Christ standing afar off and not rather dwelling in us!" said Calvin. "For we await salvation from him not because he appears to us afar off, but because he makes us, engrafted into his body, participants not only in all his benefits, but also in himself."[26]

And yet, as with Baptism, the gospel proclaimed in Eucharist and the story we tell about ourselves at the Table is incomplete apart from recognition that the Lord's Supper divides the church. Many eucharistic liturgies include the Lord's words, "They will come from east and west, and from north and south, and sit at table in the kingdom of God" (Luke 13:29). Surely they will, but for now all are not always welcome. Some churches have clear reasons for restricting access to the sacrament, while many congregations voice the words with little or no awareness of the deliberate history and unconscious practice of racial exclusion at the *Lord's* table. But no church should be content with the chasm that separates the worthy from the unworthy, and no church, no congregation, should be content with the legacy of racial homogeneity that characterizes too many Christian communities.[27]

GATHERING AND SENDING

If Word and sacrament are primary means of the church's apprehension of the presence of Christ, and therefore of our union with Christ, then Word

26. Calvin, *Institutes*, 3.2.24, 570.

27. For a searing analysis of racialized eucharistic practice in the PCUSA, see Mary McClintock Fulkerson and Marcia Mount Shoop, *A Body Broken, A Body Betrayed: Race, Memory, and Eucharist in White-Dominant Churches* (Eugene, OR: Cascade, 2015).

and sacrament cannot be reduced to worship. The trajectory of Word and sacrament reaches far beyond the Sunday assembly. If we are made one with Christ, then we are one with the risen Lord who goes before us into Jerusalem, Galilee, Samaria, and to the ends of the earth. Perhaps the author of Hebrews brings it closer to home: "Jesus also suffered outside the city gate in order to sanctify the people by his own blood. Let us then go to him outside the camp . . ." (Heb 13:12–13).

Word and sacrament. . . the presence of Christ . . . union with Christ . . . outside the camp. Word and sacrament are marks of the church because they impel the church beyond itself. Far from being interior acts of the church that encourage self-absorption, Word and sacrament send the church to be one with Christ, participating in the mission of God for the sake of the world. The waters of baptism flow into the Great Lakes, into wells dug in Ethiopia, and into water purifiers in Haiti. The bread of Eucharist is shared in Detroit homeless shelters, Syrian refugee camps, and food stamps. The Word is spoken in cries for justice and whispers of compassion. Worship and mission are not two things, but one; either without the other can easily become no thing.

Since the publication of Dom Gregory Dix's monumental study, *The Shape of the Liturgy*,[28] there has been widespread (although not unanimous) agreement that the historic structure of Christian worship is a fourfold movement centered on Word and Eucharist. Many churches express this movement as "Gathering-Word-Eucharist-Sending." In practice, however, the fourfold movement is obscured by congregational worship that is dominated by Word and sacrament (or Word alone), with gathering and sending reduced to small, decorative bookends supporting Scripture/proclamation and baptism/Eucharist. More often than not, gathering is confined to a call to worship, singing, and prayers (and announcements!), while sending is restricted to prayer, singing, and a charge/benediction. Such gatherings and sendings are not only brief liturgical jumbles; they are strictly interior to worship itself with little recognition of where worshipers are coming from and where they are going to.

Gathering begins long before the prelude, and sending endures far beyond benediction and postlude. In Karl Barth's 1922 address to a pastors' conference, he imagines a typical Sunday morning as the community makes its way to church:

28. Dom Gregory Dix, *The Shape of the Liturgy* (New York: Seabury Press, 1982).

Here are *people*, perhaps only two or three as is the case in the country, but perhaps a few hundred, who stream into this building driven by an odd instinct or will—where they seek *what*? The satisfaction of an old habit? Perhaps, but from where does this habit come? Do they seek entertainment and instruction! A very strange entertainment and instruction indeed! Edification? Yes, it is claimed, but what does edification mean? Do they know somehow? Or do they have other reasons for being here? In any case, they are here . . . and their presence already points to an event which they anticipate or appear to anticipate. . . .[29]

It is all too easy to assume that people in the pews are simply there, characterized by their sheer presence as if they came from nowhere. It is all too easy to assume that the people in the pews are committed Christians (with the occasional "seeker" mixed in). Yet the people come from diverse, specific places, out of various motivations, with assorted expectations. Scattered people are gathered, and the gathering is God's doing. When a church imagines that *it* is the gatherer, by dint of *its* attractiveness, it becomes more likely that Word will fragment into mere words and sacrament will become mere ceremony. *God* calls the congregation together from the diverse circumstances and impulses of its members, a reality that should be made clear in the "call to worship" that commences the liturgy and continues throughout the liturgy itself. Assembled worshipers are not a homogeneous mass.

Just as God gathers scattered people, calling them to worship, so God sends gathered people to bear witness to the grace of the Lord Jesus Christ, the love of God, and the communion of the Holy Spirit, rendering service to persons and societies in need. The church too often assumes that *it* sends people out into a generic "world," but it is God who sends persons into specific callings—to jobs and homes and friends and families—that may be places of fulfillment or anguish, purpose or confusion, dread or hope. It is all too easy for the church to assume that the lives of Christians are lived within *its* worship and programs, and that people will grow in faith as they give themselves to *its* activities.

Word and sacrament are primary means of the church's apprehension of the presence of Christ, and therefore of our union with Christ, but gathering and sending are necessary to the full integrity of Word and sacrament.

29. Barth, "The Need and Promise of Christian Proclamation," in *The Word of God and Theology*, trans. Amy Marga (London: T&T Clark, 2011), 109.

If Word and sacrament are to live out their dominical trajectory they must not be confined to the interior life of the church. David Buttrick makes the helpful distinction between "in-church" speaking that is addressed to the baptized faithful and "out-church" speaking that is addressed to those outside of the eucharistic communion. Proclamation of the Word of God must not be confined to worship nor become the exclusive province of pastors. "Out-church preaching is primarily the task of the laity," says Buttrick, "those who by Baptism have been ordained to a common, evangelical ministry . . . speaking *out* is the church's calling."[30] A question to be asked of in-church speaking is whether it prepares people to be sent out to speak the gospel.

Similarly, baptism and Eucharist are not exclusive "in-church" events. Baptized disciples are sent to live and speak faith as central to their diverse callings. Those who have been served at the Lord's table are sent to serve at near and distant "tables" throughout the world. Discipleship is not an "in-church" calling. Rather, because we are united with Christ in his death and new life, Word and sacrament send us "out-church."

The Word proclaimed and heard, baptism and Eucharist celebrated in accord with Christ: these are the foundational and essential characteristics of faithful churches. Yet, in no church are proclamation and sacraments "pure." Proclamation may be muddled, indistinct, muted, or misdirected. Baptism and Eucharist may be celebrated without consciousness of the ecclesial, racial, and class divisions that blemish them. While no church should be content with careless or willful neglect of flaws in its practice of Word and sacrament, their efficacy is not dependent upon human rectitude. The church is a creation of the Word, not its master, and the Word of God voiced in proclamation, baptism, and Eucharist—however imperfectly—will not return empty.

All of this may come into clearer focus by expanding the view of church beyond Word and sacrament in the congregation itself to the wider locus of proclamation, baptism, and Eucharist as God's action in the whole church. It is the character of the church as communion that will provide a wider angle of vision, bringing congregation into its proper context.

30. David Buttrick, *Homiletic* (Philadelphia: Fortress, 1987), 226.

Chapter 4

COMMUNION OF THE HOLY SPIRIT

Through the testing of this ministry you glorify God by your obedience to the confession of the gospel of Christ and by the generosity of your communion with them and with all others, while they long for you and pray for you because of the surpassing grace of God that he has given you. Thanks be to God for his indescribable gift!

2 Corinthians 9:13–15

The history of the church is very complex, very mingled. I want you to know how aware I am of that fact. These days there are so many people who think loyalty to religion is benighted. I am aware of that, and I know the charges that can be brought against the churches are powerful.

Marilynne Robinson, *Gilead*

The congregation gathered around Word and sacrament is the basic form of church, but it is not a sufficient form of church. The gathered congregation is the one, holy, catholic, apostolic church only in its essential communion with its Lord and therefore in communion with other gathered congregations. Yet ecclesial solipsism is an all-too-familiar danger for congregations. Whether a congregation is large or small, poor or wealthy, growing or declining, contentious or peaceful, the temptation to gaze inward is ever present, narrowing each congregation's perception of church to their own church. In contemporary North America, where congregations live in implicit rivalry with one another, building up the body of Christ is too often seen as enhancing one congregation—even at the expense of neighboring congregations—in the competition for attracting and maintaining members. Congregational self-absorption cannot be rationalized by recourse to an immaterial relationship with all Christians through shared faith in Christ; effortless belief that does not produce tangible consequences has little to do with lived relationships among actual congregations.

Both the New Testament and Christian tradition have something larger and more substantial in view. When Paul wrote to "the church of God that is in Corinth," his salutation assumed that there were churches of God in other places. When he wrote to the Galatians he addressed "the churches of Galatia" together, and in his letter to the Romans he greeted "all God's beloved in Rome" who were dispersed in different house churches. The letter to the church in Colossae concluded with instructions that it be shared with the church in Laodicea and that a letter from Laodicea be read in Colossae. New Testament letters are replete with references that both assume and encourage inter-relationships among Christian communities scattered throughout the Roman Empire.

As Christian faith spread throughout the Mediterranean world, multiple congregations in the same locality were linked through a common relationship to their bishop, and local clusters of churches were related through bonds among their bishops. In the sixteenth-century Reformation, some Protestant churches retained the office of bishop, while others developed regional councils. Both orders were intended to bind congregations together in common faith and life. A striking instance of ecclesial mutuality can be seen in the Preface to the Scots Confession of 1560. The newly reformed church in Scotland announced to other churches in Europe that it was pleased "to have made known to the world the doctrine which we profess and for which we have suffered abuse and danger." It was not content simply to distribute its confession of faith, however, for the Preface went on to request,

> if any man will note in our Confession any chapter or sentence contrary to God's Holy Word, that it would please him of his gentleness and for Christian charity's sake to inform us of it in writing; and we, upon our honor, do promise him that by God's grace we shall give him satisfaction from the mouth of God, that is, from Holy Scripture, or else we shall alter whatever he can prove to be wrong.[1]

1. Preface to "The Scottish Confession of Faith," in *Reformed Confessions of the Sixteenth Century*, ed. Arthur C. Cochrane (Louisville: Westminster John Knox, 2003), 165.

Similarly, the Preface to the Augsburg Confession stated that "if the other electors, princes, and estates also submit written statements of their judgments and opinions, in Latin and German, we are prepared . . . to discuss with them and their associates, in so far as this can honorably be done, such practical and equitable ways as may restore unity."[2] The seventeenth-century Synod of Dort, convened to deal with a significant theological question facing the church in the Netherlands, did not address the matter in isolation from other churches. The Dutch church invited delegations from Reformed churches throughout Europe, seating them as full, voting participants in the deliberations of the Synod.

Reformation-era mutuality (including the mutuality of expressing doctrinal and ecclesiological differences) diminished over time as denominational exclusivity became the default mode of ecclesial existence. In the contemporary church, bishops and councils are still in place but their capacity to sustain common life among congregations has been diminished by managerial bureaucratization, overlapping denominational structures, and the widespread assumption that both denominations and their congregations should be self-directed and self-sufficient. How, then, can congregations live out the reality that they are the one, holy, catholic, apostolic church—but only in their essential relationship with other gathered congregations? How can denominations understand that they are not one, holy, catholic, apostolic in and of themselves but only as they are joined to others in patterns of mutual responsibility and accountability?

COMMUNION ECCLESIOLOGY

Many American Protestant denominations are fond of referring to themselves as a "connectional church." The term is unfortunate, for even at its best-intentioned, "connectional church" has an organizational, institutional ring, signifying interrelated management structures. Scant attention is given to a more appropriate, biblical term for the church: *koinōnia*—communion. Even when the term is used, it rarely refers to congregations and their relationship to other congregations, indicating instead institutional affiliations within denominational families, such as the Anglican Communion or the World Communion of Reformed Churches.

---

2. Preface to "The Augsburg Confession," in *Creeds of the Churches*, ed. John H. Leith (Louisville: John Knox Press, 1982), 65.

Communion language does occur regularly in Catholic and ecumenical ecclesiology, however; both have given significant attention in recent decades to the church as communion. The Second Vatican Council's profound and lasting impact is felt not least in its initiation of sustained reflection on the church as communion. Although Vatican II did not articulate a fully developed understanding of the church as communion, it engendered a broad discussion of communion that has continued into the present. Lorelei Fuchs has shown that in the Council's major documents on the church—*Lumen gentium* and *Gaudium et spes*—and its decree on ecumenism—*Unitatis redintegratio*—"Church as communion is the budding ecclesiological idea guiding the council."[3]

Since Vatican II, the bud has come to flower in official Catholic Church documents and the ongoing work of Catholic theologians. J.-M. R. Tillard's *Church of Churches: The Ecclesiology of Communion* sets out a comprehensive understanding of the church as "the *communion of communions*, appearing as a *communion* of local Churches, spread throughout the world, each one being a *communion* of the baptized, gathered together into communities by the Holy Spirit, on the basis of their baptism, for the eucharistic celebration."[4] Cardinal Ratzinger also explored the matter in books and essays, stressing throughout that communion has "a theological and Christological character, one associated with the history of salvation" as well as with ecclesiology.[5]

There is a loose sense in which *koinōnia*/communion has always been central to the modern ecumenical movement. At its inception in 1948, the World Council of Churches (WCC) adopted language from the 1910 World Missionary Conference in Edinburgh, identifying itself as "a fellowship of churches." As the WCC developed, its conventional use of "fellowship" matured through biblical and theological consideration of *koinōnia* and its implications for ecumenical ecclesiology. The Council's efforts culminated in 1991 with the Canberra Assembly's adoption of "The Unity of the Church as Koinonia: Gift and Calling," a statement developed by the WCC Commission on Faith and Order. The statement declares:

3. Lorelei F. Fuchs, *Koinonia and the Quest for an Ecumenical Ecclesiology* (Grand Rapids: Eerdmans, 2008), 115.

4. J.-M. R. Tillard, *Church of Churches: The Ecclesiology of Communion* (Collegeville, MN: Liturgical Press, 1992), 29.

5. Joseph Cardinal Ratzinger, *Pilgrim Fellowship of Faith: The Church as Communion* (San Francisco: Ignatius Press, 2005), 131. See also Ratzinger, *Called to Communion: Understanding the Church Today* (San Francisco: Ignatius Press, 1996).

The unity of the church to which we are called is a koinonia given and expressed in the common confession of the apostolic faith; a common sacramental life entered by the one baptism and celebrated together in one Eucharistic fellowship; a common life in which members and ministries are mutually recognized and reconciled; and a common mission witnessing to the gospel of God's grace to all people and serving the whole of creation.[6]

Canberra's statement built upon past reflections of the church as communion, but it also set out an agenda for fulfilling *koinōnia*'s call to the churches. The Faith and Order Commission's 1993 World Conference in Santiago de Compostela, Spain, inaugurated a series of studies on communion, beginning with an appeal that urged "all churches to find ways to recognize in each other the apostolic faith."[7] Ecumenical work on *koinōnia* continues into the present, moving toward more specific challenges to the churches. The WCC's 2006 Assembly in Porto Alegre, Brazil, articulated implications of *koinōnia* for relationships among the churches:

> The relationship among churches is dynamically interactive. Each church is called to mutual giving and receiving of gifts and to *mutual accountability*. Each church must become aware of all that is provisional in its life and have the courage to acknowledge this to other churches. . . . The honest sharing of commonalities, divergences, and differences will help all churches to pursue the things that make for peace and build up the common life.[8]

Ecumenical reflection on *koinōnia* has focused primarily on meta-relationships among Catholic, Orthodox, Protestant, and Pentecostal churches. Throughout this reflection, the ecumenical call to unity has been paramount, tending to reduce *koinōnia*/communion to ecumenical shorthand for a way to conceive the desired goal of visible unity of the churches. Yet even when ecumenical "full communion" agreements among denominations—such as the Lutheran-Reformed "Formula of Agreement" and

---

6. "The Unity of the Church as Koinonia: Gift and Calling," in *The Ecumenical Movement: An Anthology of Key Texts and Voices*, ed. Michael Kinnamon and Brian E. Cope (Geneva: WCC Publications, 1997), 124.

7. Fuchs, *Koinonia*, 181.

8. World Council of Churches, "Called to Be the One Church," II.7, V.13, www.oikumene .org/resources/documents/assembly/2006-portoalegre.

the Lutheran-Episcopal "Called to Common Mission"—achieve improved denominational relationships, they fall far short of their purported aim of full communion.[9] *Koinōnia* cannot be limited to the search for church unity, nor should it be confined to denominational agreements. Moreover, its ecumenical use has had the unintended consequence of shaping *koinōnia*/communion into a verbal receptacle that is filled with a wide variety of notions and preferences. Commenting on the Catholic reception of communion, Cardinal Ratzinger noted that "no term is ever safe from misunderstanding. In the same measure as 'communion' became the current buzzword, its meaning was distorted and rendered superficial."[10]

The Word *Koinōnia*

Koinōnia is best protected from distortion and superficiality by carefully attending to the ways the term is used in the New Testament. Only then can the depth of its association with the church be appreciated, and only then can its full significance for understanding the church in our time be assessed. *Koinōnia* occurs with moderate frequency in the New Testament, variously rendered in English translations as *communion, fellowship, participation, partnership, sharing, contribution,* and *taking part.* The variety of translations suggests the richness of the term—no one English word can capture its range of meanings—yet readers who are confined to translations of the New Testament are unaware that one Greek word underlies disparate English vocabulary. This, in turn, prevents readers from noticing scriptural relationships among such seemingly dissimilar matters as Trinity, sharing money, and reconciliation. In fact, what makes the one term so suggestive is the range of contexts in which it used.

There is a sense in which *koinōnia* is untranslatable, but English Bibles must provide readers with a rendering. In addition to the multiplicity of words and phrases, translation difficulty may be illustrated by the ways the Revised Standard Version (RSV) and New Revised Standard Version (NRSV) render the apostolic benediction of 2 Corinthians 13:14—"The grace of the Lord Jesus Christ, the love of God, and the *koinōnia* of the Holy Spirit be with you all." The RSV renders *koinōnia* as *fellowship*, but

---

9. See Joseph D. Small, "What Is Communion and When Is It Full?" *Ecclesiology* 2, no. 1 (2005).

10. Ratzinger, *Pilgrim Fellowship of Faith*, 132.

with a note indicating "or *participation in.*" The NRSV has *communion*, with a note, "or *sharing in.*" While fellowship, participation, communion, and sharing are all possible renderings of *koinōnia*, they are not synonyms. The difficulty in capturing *koinōnia* with one English equivalent has led to the suggestion that it not be translated at all but simply transliterated wherever the Greek term occurs in the New Testament. However, beyond the problem of what to do with other words in the *koinōn-* family, this proposed solution carries with it the danger of reducing the breadth and depth of *koinōnia* to a blank slate that can be filled in by whatever readers bring to it.

Choices must be made, although they should not be made in abstraction from the ways that *koinōnia* and other *koinōn-* words are employed in Scripture. The full range of biblical contexts can be recognized and related to one another, however, enabling readers to appreciate scriptural usage. A small sample of New Testament usage will display the various yet coherent ways that *koinōnia* expresses qualitative dimensions of church that are suggestive for the life of contemporary Christian congregations and denominations.

Communion with God

Foundationally, *koinōnia* is used as a means of expressing the deep communion of believers with the triune God, a communion that reveals the very being of the one God—Father, Son, and Holy Spirit. Among such texts are:

> The grace of the Lord Jesus Christ, the love of God, and the *koinōnia* of the Holy Spirit be with all of you (2 Cor 13:13).

> God is faithful; by him you [plural] were called into the *koinōnia* of his Son, Jesus Christ our Lord (1 Cor 1:9).

> For all of you *synkoinōnous* [commune together] in God's grace with me (Phil 1:7). . . . If then there is any encouragement in Christ, any consolation from love, any *koinōnia* in the Spirit (Phil 2:1). . . . I want to know Christ and the power of his resurrection and the *koinōnia* of his sufferings. (Phil 3:10)

The texts portray human *koinōnia* with the triune God. God overcomes divine-human estrangement, creating deep, intimate, abiding communion between himself and a human community in acts of sovereign grace. God is God, and the community of faith is human; the essential asymmetry remains even while essential distance is overcome. The Creator graciously establishes *koinōnia* with human creatures, a relationship of such intimate depth that it embraces *koinōnia* in flesh and blood, suffering and sacrifice, life and death, new life in the Spirit's gifts. Of the possible English words used to translate *koinōnia*, only *communion* adequately conveys the intimate, enduring depth of relationship in the Spirit that comes from the love of God through the grace of Christ.

Koinōnia is a theological reality before it is an ecclesiological possibility; communion is a statement about God and God's way in the world before it is a statement about the church and its way in the world. Understanding communion and full communion relationships among churches begins with contemplating the mystery of divine-human *koinōnia*. Only then can understanding of communion's ecclesial and ecclesiastical implications be faithful to the apostolic witness and fruitful in the lives of the churches.

Communion among Believers

The communion of believers with God takes shape in a communion among believers that bears the marks of communion with Father, Son, and Holy Spirit.

> We declare to you what we have seen and heard so that you [plural] also may have *koinōnia* with us; and truly our *koinōnia* is with the Father and with his Son Jesus Christ. (1 John 1:3)
>
> The cup of blessing that we bless, is it not a *koinōnia* in the blood of Christ? The bread that we break, is it not a *koinōnia* in the body of Christ? Because there is one bread, we who are many are one body, for we all partake of the one bread. (1 Cor 10:16–17)
>
> I thank my God every time I remember you [plural], constantly praying with joy in every one of my prayers for all of you, because of your *koinōnia* in the gospel from the first day until now. (Phil 1:3–5)

Koinōnia's theological foundation is the basis of communion among the men and women who have been drawn into communion with the one God—Father, Son, and Holy Spirit. The *koinōnia* of the community of faith is not established by attractions and associations with one another. Human affinities and human efforts of whatever kind do not create *koinōnia*, for relationships within the community grow from our common *koinōnia* with God through Christ in the power of the Holy Spirit. Because God draws us into communion with himself, we are drawn into *koinōnia* with one another.

The texts display the depth of relationship that is our *koinōnia*. *Koinōnia* in Christ's body and blood is *koinōnia* in the ecclesial body, characterized by joyous faith, hope, and love. *Communion* conveys the character of the Christian community's intense, enduring relationships that emerge from the grace of the Lord Jesus Christ, the love of God, and the communion of the Holy Spirit.

It is not mere coincidence that *communion* is a word commonly used for the Eucharist, particularly for the sharing of bread and wine. St. John of Damascus sets out clearly the church's understanding of ecclesial communion that is grounded in eucharistic communion that is grounded, in turn, in the gracious communion generated by God through Christ in the Spirit.

> It [the Eucharist] is called *koinōnia* because through it we *koinōnein* in the divinity of Jesus. It is also called *koinōnia*, and truly is, because of our having *koinōnia* through it with Christ and partaking both of His flesh and His divinity, and because through it we have *koinōnia* with and are united to one another. For because we all eat one loaf we become one body and one blood of Christ and members of one another; we may be said to be embodied with Christ.[11]

Communion in the Truth of the Gospel

Communion within the community is even more than intimate and abiding relationships. *Koinōnia* encompasses shared fidelity to the truth about God and God's way in the world as well as shared fidelity to truthful living. The New Testament expresses this both positively and negatively: *koinōnia* in the truth and in truthful living also means that there is to be no *koinōnia* in falsehood, no *koinōnia* in immorality.

> This is the message we have heard from [Christ] and proclaim to you, that God is light and in him there is no darkness at all. If we say that we have

11. John of Damascus, "Orthodox Faith," IV.13, in *The Fathers of the Church*, vol. 37, trans. Frederick Chase, Jr. (Washington, DC: The Catholic University of America Press, 1958), 361.

koinōnia with [God] while we are walking in darkness, we lie and do not do what is true; but if we walk in the light as he himself is in the light, we have *koinōnia* with one another. (1 John 1:5–7)

When I remember you in my prayers, I always thank my God because I hear of your love for all the saints and your faith toward the Lord Jesus. I pray that the *koinōnia* of your faith may become effective when you perceive all the good that we may do for Christ. (Philem. 4–6)

Do not *synkoinōneite* [commune with/participate in] the unlawful works of darkness, but instead expose them. (Eph 5:11)

Koinōnia within the community is not characterized by indeterminate affections, indistinct convictions, or indifferent actions. The church's *koinōnia* is in the gospel, the good news of the Father's sending of the Son in the power of the Spirit, and so the church is called to live its *koinōnia* in fidelity to *this* way, *this* truth, *this* life. Our communion in the truth is not only communion in faithful belief, although it certainly includes integrity of shared Christian conviction. *Koinōnia* in truth is also *koinōnia* in truthful living characterized by peace, light, love, forbearance, and doing good. *Koinōnia* in the truth of the gospel within the church entails deep, intimate, abiding mutuality in the truth of the gospel. Communion in truth necessitates agreement, living in peace, and having the same mind. These characteristics of *koinōnia* enable the community to resist mistaken belief and misguided action.

Communion and Reconciliation

Communion expresses reconciled agreement between diverse forms of fidelity to the gospel and differing forms of communal life. It also expresses reconciliation of sinners to the community.

And when James and Cephas and John, who were acknowledged pillars, recognized the grace that had been given to me, they gave to Barnabas and me the right hand of *koinōnia*, agreeing that we should go to the Gentiles and they to the circumcised. (Gal 2:9)

If then there is any encouragement in Christ, any consolation from love, any *koinōnia* in the Spirit, any compassion and sympathy, make my joy complete: be of the same mind, having the same love, being in full accord and of one mind. Do nothing from selfish ambition or conceit, but in humility regard others as better than yourselves. Let each of you look not to your own interests, but to the interests of others. Let the same mind be in you that was in Christ Jesus. (Phil 2:1–5)

My friends, if anyone is caught in a transgression, you who have received the Spirit should restore such a one in a spirit of gentleness. Take care that you yourselves are not tempted. Bear one another's burdens, and in this way you will fulfill the law of Christ. . . . Those who are taught the word must *koinōneitō* in all good things with their teacher. (Gal 6:1–2, 6)

Just as *koinōnia* expresses the good news that God has reconciled us to himself in Christ, establishing communion with us, so also *koinōnia* expresses the ministry of reconciliation that is central to the life of the community, establishing communion among us. The reconciliation that is a central feature of communion's actuality is not confined to dramatic instances of real or threatened division; it also encompasses the daily search for generosity of spirit, harmony, and love. In both cases, reconciliation within the community is not bourgeois tolerance or the simple confirmation of diversity. Reconciliation is generated by the *koinōnia* of the Spirit.

Communion in Resources

Communion among various local communities is characterized by mutual responsibility that finds expression in sharing resources.

For, as I can testify, they voluntarily gave according to their means, and even beyond their means, begging us earnestly for the privilege of *koinōnian* in this ministry to the saints—and this, not merely as we expected; they gave themselves first to the Lord and, by the will of God, to us. (2 Cor 8:3–4)

Through the testing of this ministry you glorify God by your obedience to the confession of the gospel and by the generosity of your *koinōnia* with them and with all others, while they long for you and pray for you because of the surpassing grace of God that he has given you. (2 Cor 9:13–14)

At present, however, I am going to Jerusalem in a ministry to the saints; for Macedonia and Achaia have been pleased to *koinōnian* their resources with the poor among the saints at Jerusalem. They were pleased to do this, and indeed they owe it to them; for if the gentiles have come to *ekoinōnēsan* their spiritual blessings, they ought also to be of service to them in material things. (Rom 15:25–27)

Communion is a reality among communities of faith as well as within them. Communion among churches goes far beyond thinking well of each other, or establishing diplomatic relationships, or even joining together in conciliar relationships. Deep patterns of mutual responsibility and accountability find material expression in the generous sharing of resources. Distributing money was the issue at hand in the early church, and it may be a mark of communion's actuality, but communion in material resources is only one tangible verification of genuine *koinōnia* in the communities' full resources of energy, intelligence, imagination, and love.

Sharing is too frail a word for the commonality of resources among churches. Even at its best, it implies charity between haves and have-nots rather than communion that has its origin in "the generous act of our Lord Jesus Christ, that though he was rich, yet for our sakes he became poor, so that by his poverty [we] might become rich" (2 Cor 8:9). *Communion* better expresses the quality of relationships that are to characterize the *koinōnia* among communities of faith, although these relationships are seldom characterized by consistently sharing material resources.

The Communion of the Holy Spirit

Koinōnia is the character, the gift, and the work of the Holy Spirit. As the church "receives the Holy Spirit" (John 20:22), it receives the gift of communion and is drawn into the Spirit's work of communion. The church's rule of faith, expressed in the Nicene and Apostles' Creeds, declares that the Holy Spirit, the Lord and Giver of life, gives life to the one, holy, catholic, apostolic church. Communion is the shape of that life, animating the church within itself and sending the church beyond itself in service to the world.

At the conclusion of the Council of Nicaea in 325, the "third article" of the creed said simply, "and the Holy Spirit." It was left to the Council of Constantinople, nearly sixty years later, to complete the task. The third articles of the Nicene-Constantinopolitan Creed and the later Apostles' Creed may give the impression of affirming a list of doctrinal leftovers, but the impression is mistaken. Like the articles on God the Father and God the Son, the third article is a coherent narrative of the being and work of God the Holy Spirit. The Holy Spirit is the giver of life to the church, moving over the waters of baptism and vivifying the communion of the saints as a forgiven and forgiving community. The Holy Spirit illuminates the Scriptures and leads the church in hope. The church is a communion because it is shaped in the *koinōnia* of the Holy Spirit.

The risen Christ breathed on his disciples, saying "Receive the Holy Spirit" (John 20:22). The Spirit imparted by the Lord is the Spirit of truth—the Spirit of *the* Truth, Christ himself—the Spirit who will guide the church into all truth about the Truth (John 14:16–17, 26; 16:13–15), the Spirit who empowers the church to bear faithful witness to the Truth of God's way in the world (John 15:26–27; 16:8–11). The Holy Spirit blows across the earth, gathering the church from near and far, drawing the peoples of the earth into the communication of communion (Acts 2:1–13). In breath and in wind, the Holy Spirit is the Lord, the giver of the communion.

Koinōnia is not the church's accomplishment, as if it were a strategy to be devised or a program to be carried out. Yet the Spirit's gift and work of *koinōnia* do not occur automatically. The church is called into the communion of the Holy Spirit, called to live that communion, and called to bear witness to that communion. The church is continuously called because the church is as likely to decline the gift as to receive it, as prone to live in separation as in communion, as disposed to hoard its gift as to share it. Ecclesiology must move beyond Scripture's depiction of *koinōnia* to open its reality in the life of the contemporary church.

ECCLESIAL COMMUNION

The small sample of *koinōnia* in the New Testament suggests the character and quality of relationships that are to characterize the life of the church. Even a limited survey displays an ecclesial *koinōnia* that is deep, intimate, and abiding—a *koinōnia* of the triune God with his people, a *koinōnia* among God's people, and a *koinōnia* among communities of God's people. Communion expresses ecclesial relationships that embody:

communion with the triune God
   communion in faith, hope, and love
      communion in sacraments
         communion in the truth of the gospel
      communion in faithful living
   communion in the reconciliation of differences
communion in patterns of mutual responsibility and accountability

Ecclesial communion is not a list of discrete items but life together formed by lived engagement in an interrelated whole. Communion in the truth of the gospel is false without communion in faithful living; communion in patterns of mutual responsibility and accountability is hollow when divorced from communion with the triune God; communion in reconciliation is illusory apart from communion in faith, hope, and love. The church can only live *koinōnia*'s richness holistically.

"We-ness"

The unified vision of *koinōnia* in the life of the church may be illustrated through its entrance into English by way of its Latin equivalent, *communio*. Oliver O'Donovan notes the ways in which English nouns render *communio* in everyday speech: "concrete 'community' on the one hand, dynamic 'communion' or 'communication' on the other." To communicate, to commune, says O'Donovan, "is to hold some thing as common, to make it a common possession, to treat it as 'ours' rather than 'yours' or 'mine.' The partners to a communication form a community, a 'we' in relation to the object in which they participate."[12]

"We-ness" is at the heart of *koinōnia*—overcoming distance, ending partition, ceasing detachment, dwelling in mutuality—all in faith, hope, and love of God through Christ in the Spirit. A similar point is made by Frances Fitzgerald in her analytical history of the American experience in Vietnam. "In the Vietnamese language there is no word that exactly corresponds to the Western personal pronoun *I, je, ich*. When a man speaks of himself, he calls himself 'your brother,' 'your nephew,' 'your teacher' depending upon his relationship with the person he addresses. . . . The Vietnamese did not see himself as a totally independent being . . . but rather as a system of relationships."[13]

It is "we-ness," spoken and enacted relationships within and among congregations, denominations, and global families of churches, that is *koinōnia*'s substance and aim. The congregation is a communion of persons born in the waters of baptism and nurtured at the eucharistic table. Each congregational communion of persons is called to ecclesial communion

---

12. Oliver O'Donovan, *The Ways of Judgment* (Grand Rapids: Eerdmans, 2005), 242.

13. Frances Fitzgerald, *Fire in the Lake: The Vietnamese and the Americans in Vietnam* (Boston: Little, Brown and Company, 1972), 23.

with other congregations in its locality. Local and regional communions are called to broader patterns of denominational communion that lead toward ecumenical communion in the church catholic. In every instance, genuine communion is more than a pattern of institutional arrangements, for *koinōnia*'s actuality is found in deep, intimate, abiding mutuality that has its source in the limitless grace of the Lord Jesus Christ, the overflowing love of God, and the all-embracing communion of the Holy Spirit.

But, of course, it is all too obvious that actual churches do not display the fullness of *koinōnia*. Congregations are always jumbles of equivocal faith, uncertain faithfulness, and hesitant relationships. Interactions among congregations are episodic, and too often marked by indifference or by subtle, sometimes shameless, competition. Distance among neighboring congregations is, in part, a function of their partition into separated denominations and associations. Detachment of denominations, even those of the same tradition, is often a consequence of their confinement within national borders. Perhaps all of this is unsurprising, for the New Testament itself presents *koinōnia* as a calling, a way of ecclesial existence that must be urged, rather than as an assumed state of affairs.

Denominations and Denominationalism

Separation, not communion, us-ness rather than we-ness, is the apparent character of churchly existence. Intra-denominational fractures and inter-denominational distance are visible features of church life in America. Over sixty years ago, Charles Clayton Morrison named the root issue with a bold economy of words: "A denomination is a part of the Church of Christ existing in a structure of its own and exercising by itself those functions which belong to the unity of the whole church of Christ."[14] Each separated denomination understands itself as living out the fullness of the triune God's love, grace, and communion. Moreover, each has shaped a structure that expresses its understanding of fullness. Therefore, communion with the other churches is seen as an option, not a mandate of the gospel. Even when the option is exercised in so-called "full communion" relationships, it depends upon negotiated agreements in which participating denominations maintain their cherished institutional independence

---

14. Charles Clayton Morrison, *The Unfinished Reformation* (New York: Harper & Brothers, 1953), 56.

and their distinct ways of exercising by themselves those functions that belong to the whole church.

H. Richard Niebuhr saw "denominationalism" as "an unacknowledged hypocrisy . . . a moral failure . . . evil." He was convinced that its sources lie, not in differences of doctrines and practices, but "in the failure of the churches to transcend the social conditions which fashion them into caste-organizations, to sublimate their loyalties to standards and institutions only remotely relevant if not contrary to the Christian ideal, to resist the temptation of making their own self-preservation and extension the primary object of their endeavor."[15] Niebuhr contended that these "social sources of denominationalism" are responsible for the history of schism in the church that, in his view, is nothing less than "a history of Christianity's defeat."[16]

And yet, denominations are a fact of ecclesial existence. No matter how deeply we may rue the fracturing of the church, we have lived within the reality of the great schism of East and West for a millennium, and within the rubble of the Western church's fragmentation for an additional half of that. Is it possible to provide an account of this reality that moves beyond historical-sociological description? Barry Ensign-George wishes to provide a theological understanding of denomination as an ecclesiological category. For Ensign-George, denominations are neither a manifestation of ecclesial hypocrisy, nor a moral failure, nor an evil. Instead, "denomination is potentially one of God's good gifts to the church . . . a form in which Christians can live out varying understandings of faith in Jesus Christ and of what that faith requires in terms of right belief and right practice."[17] In Ensign-George's view, the "varying understandings" of denominations are not simply historical or sociological diversities, but rather multiple patterns of faith and life generated by the richness of the gospel. Denominations provide persons and their congregations with the means to live out different forms of faithful Christian life.

Ensign-George acknowledges, however, that the current capacity of Protestant denominations to provide cohesive descriptions of what faith requires is not apparent. "Unable to provide a compelling account of their own existence to their members," he writes, "denominations find they have no meaningful internal coherence, and they are unable to resist centrifugal

15. H. Richard Niebuhr, *The Social Sources of Denominationalism* (New York: Living Age/ Meridian, 1960), 21.

16. Niebuhr, *Social Sources of Denominationalism*, 264.

17. Barry Ensign-George, "Denomination as an Ecclesiological Category," in *Denomination: Assessing an Ecclesiological Category*, ed. Paul M. Collins and Barry Ensign-George (London: Bloomsbury/T&T Clark, 2011), 3.

forces appearing within."[18] The seemingly inevitable result of these centrifugal forces is the spinning off of fragments that become . . . more denominations. The positive potential of denomination that Ensign-George articulates remains just that—potential, not realization.

The endless fracturing and multiplication of denominations bears witness to their internal incoherence. It also displays the tendency of varying understandings of what faith in Christ requires to devolve into disconnected institutional enclaves. The presenting ecclesiological problem with denominations is their propensity for structural isolation. To the extent that denominations retain a residual sense of their theological, moral, and missional *raison d'être*, they express a defining presumption of self-sufficiency. To the extent that they lack theological, moral, and missional coherence, they rely on structural systems to maintain organizational identity. The absence of deep and abiding communion *within* denominations is both effect and cause of the lack of genuine communion between and among denominations.

Ensign-George's theological account of denomination as a central ecclesiological category includes the observation that "Denomination is inherently 'interdependent' in that any given denomination depends on the existence of other denominations for the fullness of Christian life and witness to be embodied in the world."[19] Such interdependence is only conceptual, however. While an observer might appreciate the fullness of ordering church life in the diversity of episcopal, conciliar, and congregational systems, for instance, lived patterns of actual ecclesial interdependence, resulting in mutual recognition and reconciliation of various church orders, is rare. While an observer might appreciate the fullness of Eucharist in Free Church memory of Jesus's death and resurrection, Catholic insistence on the actuality of Christ's body and blood, and Orthodox foretaste of *theosis*, actual patterns of lived eucharistic practice among these traditions is virtually nonexistent. Denominations are only potential, theoretical models of relationship, interdependence, mutuality, we-ness, communion.

ECCLESIAL COMMUNION

There was a time when the ecumenical goal of the church's visible unity centered on the effort to bring about institutional consolidation. Ecu-

---

18. Ensign-George, "Denomination as an Ecclesiological Category," 3.
19. Ensign-George, "Denomination as an Ecclesiological Category," 6.

menism's goal of organizational oneness has now given way to the goal of ordered relationships among denominations, relationships that embrace diverse patterns of ecclesial life within patterns of mutual responsibility and accountability—communion. Ecumenism does not dream of a "super church," but rather hopes for deep communion among churches.

Denominational institutionalization dampens hope. Lacking theological coherence, denominations rationalize their existence by offering organizational competence in the delivery of religious goods and services. Yet self-justifying efforts run up against a cultural moment characterized by distrust of all institutions and little confidence in their capacity to reform themselves. Even so, Barry Ensign-George calls upon denominations to understand themselves theologically—not only historically and sociologically, and certainly not only organizationally—in order to develop compelling accounts of their existence to a watching world. How might this come about?

Communion ecclesiology is invariably expressed vertically and clerically. Congregations (themselves communions) are in communion with one another in a judicatory, although in practice this occurs through the communion of priests and ministers with one another through a bishop or regional council. The ostensible ministry of this communion of priests/bishop or pastors/council is to bind congregations together in faith and life. This ministry of oversight and unity is then furthered by communion among bishops and regional denominational structures. Communion ecclesiology is thus marked by ascending relationships of clergy—pastors, priests, and bishops—who exercise a ministry of *episcopé*. This essentially "episcopal" arrangement, whether expressed personally or corporately, is worked out differently in various ecclesial traditions, yet in most instances bonds of communion weaken as distance from the congregation increases.

Despite these weak bonds of communion, denominational distinctives in the exercise of *episcopé* are so fundamental to denominational self-understanding that they are regularly played out in ecumenical impasse. It is widely recognized that "these different attitudes toward the function of *episcopé* constitute one of the basic obstacles to Christian unity."[20]

---

20. Groupe des Dombes, "The Episcopal Ministry," in *For the Communion of the Churches: The Contribution of the Groupe des Dombes*, ed. Catherine E. Clifford (Grand Rapids: Eerdmans, 2010), 38.

Congregational Communion

Communion ecclesiology, whether episcopal or conciliar, invariably neglects possibilities of lived *koinōnia* among congregations. Missing from communion ecclesiology is horizontal communion that embodies the ministry of the whole people of God by urging forms of *koinōnia* among congregations and among local bishops and councils. Congregations alone are not sufficient forms of the church, yet lived relationships among congregations are thin, fragile, and sporadic. Interactions among congregations of the same denomination, as well as among neighboring congregations of different denominations, are generally limited to irregular relationships among some pastors and shared support of some local ministries. Most congregations live their ecclesial lives in comfortable isolation from other congregations.

Lived full communion among congregations is so exceptional and irregular that it seems difficult to imagine ways in which it might be established. Perhaps the most basic and faithful form of communion is so obvious that it is easily overlooked: disciplined congregational prayer for other congregations. Each Lord's Day, praying by name for other congregations in the same denomination and neighboring churches of other denominations, provides the foundation for building communion.

Growing from prayer, a further way forward comes from an unanticipated source—the 1952 World Conference of the World Council of Churches' Commission on Faith and Order in Lund, Sweden. The WCC seems remote to most Christians, while its Faith and Order Commission is generally unknown. However, a widely praised (although ignored in practice) statement emerged from the Lund Assembly that challenges customary patterns of congregational and denominational self-sufficiency. Lund's phrasing is cautious and somewhat convoluted, but it remains powerful.

> There are truths about the nature of God and His Church which will remain forever closed to us unless we act together in obedience to the unity which is already ours. We would, therefore, earnestly request our Churches to consider whether they are doing all they ought to do to manifest the oneness of the people of God. . . . Should not our Churches act together in all matters except those in which deep differences of conviction compel them to act separately? Should they not acknowledge the fact that they often allow themselves to be separated from each other by

secular forces and influences instead of witnessing together to the sole Lordship of Christ who gathers His people out of all nations, races, and tongues?[21]

The center of this excerpt has become known as "The Lund Principle"—"Should not our churches act together in all matters except those in which deep differences of conviction compel them to act separately?" The question was addressed to denominations and world communions, and has gone largely unanswered. It is at the level of congregations that Lund's question may have the best possibilities for affirmative response.

Put positively, we might say, "Christian *koinōnia* requires that neighboring congregations act together in all matters except those in which deep differences of conviction compel them to act separately." Given all that has been said about congregational competition, this may appear unlikely, but an admittedly weak basis exists in many places. Ministerial associations, mutual mission projects, cooperative community ministries, and limited covenants are not uncommon. Although these arrangements are rarely robust, they provide forums in which new, deeper, more comprehensive possibilities could be imagined, discussed, planned, and executed.

Possibilities for lived *koinōnia* among congregations range from mutually funded and regularly implemented community mission and ministry activities, through collaborative educational offerings, to regular occasions for prayer and worship. Lund's "all matters" can begin with "some matters," giving space for growth from "some" to "all." Smaller congregations may lead the way in establishing concrete forms of communion, for ministries and mission that are beyond the capability of one congregation are possible for two or more congregations acting together. While large congregations imagine that they are self-sufficient, small congregations' awareness that they are not self-sufficient could lead to a broader awareness that no congregation is or should attempt to be self-sufficient.

Few congregations, small or larger, will readily embrace the possibilities suggested in Lund. Yet congregations and their pastors cannot easily escape the question: shouldn't churches act together in all matters unless deep differences of theological and ecclesiological conviction compel them to act separately? If not, why not? What matters of deep conviction prevent acting together? Deep differences are most likely to arise regarding

21. Kinnamon and Cope, eds., *The Ecumenical Movement: An Anthology of Key Texts and Voices*, 462–63.

Word and sacrament, but taking Lund seriously suggests that even when deep conviction compels separation, the churches—both denominations and their congregations—are compelled to articulate those convictions in serious, sustained dialogue with others. In any event, beginning with differences is not the soundest starting point. On the other hand, neither is mutual action—however extensive—the desired ending point. Lived *koinōnia*, urged on the churches by the apostolic witness, is more than a matter of convenience or strategy. Remember the opening to Lund's questions: "There are truths about the nature of God and His Church which will remain forever closed to us unless we act together in obedience to the unity which is already ours." *Koinōnia* envisions a mutuality that is grounded in the gospel's truth about God and ourselves.

Reality and Possibility

The World Council of Churches' Canberra statement on the church as *koinōnia* is suggestive. Can we imagine relationships among congregations that embody "a koinonia given and expressed in the common confession of the apostolic faith; a common sacramental life entered by the one baptism and celebrated together in one eucharistic fellowship; a common life in which members and ministries are mutually recognized and reconciled; and a common mission witnessing to the gospel of God's grace to all people and serving the whole of creation?"[22] Theology and church law sometimes limit, but rarely prohibit such forms of inter-congregational communion. What may be difficult for us to imagine is, nevertheless, what the biblical witness urges:

> We declare to [one another] what was from the beginning, what we have heard, what we have seen with our eyes, what we have looked at and touched with our hands, concerning the word of life—this life was revealed, and we have seen it and testify to it, and declare to [one another] the eternal life that was with the Father and was revealed to us—we declare to [one another] what we have seen and heard so that [we] also may have *koinōnia* . . . ; and truly our *koinōnia* is with the Father and with his Son Jesus Christ. (1 John 1:1–3)

22. "The Unity of the Church as Koinonia: Gift and Calling," 124.

It would be naïve to think that such communion among congregations is a real and present possibility throughout the church. Currently, the real and present actuality throughout much of the church is a lack of vital and faithful forms of inter-congregational relationships. Rather than providing a measure of communion among churches, judicatories have taken on a life of their own that is distant from the lives of congregations and so are withering for lack of resources and commitment.[23] National denominational structures are experienced as regulatory agencies rather than contributors to congregational health and inter-judicatory communion and so are resented. In many denominations, the current pattern of vertical ecclesial relationships is only marginally operational. The consequence of our "connectional" breakdown is congregational hyper-autonomy accompanied by both formal and de facto departure from denominational structures.

If denominations and their judicatories are to recover a coherent sense of identity, it will not begin with mission statements and strategic plans developed at the top and regularly ignored by pastors and their congregations. Paul and other scriptural witnesses urged small gatherings of mid-first-century Christians to live the fullness of *koinōnia*. His urging is more than an ancient message addressed only to historical communities, however. The scriptural call to *koinōnia* comes now to local, regional, national, and global gatherings of Christians in congregations, judicatories, and denominations. Unlike most articulations of contemporary communion ecclesiology, the call is addressed first and foundationally to congregations, urging communion within their communal life and communion with other congregations. Full communion in the church can best be built from congregations upward.

The responsibility of the churches at all levels of ecclesial life is to hear the urgent call to *koinōnia*, expressed throughout Scripture, in all aspects of their lives. Communion in deep patterns of mutual responsibility and accountability is at the heart of the church's calling. For as the apostle says, "If then there is any encouragement in Christ, any consolation from love, *any* koinōnia *in the Spirit* . . ." (Phil 2:1).

---

23. For a discussion of how this plays out in one denomination, see Joseph D. Small, "The Travail of the Presbytery," in *A Collegial Bishop? Classis and Presbytery at Issue*, ed. Allan J. Janssen and Leon van den Broeke (Grand Rapids: Eerdmans, 2010).

THE BODY OF THE CHURCH

Koinōnia is not the church's accomplishment. There are many things the church does to weaken *koinōnia,* even to the point of its near absence, but there are many things the church could do to strengthen *koinōnia.* Even so, ecclesial communion is less a product of ecclesial effort than it is a gift of the church's Lord that can either be embraced or neglected. Appreciation of the church's dynamic, God-given character and of the possibilities that this presents for ecclesial communion may be enhanced by looking closely at scriptural ways of picturing the church's intimate relationship with the one God—Father, Son, and Holy Spirit. The following four chapters will explore aspects of the church's Christological, pneumatological, and theological reality.

Chapter 5

BODY LANGUAGE

. . . we, who are many, are one body in Christ, and individually we are members one of another.

Romans 12:5

At this point I departed from my text to say that an old pastor's anxiety for his church is likewise a forgetfulness of the fact that Christ is himself the pastor of His people and a faithful presence among them through all generations.

Marilynne Robinson, *Gilead*

Nearly two generations ago, Paul Minear published *Images of the Church in the New Testament*, a significant study that became influential beyond its stated purpose of achieving "a fuller comprehension of the many ways in which the New Testament writers thought and spoke about the church."[1] He identified thirty-two minor images of the church in the New Testament, ranging from "Ambassadors" to "Wine," and four major images: "People of God, New Creation, Fellowship in Faith, and Body of Christ." Minear cautioned that an effort to choose one image as the key to the others was futile because Scripture's pluriform witness required that all the images be thought of together, and that each image should be seen in context with the others. Minear maintained that "through all the analogies the New Testament writers were speaking of a single reality, a single realm

---

1. Paul S. Minear, *Images of the Church in the New Testament* (Philadelphia: Westminster, 1960), 11.

of activity, a single magnitude."[2] Yet, despite Minear's understanding, his book has contributed to the widespread belief that various images point to different, even divergent understandings of the church, encouraging the current tendency to favor one or another image as decisive for how the church should be understood.

A decade and a half after Paul Minear's survey of images, Avery Dulles published a more theological study, *Models of the Church.* He proposed five models, deduced from the writings of major ecclesiologists: Institution, Mystical Communion, Sacrament, Herald, and Servant. Like Minear, Dulles makes it clear that "a balanced theology of the Church must find a way of incorporating the major affirmations of each basic ecclesiological type. Each of these models calls attention to certain aspects of the Church that are less clearly brought out by the other models."[3] He goes on to note that "it should be scarcely necessary to point out that no good ecclesiologist is exclusively committed to a single model of the church."[4]

It is apparent, however, that both professional and amateur ecclesiologists are likely to favor some images and models over others. The image People of God currently enjoys ascendance over Body of Christ, while the model of Servant is far more popular than Sacrament or Mystical Communion. Lost in the preference for some at the expense of others is Minear's insight that all point to a single reality. Perhaps more important is the obvious point that Minear's images and Dulles's models are not intended as empirical descriptions, but rather as metaphors (an exceptionally complex trope) or as heuristic devices. To transform them into objective accounts, privileging some while dismissing others, is to miss the scriptural and theological point.

Nevertheless, it is important to give careful attention to a particular New Testament image for the church: *body of Christ.* It is important to deal with *body of Christ* because it is commonly used and even more commonly misunderstood, thus skewing the ways we think about the shape and life of the church. Moreover, exploring the way *body of Christ* is treated in the New Testament will open new perspectives on the action of the Holy Spirit in the life of the church, as well as prepare the way for later treatment of *people of God.*

2. Minear, *Images of the Church,* 222.
3. Avery Dulles, *Models of the Church* (Garden City, NY: Doubleday, 1974), 7.
4. Dulles, *Models of the Church,* 9.

YOU ARE THE BODY OF CHRIST

The *body of Christ* texts—1 Corinthians 12, Romans 12, Ephesians 1 and 4, and Colossians 1—have long been a principal source for understanding Christian community, with potential to provide new insight into the life of the contemporary church. Each text, in ways familiar to most Christians, presents the church as the body of Christ. Yet customary acquaintance with the New Testament's *body of Christ* language may diminish our capacity to understand it, much less to live it. Although familiarity does not breed contempt, it may generate indifference. *Body of Christ*, Scripture's shocking metaphor, has become a cliché.

"Human organizations are like the human body," is a modern truism. The comparison is embedded in everyday references to "the body politic," "a body of troops," and "legislative bodies," not to mention less obvious allusions such as "corporation" and "corporate life." Unfortunately, such conventional uses of the figure of speech—both organizations and bodies are composed of different yet interdependent parts—shape the way New Testament *body of Christ* texts are understood in the church. "Each of us has something to contribute to the whole church (so the story goes) and the church is incomplete without the diverse gifts of its members. The church cannot be whole without all of its members, and none of its members can go it alone." Whether in its congregational form (singers, organizers, educators, kitchen workers, preachers, and caregivers are all needed to make the church's life whole), or in its denominational form (liberals and conservatives, evangelists and social activists, bureaucrats and pastors, need each other in order to be complete), or in its ecumenical form (different ecclesial traditions have gifts to share that enrich the life of the church catholic), the comparison of the church to the body is a commonplace.

The standard way of understanding *body of Christ* transforms it into "body of church," with "Christ" as a mere modifier. The apparent point is the celebration of diversity, ensuring that the worth of each is recognized and that the incorporation of all is guaranteed. Correlation between an organization and the human body is not only a modern cliché it was already a platitude in the first century. The human organization as body was a well-known Hellenistic figure of speech used to describe the *polis*, the family, and other associations and institutions.[5] If Paul had done nothing

---

5. *Theological Dictionary of the New Testament*, vol. 7, ed. Gerhard Kittel and Gerhard

more than note that diverse persons in the church function together as a unified whole, just as eyes, ears, nose, and throat function together in the human body, readers of his letters might have dismissed his body language as a simple truism. Comparing any organization, even the church, to the human body was little more than first-century conventional wisdom. But Paul was not being trite.

THE BODY IS CHRIST'S

A close look at the *body of Christ* passages in 1 Corinthians, Romans, Ephesians, and Colossians quickly moves beyond conventional understandings. The texts do far more than compare the diverse organization, the church, to the one-yet-differentiated human organism, the body. Neither 1 Corinthians nor Romans nor Ephesians nor Colossians says simply that the church is *like* the body. Instead, they make the startling claim that the church *is* the body *of Christ*. It is as the body *of Christ* that the church is one, and it is as the body *of Christ* that the church's diversity is experienced.

> For just as the body is one and has many members, and all the members of the body, though many, are one body, *so it is with Christ*. . . . Now you are the body *of Christ*, and individually members of it. (1 Cor 12:12, 27)
>
> For as in one body we have many members, and not all the members have the same function, so we, who are many, are one body *in Christ*, and individually we are members one of another. (Rom 12:4–5)
>
> [God] has put all things under [Christ's] feet and has made him the head over all things for the church, which is *his body*, the fullness of him who fills all in all. (Eph 1:22–23)
>
> There is *one body* and one Spirit, just as you were called to the one hope of your calling, one Lord, one faith, one baptism, one God and Father of all, who is above all and through all and in all. . . . We must grow up in every way into *him who is the head*, into *Christ*, from whom the *whole body*, joined and knit together by every ligament with which it is equipped, as each part is working properly, promotes the body's growth in building itself up in love. (Eph 4:4–6, 15–16)

Friedrich (Grand Rapids: Eerdmans, 1971), 1038–39. see also J. A. T. Robinson, *The Body*, Studies in Biblical Theology, 5 (London: SCM, 1952), 59–60, note 1.

[Christ] himself is before all things, and in him all things hold together. *He is the head of the body*, the church; he is the beginning, the firstborn from the dead, so that he might come to have first place in everything. . . . I am now rejoicing in my sufferings for your sake, and in my flesh I am completing what is lacking in Christ's afflictions for the sake of *his body*, that is, the church. (Col 1:17–18, 24)

The jarring element in these texts is not that the church can be likened to the body but rather that the church-body is the body *of Christ*, the body *in Christ*, the body whose *head is Christ*! The church-body is not its own body, composed simply of its various members, but *Christ's* body. Conversely, Christ's body is not restricted to Christ alone, for *the church* is also the body of Christ! Clearly, Paul's language is not mere simile: "the church is like a body." Rather, it is a rich metaphor in which two disparate terms, church-body and Christ-body, are brought together in a way that discloses an altogether new reality. Church-body and Christ-body are each intelligible separately, but *church-body-of-Christ* goes far beyond ordinary usage, stretching language to the breaking point, creating a startling apprehension of an unexpected actuality.

If it is a mistake to understand the church as the body of Christ to be a mere comparison, it is also an error to take the language literally, as if the church is Christ's continuing presence in the world. J. A. T. Robinson's study of Paul's theology of the body claims that "Paul uses the analogy of the human body to elucidate his teaching that Christians form Christ's body. But the analogy holds because they are in literal fact the risen organism of Christ's body in all its concrete reality. . . . It is almost impossible to exaggerate the materialism and crudity of Paul's doctrine of the Church as literally now the resurrection *body* of Christ."[6] Taking "the church is the body of Christ" as a simple statement of literal fact does more than assert an implausible appraisal of the church. It also collapses the distinction between human and divine. To equate the continuing presence of the risen Christ to the all-too-human Christian community is to displace God's transcendence, identifying Christ with ourselves in our ecclesial existence. Robinson asserts that Christians form Christ's body; the texts proclaim that Christ forms Christian community.

The mistake of understanding *body of Christ* as a simile (the church can be compared to the human body) and the mistake of literal under-

---

6. Robinson, *The Body*, 51.

standing (the church is the earthly presence of the risen Christ) have the effect of pushing Christ to the sidelines. In both mistakes, the focus is on the church alone, either as sociologically available institution or as theologically available concept. In the former, Christ serves merely as an identifier of a particular organization called "church." In the latter, Christ is subsumed within an abstract theological conception of an immaterial church.

In Paul's discourse, *body of Christ* is metaphorical language. Metaphor is not a simple trope, an ornamental figure of speech used to embellish a subject—in this case "church." Metaphors are innovative uses of language that redefine reality. Paul Ricoeur calls metaphor "a calculated error. It consists of assimilating things which do not go together. But precisely by means of this calculated error, metaphor discloses a relationship of meaning hitherto unnoticed. . . . In short, metaphor says something new about reality."[7] Metaphors, like symbols, "give rise to thought." Church as the body of Christ brings together two distinct elements, not naturally associated, in a manner that engenders a new way of thinking, both about the church and about the presence of Christ.

At the most obvious level, the metaphor discloses that the church is not its own. Because the church is the body *of Christ* it is not self-generated or self-sustaining or self-directed. The church is not its own, for the church belongs to another, to Christ, precisely as Christ's body. As *Christ's* body, then, the church is not master of its own life, able to determine its own nature or purpose; the church belongs to Christ alone. But, of course, the church is continuously tempted to claim its life as its own. Congregations, denominations, and world communions seek to organize their lives around their own strategic plans, management structures, initiatives, and programs. The foundational sense of "the church is the body of Christ" is overlooked as churches regularly assert themselves as masters of their own present and future.

The church is not its own, and yet the bond of *church* and *body of Christ* is not a natural one, as if the church were the actual form of the risen Christ's earthly presence, or as if the church were installed in the ascended Christ's heavenly presence. The metaphor neither confines Christ within the church nor collapses the church into divinity. As the *body of Christ*, the church exists as a visible collection of ordinary people that, nevertheless,

---

7. Paul Ricoeur. "The Metaphorical Process," in *Semeia 4: An Experimental Journal for Biblical Criticism* (Missoula MT: Society of Biblical Literature, 1975), 79–80.

is the locus of the real presence of Christ and thus a collection of people who have a Master.

It is not coincidental that the other striking New Testament use of *body of Christ* also discloses Christ's real presence. "This [bread] is my body," says Jesus. Bread is Christ's body; church is Christ's body. Bread remains ordinary bread and church remains an ordinary collection of people, yet both bread and church are the locus of Christ's presence. "Jesus gives us in the Supper the real substance of his body and blood," says Calvin, "so that we may possess him fully, and, possessing him, have part in all his blessings."[8] Christ's real presence in eucharistic bread and wine nourishes the body of Christ, constituting and manifesting the real presence of Christ in the church.

THE BODY IS WOUNDED

As if this were not enough—*we* are the body *of Christ, we* are one body *in Christ, we* are the body whose *head is Christ*—the texts suggest that the church is Christ's *wounded* body, even Christ's *crucified* body. The suffering, executed, dead, and buried Jesus has been raised to new life, of course, but resurrection does not eradicate crucifixion. It is the crucified One who is raised, and the resurrected One is none other than the crucified. As the body *of Christ,* the church is not a glorified body, no matter how presumptuous and pretentious it may be. Because the church is the body of the crucified-risen Christ, the church lives with nail marks in its hands and a gash in its side (John 20:24–29), as a slaughtered lamb (Rev 5), and as the body whose hands and feet remain pierced (Luke 24:36–49). Peter writes, "Beloved, do not be surprised at the fiery ordeal that is taking place among you to test you, as though something strange were happening to you. But rejoice insofar as you are sharing Christ's sufferings" (1 Pet 4:12–13). Yet the church continues to be surprised and disappointed by anything short of success.

The church does not live in triumphant glory, although it often pretends to itself and others that it is a powerful, victorious force in the world. The pretense is impossible to maintain in too many places in the world where churches suffer deprivation, repression, or persecution. The church is

---

8. John Calvin, "Short Treatise on the Lord's Supper," in *Calvin: Theological Treatises,* ed. J. K. S. Reid (Philadelphia: Westminster, 1954), 148.

composed of ordinary men and women whose collective suffering is the church's suffering. The pretense of the triumphant church is even difficult to maintain among the rich and comfortable churches of North America. Pervasive secularization, religious diffusion, the interiorizing of spirituality, and the church's cultural disestablishment push the church to the edges of the public square and the margins of private life. Nostalgia and wishful thinking are ever present, however, shielding the churches from the realities of the current era. The New Testament *body of Christ* texts draw the church back to the cross as they proclaim the Lord's death until he comes. The church is made Christ's body through baptism into Christ's death, "for in the one Spirit we were all baptized into one body" (1 Cor 12:13). The church has been united with Christ in a death like his, and the fullness of resurrection is not yet its possession (Rom 6:5). The church's bodily existence in suffering is not an unfortunate necessity, but the God-given shape of its life as the *body of Christ*.

The pretense of a triumphant church also desensitizes the church to its self-inflicted wounds. Remember Calvin's lament: "This other thing also is to be ranked among the chief evils of our time, that the Churches are so divided, that human fellowship is scarcely now in any repute among us. . . . Thus it is that the members of the Church being severed, the body lies bleeding."[9] Paul's rhetorical question—"Has Christ been divided?"— is meant to be answered in the negative, yet the *body of Christ* has been divided and subdivided repeatedly. His question is more than rhetorical and the answer remains uncertain. From first-century Corinth through Christian communities spanning twenty centuries, the grotesque reality is that the suffering body of Christ is lacerated and torn by the very disciples of Christ.

Douglas John Hall's recovery of Luther's *theologia crucis*—theology of the cross—has its necessary counterpart in *ecclesia crucis*.[10] Luther's theological theses in the Heidelberg Disputation include propositions about persons that, with a minor adjustment, refer equally to the church:

- *The church* that believes it can obtain grace by doing what is in it adds to sin so that it becomes doubly guilty.

9. John Calvin, "Letter to Cranmer" (1552), in *Selected Works of John Calvin: Tracts and Letters*, ed. Henry Beveridge and Jules Bonnet (Carlisle, PA: Banner of Truth Trust, 2009), 5:347–48.

10. See Douglas John Hall, *Lighten Our Darkness: Towards an Indigenous Theology of the Cross* (Philadelphia: Westminster, 1976).

- It is certain that *the church* must utterly despair of its own ability before it is prepared to receive the grace of Christ.
- It does not deserve to be called *a church* that looks upon the invisible things of God as though they were clearly perceptible in those things which have actually happened.
- It deserves to be called *a church*, however, that comprehends the visible and manifest things of God seen through suffering and the cross.
- A *church* of glory calls evil good and good evil. A *church* of the cross calls the thing what it actually is.[11]

As the body of Christ, the church's life is not lived in power and glory but amid uncertainty, danger, and suffering. The church's place in the world is marked less by metrics to gauge effectiveness than by union with Christ in his suffering. The author of Hebrews puts the matter graphically: "Therefore Jesus also suffered outside the city gate in order to sanctify the people by his own blood. Let us then go to him outside the camp and bear the abuse he endured" (Heb 13:12–13).

THE BODY OF THE ONE CHRIST

In contemporary North American churches, *body of Christ* texts are employed to celebrate diversity, calling for recognition, approval, and inclusion of the rich variety of persons and groups in the church. But while it is generally assumed that the *body of Christ* texts promote diversity, Paul does not use the metaphor to celebrate or mandate multiplicity. Rather, he uses it when God-given diversity leads to disagreement that breeds antagonism that results in estrangement. Because Christ's body should not be marked by discord, hostility, and separation, Paul employs *body of Christ* to urge *unity*.

The opening of 1 Corinthians is typical: "Now I appeal to you, brothers and sisters, by the name of our Lord Jesus Christ, that all of you be in agreement and that there be no divisions among you, but that you be united in the same mind and the same purpose" (1 Cor 1:10). Paul appeals for agreement and an end to divisions precisely because unity is noticeably absent. In the contemporary church, vague unity is assumed while palpa-

11. Martin Luther, "Heidelberg Disputation" [altered], in *Martin Luther's Basic Theological Writings,* ed. Timothy F. Lull, 2nd ed. (Minneapolis: Fortress, 2005), 49.

ble diversity is promoted, even mandated. In the first-century church, both natural and God-given diversity are assumed while unity must be urged and striven for. But the unity that Paul consistently exhorts is a unity *of* diverse members, not a unity imposed *upon* diverse members. "For as in one body we have many members, and not all the members have the same function, so we, who are many, are one body in Christ, and individually we are members one of another. We have gifts that differ according to the grace given to us" (Rom 12:4–6).

Body of Christ is used throughout the New Testament at points of conflict and division. First Corinthians is laced with recognition of dissensions, quarreling, factionalism, and strife. The conflict within the community demonstrates dramatically that members of the body of Christ have a common need for diverse gifts. Recognition of this reality leads to "care for one another" (1 Cor 12:25) in the "more excellent way" (1 Cor 12:21) that "does not insist on its own way" (1 Cor 13:5). The split between Jewish Christians and gentile Christians in Rome leads Paul to use *body of Christ* again, bracketed by admonitions that no one should "think of himself more highly than he ought to think" (Rom 12:3) and exhortations to "love one another with brotherly affection" (Rom 12:10) and to "live peaceably with all" (Rom 12:18). Even the stately letter to the Ephesians acknowledges the continuing division of Jews and gentiles, coupling "one body" with the plea to live "forbearing one another in love . . . maintaining the unity of the Spirit in the bond of peace" (4:2–3). In Colossians, the link between Christ's suffering and the church's suffering is explicit: "I am now rejoicing in my sufferings for your sake, and in my flesh I am completing what is lacking in Christ's afflictions for the sake of his body, that is, the church" (Col 1:24).

The church is a fully human community, but it is not merely a human community with the brand name "Christian." Christ is so present in this body that the body is no longer its own, but Christ's. This reality is neither natural nor comfortable, however, so the church must be urged to live its unity in Christ. Ephesians 4 begins with striking urgency: "I *beg* you to lead a life worthy of the calling to which you have been called . . . *forbearing* one another in love, eager to *maintain* the unity of the Spirit in the bond of peace." The unity of the Spirit is the overarching *telos* of the body that matures through the appropriate exercise of diverse gifts. At every level of the church's life—congregations, judicatories, denominations, world communions—the body that is Christ's is called to be one.

GIFT AND CALLING

The church is called to live as the unified *body of Christ* in the harmonious interplay of its indispensable parts precisely because that is *not* the way it lives. Far from a hackneyed convention to be trotted out in celebration of the church's unity or its multiplicity, *body of Christ* is a disturbing rebuke to the church's self-inflicted wounds of division. Church division is not only the reality of separated Orthodox-Catholic-Protestant-Pentecostal Churches. It is also the reality of conservative-liberal, traditional-reformist, and evangelical-progressive factional divisions within the separated churches. It is also the existence of racial, ethnic, class, and national partitions in denominations and their congregations. It is also the dissection of the body by gender, age, and a host of other human characteristics. If the *body of Christ* texts are to be rescued from banality, the church must feel their rebuke before receiving the new possibilities they present.

The unity of the church is never our achievement. The church's unity is both gift and calling, but the call proceeds from the gift. The church cannot create, legislate, or command unity, for the unity of the body of Christ is Spirit-given. The texts are clear that our embodiment in Christ is a given: "We, who are many, *are* one body in Christ" (Rom 12:5); "now you *are* the body of Christ" (1 Cor 12:27); "There *is* one body and one Spirit" (Eph 4:4). The church is not burdened with self-devised striving for its own achievement of equilibrium or uniformity, for the church's unity is a gift of its Lord. Yet the church regularly squanders its inheritance and buries its gift, so the Spirit's gift it is also the church's calling. "If then there is any encouragement in Christ," says Paul, "any consolation from love, any sharing in the Spirit, any compassion and sympathy, make my joy complete: be of the same mind, having the same love, being in full accord and of one mind" (Phil 2:1–2).

The diversity of the church is never our achievement. The diversity of the *body of Christ* is not an ecclesial capability, for the church is more than a mosaic of natural human variety. The diversity of *Christ's body* grows from "manifestations of the Spirit" (1 Cor 12:7); it is not limited to an assortment of abilities or demographic constituencies. The church's diversity flourishes from the overflowing generosity of the Spirit's variety of gifts. "We have gifts that differ according to the grace given to us" (Rom 12:6); "Now there are varieties of gifts, but the same Spirit; and there are varieties of services, but the same Lord; and there are varieties of activities, but it is the same God who activates all of them in everyone" (1 Cor 12:4–6);

"But each of us was given grace according to the measure of Christ's gift" (Eph 4:7). The church is not called to manufacture, legislate, or brandish diversity, imagining that it is an ecclesial achievement rather than the gift of the Holy Spirit. The church may idolize its gifts or isolate its endowments, but the fundamental ecclesial reality is the richly gifted multiplicity of the one *body of Christ*. Yet the church regularly mistakes the Spirit's gifts for human attainments, confuses variety with classifications, and lives comfortably with reductions in the richness of the Spirit's *charismata*. Thus, the Spirit's gifts are also the Spirit's calling. "We have gifts that differ according to the grace given to us," says Paul, and we are to use them (Rom 12:6–8).

A striking feature of *body of Christ* texts is that unity and diversity are not seen as alternatives but as intimately related, mutually indispensable aspects of an organic whole. The unity of the church cannot be conceived apart from the variety of gifts that flourish within the whole, and diversity within the church makes no sense apart from the life-giving unity of the whole. The unity of the *body of Christ* is comprised of the variety of gifts, and the variety of gifts compose the whole. Apart from diversity, the church's unity quickly degenerates into uniformity. Apart from unity, the church's diversity quickly fragments in disarray. Celebrants of diversity may be right to fear oppressive orthodoxy, for it is a danger to the freedom that grows from the Holy Spirit's gifts. What may be less apparent is that attempts to achieve rigorous uniformity are a clear and present threat to unity as well. Without variety, the church will cease to be a living body, much less the body of Christ. On the other hand, champions of unity are quite right to fear promiscuous pluralism, for it is a danger to the harmony that grows from wholeness. Again, what may be less apparent is that indiscriminate variation is destructive of diversity as well. Without unity or without diversity the church will cease to be a body at all, surely not the *body of Christ*.

CREATION OF THE SPIRIT

Because the church is not *a* body, but *Christ's* body, the community of Christ's people derives its bodily identity from Christ. Because "the way one thinks about Christ is the way one thinks about the church," neither Christology nor ecclesiology can be detached from pneumatology.[12]

---

12. Jurgen Moltmann, *The Church in the Power of the Spirit: A Contribution to Messianic Ecclesiology* (Minneapolis: Fortress Press, 1993), 66.

Throughout the New Testament, the identity of Jesus is intimately linked to the generative action of the Holy Spirit. And just as Christ was conceived by the Holy Spirit, so the church's bodily identity is engendered by the Holy Spirit. The church is not merely a historical-sociological phenomenon or an idealized theological construct but is, like Christ, a Spirit-conceived, Spirit-anointed, Spirit-sent, Spirit-breathing, Spirit-enlivened body. Moltmann's formulation can be supplemented by Reinhard Hütter's dictum concerning the relationship between the Holy Spirit and the church: "pneumatology without ecclesiology is empty, ecclesiology without pneumatology is blind."[13] Without the church, the Spirit can be confined to individual interiority, and without the Spirit, the church is reduced to making its own way in the dark.

Incarnation

The angel Gabriel appeared to Mary, announcing, "The Holy Spirit will come upon you, and the power of the Most High will overshadow you; therefore the child to be born will be holy; he will be called Son of God" (Luke 1:35). As the child conceived in Mary's womb was from the Holy Spirit, so the church is generated by the Spirit. As the Holy Spirit came upon Mary and the child to be born was holy, so the Holy Spirit filled disciples at Pentecost and a communion of *hagioi* (holy ones/saints) was formed. The Holy Spirit generated the nascent church's composition and mission by empowering God's mighty deeds in Christ to be proclaimed to people from across the world in language that all could understand. The body of Jesus Christ was conceived by the Holy Spirit; the church as the *body of Christ* is conceived by the Holy Spirit.

Although the *body of Christ* is Spirit-conceived, the church continues to be "amazed and perplexed, saying to one another, 'What does this mean?'" (Acts 2:12). Protestants seem to have ceded the Holy Spirit to Pentecostals and charismatics, reducing "the Spirit" to a surd that is employed to validate church decisions, animate appealing forms of worship, or inspire a vast range of spiritualities. In the meantime, Pentecostalism itself is largely ignored or treated as an aberration. Contemporary Pentecost celebrations of "the birthday of the church" lack an embodied sense that the Holy Spirit,

---

13. Reinhard Hütter, *Suffering Divine Things: Theology as Church Practice* (Grand Rapids: Eerdmans, 2000), 127.

"the giver of life," continues to animate the *body of Christ*, providing the breath without which it suffocates. The Holy Spirit continues to enliven the church with gifts that produce the fruit of love, joy, peace, patience, kindness, goodness, faithfulness, and self-control. Yet Christ's call to the church to "receive the Holy Spirit" awaits the church's response: "If we live by the Spirit, let us also walk by the Spirit" (Gal 5:25).

Baptism

The child who was conceived by the Holy Spirit and born of the Virgin Mary grew to be a man who traveled to the River Jordan to be baptized by John. "And just as he was coming up out of the water, he saw the heavens torn apart and the Spirit descending like a dove on him. And a voice came from heaven, 'You are my Son, the Beloved; with you I am well pleased'" (Mark 1:10). John the Baptizer said of Jesus, "I have baptized you with water, but he will baptize you with the Holy Spirit" (Matt 3:11). Anointed by the Spirit, the embodied risen Christ baptized the church, *his body*, with the Holy Spirit: "[Jesus] breathed on them and said to them, 'Receive the Holy Spirit'" (John 20:22). The risen Christ then proclaimed to his disciples, "John baptized with water, but you will be baptized with the Holy Spirit" (Acts 1:5), and thus, at Pentecost, the Spirit was "poured upon all flesh" (Acts 2:17).

Baptism continues to form the *body of Christ*. Most denominations and world communions acknowledge that persons are baptized "into Christ" and therefore into the holy, catholic church, not into the narrow confines of a particular denomination or congregation. Baptismal practice in too many congregations shrinks the sacrament into a local celebration, however. This reduction minimizes the catholicity of baptism, not only by ecclesiastical contraction, but also by an absence of broad human multiplicity. Practical confinement of baptism is further restricted by its seclusion within too many congregations that are racial, ethnic, and class enclaves. Paul announced the church's baptismal identity: "in the one Spirit we were all baptized into one body—Jews or Greeks, slave or free—and we were all made to drink of one Spirit" (1 Cor 12:13). *One* Spirit . . . *one* body . . . *all* of us . . . *one* Spirit. In 1 Corinthians Paul specifies *all* by reference to ethnic and economic inclusion, just as in Galatians he specifies baptismal inclusion in terms of gender as well as ethnicity and economic status (Gal 3:27–29). The church's enduring failure to fulfill baptismal catholicity is due, in large measure, to understanding baptism as something *it* does, rather than as an act of the Holy Spirit.

Temptation

Immediately after the Holy Spirit anointed Jesus in baptism the Spirit drove Jesus into a wilderness of temptation. Jesus fasted for forty days and forty nights, and at the end of this ordeal, he was hungry, tired, and weak. At Jesus's baptism, the voice from heaven had announced, "This is my Son, the Beloved, with whom I am well pleased." In the wilderness, the seducing voice of temptation began, "*If* you are the Son of God . . ." The doubt-provoking, suggestive *if* hangs over all three temptations: *if* you are the Son of God command these stones to become loaves of bread; *if* you are the Son of God throw yourself down from the pinnacle of the temple, for angels will bear you up; I will give you all the kingdoms of the world *if* you will worship me. Jesus countered the Tempter's *if* with the certainty of God's word. "Then the devil left him."

The church prays, "lead us not into temptation," but temptation always comes to the *body of Christ* most seductively when the church finds itself in the wilderness. Not that long ago the church in America was respected by all and admired by many, but its ongoing cultural disestablishment has left it susceptible to the tempting fantasy of return to the imagined glory of days gone by. *If* we are the church, let us feed people with whatever they hunger for, and then they will approve of us . . . *if* we are the church, let us dazzle people with entertainments, for then they will be attracted to us . . . *if* we are the church, let us do whatever it takes to bring people back—to *us*. Jesus's response to his wilderness temptation was to return to Galilee where he proclaimed *God's* good news, "The time is fulfilled, and the kingdom of God is at hand; repent, and believe the gospel" (Mark 1:15). As the body of Christ, the church is called to proclaim, not itself, but to announce the gospel to itself and to the world: "God's time is flowing into this time, and God's new Way in the world is touching 'the way things are'; turn around, walk in the direction of God's Way. Believe that this news is good, trust it, and remain steadfast in it" (Mark 1:15, author's paraphrase).

Ministry

Jesus emerged from wilderness temptation to proclaim the reign of God, fulfilling in himself the prophecy, "The Spirit of the Lord is upon me, because he has anointed me to bring good news to the poor. He has sent me to proclaim release to the captives and recovery of sight to the blind, to let the oppressed go free, to proclaim the year of the Lord's favor" (Luke 4:18–19). And so he did, from Galilee to Jerusalem. As word spread, John the Baptizer needed confirmation of his initial assessment, so he sent some of his disciples to ask Jesus, "Are you the one who is to come, or are we to wait for another?" Jesus answered, "Go and tell John what you have seen and heard: the blind receive their sight, the lame walk, the lepers are cleansed, the deaf hear, the dead are raised, the poor have good news brought to them" (Luke 7:22). Matthew testified that Jesus was the fulfillment of God's words given through Isaiah: "Here is my servant . . . I will put my Spirit upon him, and he shall proclaim justice to the Gentiles" (Matt 12:18). What Jesus said was as dramatic as what he did. He proclaimed a righteousness that was at odds with conventional Jewish wisdom, and he proclaimed it for gentiles as well as Jews.

If the church is asked if it is what people have been waiting for, or if they should look elsewhere, what can the church say? Do people hear the church, the body of Christ, proclaim *God's* justice? Do people see the church living out God's unexpected transformation of the way things are? The body of Christ, upon whom the Holy Spirit has been poured out, is called to bring the good news of God's new way in the world to those who are poor in spirit and to those who are just poor, to those who mourn and to those who weep, to those who hunger and thirst for righteousness and to those who are simply hungry (Matt 5 and Luke 6). Obedience to the call is unlikely to be rewarded by regained cultural approval, but the body of Christ is promised that even when it is excluded, reviled, and cast out on Christ's account, its reward will be found in God's presence.

Churches in America are more likely to talk about their programs, facilities, and friendly welcome than about God's justice in the world. Churches may be more concerned with good news for themselves and their members than with *God's* good news for people who are poor, for prisoners, for all who suffer, for outcasts. The church's proclamation may feature encouragement for insiders rather than reconciliation for outsiders, and its action may focus on programs for members rather than justice for those on the margins of society's norms. Christ's announcement in the synagogue and his response to John's inquiry are not mere historical accounts of Jesus's ministry; they call the body of Christ to its ministry as well.

Cross

The New Testament Gospels present themselves as Passion narratives with extended introductions. From the entrance into Jerusalem to the agony of the cross, Jesus's last days are narrated as the climax and the meaning of all that went before. What had seemed to disciples as unspeakable tragedy came to be understood as fulfillment of Israel's hope and the heart of the gospel itself. The Gospels of Matthew, Luke, and John conclude their accounts of Jesus's death on the cross with matter-of-fact statements that may carry a double meaning: "Then Jesus . . . let go the spirit [*aphēken to pneuma*]" (Matt 27:50); "Father, into your hands I give over/entrust my spirit [*paratithemai to pneuma mou*]" (Luke 23:46); "he bowed his head and handed over the spirit [*paredōken to pneuma*]" (John 19:30). These texts are generally taken to mean simply that Jesus died (thus the NRSV rendering of Matthew as "and breathed his last"), but some commentators note the possibility that in these texts *to pneuma* may not refer simply to Jesus's human spirit/breath, but to the Holy Spirit.[14] Thus, "Jesus let go the Spirit . . . into your hands I give over the Spirit . . . he handed over the Spirit." Perhaps it is not necessary to choose one or the other possibility. The ambiguity of *pneuma*—spirit, breath, wind— may indicate why the evangelists described Jesus's death with this particular idiom, indicating both the end of Jesus's life and the end of the Holy Spirit's presence in his earthly life. At any rate, the Spirit was as present at the end as at the beginning. The writer of Hebrews knew the crucified Jesus as the high priest who entered the Holy of Holies by his own sacrifice, offering himself on the cross "through the eternal Spirit" (Heb 9:14).

Martin Luther's catalogue of the seven marks of the church concludes with ecclesial cross-bearing: "the holy Christian people are externally recognized by the holy possession of the sacred cross . . . in order to become like their head, Christ." Luther bases his brief comments on the conclusion to the Beatitudes in the Sermon on the Mount: "And the only reason [the Christian people] must suffer is that they steadfastly adhere to Christ and God's word, enduring this for the sake of Christ."[15] The Gospels locate cross-bearing at a different point, directly following Peter's confession and Jesus's announcement that he must suffer and die. With minor adjustments, his words to the crowd as well as to the disciples are his call to the church now: "If any *church* wants to become my follower, let *it* deny *itself* and take up *its* cross and follow me. For the *church* that wants to save *its* life will lose it, and the *church* that loses *its* life for my sake, and for the sake of the gospel, will save it" (Mark 8:34–35, altered).

14. Cf. C. K. Barrett, *The Gospel According to St. John* (London: SPCK, 1962), 460.

15. Martin Luther, "On the Councils and the Church," in *Martin Luther's Basic Theological Writings*, ed. Timothy F. Lull, 375.

The church is called to take up its cross and follow the crucified and risen Christ. Yet the church, like the young Peter, is accustomed to fastening its own belt and going wherever it wishes rather than being taken where it does not want to go, to the cross (cf. John 21:18). The church is called by its Lord to abandon churchly efforts to ensure its standing in the eyes of the world, and to "steadfastly adhere to Christ and God's word." The church takes up its cross by acting, not by being acted upon. Yet Luther is also right in saying that when it takes up its cross the church should be prepared to be reviled and even persecuted. American churches have experienced centuries of comfort in a hospitable land. It may be, however, that the cultural movement away from the church is a harbinger of hard times to come, when cross-bearing will be imposed rather than chosen.

Resurrection

Death was not the end. Jesus Christ was "declared to be Son of God with power according to the Spirit of holiness by resurrection from the dead" (Rom 1:4). The risen Christ commissioned his disciples, breathing on them, "Receive the Holy Spirit" (John 20:22). The living Lord charged disciples to go into the whole world to make more disciples, "baptizing them in the name of the Father and of the Son and of the Holy Spirit" (Matt 28:19), assuring them and us that he is with us always.

From beginning to end to new beginning, Jesus Christ is conceived by the Holy Spirit. "It is impossible to talk about Jesus without talking about the workings of the Spirit in him," says Moltmann. "The historical account of his life is from the very beginning a theological account, for it is determined by his collaboration—his co-instrumentality—with the Spirit and 'the Father.' His life history is at heart a 'Trinitarian history of God.'"[16] His risen life is also at heart a continuing Trinitarian history of God. And so Paul declares to the church, "you are in the Spirit, since the Spirit of God dwells in you. Anyone who does not have the Spirit of Christ does not belong to him. But if Christ is in you, though the body is dead because of sin, the Spirit is life because of righteousness" (Rom 8:9–10). *Spirit . . . Spirit of God . . . Spirit of Christ . . . the Spirit is life.*

Like the embodied Christ whose body we are, the church becomes the

16. Jürgen Moltmann, *The Way of Jesus Christ* (San Francisco: HarperSanFrancisco, 1990), 74.

body of Christ in the power of the Holy Spirit. From Pentecost on, it is the Holy Spirit of God who gives birth and life to the church as the body of Christ.

A LIVING BODY

Living bodies are not inert. Healthy bodies do things. And so, precisely as the body of Christ the church is called to do things, to act in particular ways. The call is not to imitate Christ, much less merely to embrace his memory as a moral example. Christ is present with and for the church, his body, as the One who calls the church to follow where he leads. The Holy Spirit is present with and for the church, animating the body of Christ and giving the church ears to hear Christ's call. "Jesus Christ is the same yesterday and today and forever. . . . So Jesus also suffered outside the gate in order to sanctify the people through his own blood. Therefore, let us go forth to him outside the camp . . ." (Heb 13:8, 12–13).

As the *body of Christ*, the church does not exist for its own sake but for the sake of the world. Just as Christ gave his body on the cross and in the bread, so the church is to give itself in sacrificial service. The consistent use of the formulary—*took . . . blessed . . . broke . . . gave*—makes it clear that the earliest witnesses understood the feeding of the thousands in eucharistic terms. Faced with a crowd of hungry people, severely limited resources, and Jesus's directive to feed the multitude, the disciples had no idea what to do. Jesus *took* the few available loaves and some fish, *blessed/gave thanks*, *broke* the bread, and *gave* the food to his disciples, telling them to feed the hungry crowd.

The Gospel of John's narrative of the risen Christ's final appearance also features a meal of bread and fish. After the disciples had finished breakfast, Jesus asked Peter three times, "Do you love me?" Peter replied, "Yes, Lord. You know that I love you." After each of Peter's declarations, the Lord said, "Feed my lambs. . . . Tend my sheep. . . . Feed my sheep" (John 21:9–17). As the *body of Christ* now receives Christ's body and blood in bread and wine, the Lord's call still sounds—"You give them something to eat . . . set a meal before the people . . . distribute the food . . . feed my sheep." Blessed are those who hunger and thirst for righteousness, and blessed are those who are simply hungry, and so the *body of Christ* is called to do something, to distribute to the multitudes what they need, to feed all the sheep with Christ who is the bread of life *and* with their daily bread. Christ's presence in the bread of life and the cup of salvation is not an insider ritual but the commencement of the church's life in the world.

Chapter 6

CALL AND RESPONSE

For as the rain and snow come down from heaven, and do not return there until they have watered the earth, making it bring forth and sprout, giving seed to the sower and bread to the eater, so shall my word be that goes out from my mouth; it shall not return to me empty, but it shall accomplish that which I purpose, and succeed in the thing for which I sent it.

Isaiah 55:10–11

It's strange the way everybody has their own pet notion about Jesus, and nobody's pet notion seems to agree with anybody else's. Grandawma, for instance, says He's "just a defunct social reformer." Then there's Papa, who once said He's God's Son all right, and that He survived the crucifixion just fine, but that the two-thousand-year-old funeral service His cockeyed followers call Christianity probably made Him sorry He did. Meanwhile there's Freddy, who's six now, and who told me she saw Christ hiding under her bed one night, but all He'd say to her was, "Pssst! Shhh! Pharisees!"

David James Duncan, *The Brothers K*

The gathered congregation is the basic form of church, but it is not a sufficient form of church. The gathered congregation is the one, holy, catholic, apostolic church only in its essential communion with other gathered congregations. But there is more to be said. All forms of ecclesial communion derive from the church's communion with the Lord of the church. But who is this Lord of the church? Jürgen Moltmann's ecclesiological axiom—"The way one thinks about Christ is also the way one thinks about the church"—is essential to a theological understanding of the actual church, but it complicates matters as well as clarifying them.[1]

Christology has been contested from the beginning. "Who do people say that I am?" Jesus asks his disciples. Their reply makes it clear that "the people" are not of one mind, so the question intensifies as Jesus then asks, "But who do *you* say that I am?" (Mark 8:27–29). The New Testament answers that question in a multitude of ways: Messiah, Lord, Savior, Servant, Son of God, Son of Man, Last Adam, Wisdom, Word, Alpha and Omega . . . the answers tumble over one another in a cascade of depictions. The effect is not confusion, however, as if each indicates a discrete Christological option. Rather, the profusion of portrayals leads us to the one who is not reduced to the possibilities contained in any of them. The multiplicity of Christological "titles" all indicate a single reality—"This Jesus God raised up" (Acts 2:32). Moreover, each of the so-called titles derives its meaning from the one to whom it refers; the titles do not define Jesus.

Even when multiple Christological perspectives are understood to focus on the singular Jesus Christ, a fundamental issue remains: how do we answer Jesus's question now? Is it an old question that can only be answered by saying who he *was*? No. The right question is, "who is Christ actually for us today?"[2] Dietrich Bonhoeffer asked the question in the waning days of the Third Reich, amid the horrors of war and holocaust, after a year of imprisonment, and within days of his execution. These circumstances also led him to wonder, "if we eventually must judge even the Western form of Christianity to be only a preliminary stage of a complete absence of religion, what kind of situation emerges for us, for the church?"[3] Bonhoeffer's self-interrogation may prompt a similar examination in our time, leading to pointed questions: Who is Jesus Christ for us today? Who are we for Jesus Christ today? In a secular age of churchly decline, what kind of situation emerges for our churches?

---

1. Jurgen Moltmann, *The Church in the Power of the Spirit: A Contribution to Messianic Ecclesiology* (Minneapolis: Fortress Press, 1993), 66.
2. Dietrich Bonhoeffer, "Letter to Eberhard Bethge," in *Letters and Papers from Prison*, vol. 8 of *Dietrich Bonhoeffer Works* (Minneapolis: Fortress, 2009), 362.
3. Bonhoeffer, "Letter to Eberhard Bethge," 363.

THE REAL PRESENCE OF CHRIST?

If the risen, living Christ is present now, it must be admitted that his presence is of an odd sort, diverging from the way we usually talk about a person being present to us. Hans Frei begins his inquiry into the identity of Jesus Christ by noting that "one way or another there has been a Christian belief that Jesus Christ is a contemporaneous person, here and now, just as he spans the ages." But, Frei goes on to say, "to the non-Christian and the 'natural' unbelieving person in us, all this is, of course, a very difficult claim at best."[4] The complexity of Christ's presence is exponential—one way or another . . . a belief . . . a very difficult claim . . . at best. And yet, Christian confession of the real presence of Christ has been central to the faith of the church from the outset.

Bonhoeffer began his University of Berlin lectures on Christology with the stark assertion that "Jesus is the Christ present as the Crucified and Risen One. That is the first statement of Christology. 'Present' is to be understood in a temporal and spatial sense, *hic et nunc*."[5] Lest there be any doubt about his meaning, Bonhoeffer immediately proceeded to identify two "severe misinterpretations" of the presence of Christ: first, "It is not Christ himself who is present, but his effective historical influence," and second, "a picture of Christ which is outside history, whether it is the idealistic picture drawn by those of the Enlightenment or the spiritual picture of the inner life of Jesus." Common to both is the idea that Christ is not now present as a person but only as an influence, a force in people's lives. "Hidden in the background of this idea of Christ," said Bonhoeffer, "there lies the fact that it does not deal with the resurrection, but only with Jesus up to the cross, with the historical Jesus. This is the dead Christ."[6] The current popularity of various "Jesus of history" books indicates that this is one misinterpretation that will not die.

There is a sense in which misinterpretations are understandable, however, even among those who affirm the bodily resurrection of Jesus. For centuries, Christians have confessed the creedal statement that the risen Christ "ascended into heaven and is seated at the right hand of the Father" and that "he will come again." This seems to imply that if Christ is

---

4. Hans W. Frei, *The Identity of Jesus Christ: The Hermeneutical Bases of Dogmatic Theology*, expanded ed. (Eugene, OR: Cascade, 2013), 27.

5. Bonhoeffer, *Christ the Center* (New York: Harper & Row, 1966), 43.

6. Bonhoeffer, *Christ the Center*, 44.

in heaven, then he is not here, and if he will come again, that he is now absent.

Centuries of elaborate Christian art depict Christ's ascension as a dramatic, majestic ascent, as he is borne aloft on a carpet of clouds. But Luke's account of the ascension, so reminiscent of the Transfiguration, says simply that the risen Christ was lifted up, exalted, hidden from sight by a cloud—*cloud* being the Bible's normal way to speak of the presence of God's glory. The striking element in the narrative is not the logistics of the Son of God's ascent, but the reception of the risen Christ into the full glory of God. Yet this only intensifies the stark impression that Jesus was taken away from humans. The ascension appears to be the beginning of the real absence of Christ.

Does Christ now dwell only in scriptural and liturgical memory, and will he come again someday, now enduring only in our hope? If that is all there is, then Christ's real absence will lead to a fading of memory and a withering of hope. Scripture and creed have something more in mind. T. F. Torrance puts the Christological and ecclesiological implication of the doctrine of the ascension succinctly: "In the doctrine of the Church as the body of Christ everything turns on the fact of the resurrection of Jesus Christ in Body and His ascension in the fullness of His Humanity. To demythologize the ascension (which means, of course, that it must first of all be mythologized) is to dehumanize Christ, and to dehumanize Christ is to make the Gospel of no relevance to humanity, but to turn it into an inhospitable and inhuman abstraction."[7]

The ascension is a central element in the foundational creeds because it expresses the continuing solidarity of the incarnate, crucified, and resurrected Jesus with us "in the fullness of His Humanity," while simultaneously expressing his absence from localized presence. Ascension is not Christ's evaporation into a disembodied spiritual realm, but rather the entrance of Jesus—son of Mary, Jew from Nazareth, crucified, dead and buried, raised—into the glory of God. He is taken from our sight, but he is not taken from solidarity with us. He is "seated at the right hand of the Father," not as one who is finished with us, but as the exalted One who is Lord over all and Lord of the church.

The church lives in the tension between the real absence and the real presence of Christ. Ours is a time, like all the church's times, when we feel both the ache of Christ's departure from us and the reassurance of his

7. T. F. Torrance, *Royal Priesthood*, 2nd ed. (Edinburgh: T&T Clark, 1993), 43–44.

presence with us. No longer with us in localized flesh, yet present to us in his humanity; no longer with us as an itinerant rabbi, yet present to us as Lord. The church knows the presence of the ascended Lord even as it suffers his absence and yearns for his coming again.

ASCENSION AND ECCLESIA

Douglas Farrow begins his inquiry into the significance of the doctrine of the ascension for ecclesiology by stating boldly that, "since it is only Christ who can make the church the church, perhaps the best way is to point directly to the central paradox of the *Christus praesens* and the *Christus absens*. . . . Is there anything about the church that is unaffected by this peculiar ambiguity at its very heart?"[8] Farrow goes on to say that "the ascension forces us to grapple with the inner logic of the church in a way that highlights its paradoxical situation, a thorough understanding of which is essential to its welfare and its mission."[9]

Perhaps this is true. But far too often the church sidesteps the peculiar ambiguity at its heart by failing to grapple with the inner logic of its paradoxical situation. Sidestepping to the left, the church consigns Jesus to the distant past, trapping "the historical Jesus" in one or three years of his life in Galilee, Samaria, and Judea. This allows the church to pick and choose the historical Jesus it prefers, paying homage to its founder while proceeding to self-determine the shape of its institutional life. Sidestepping to the right, the church presumes Christ's spiritual presence, trapping him in the immateriality of believers' hearts. This permits the church to claim Christ's warrant for the shape of its world-avoidance amid its worldly pretentions. Only when the church understands its life within Christ's absent presence and Christ's present absence can the church know that "it is not its own, but that it belongs, body and soul, in life and in death, to its faithful Savior, Jesus Christ."[10]

Separated from the ascension, resurrection is easily reduced to a point in time, a past event of limited consequence in the everyday lives of Christians and of limited importance to the churches as they shape their insti-

---

8. Douglas Farrow, *Ascension and Ecclesia* (Grand Rapids: Eerdmans, 1999), 3.

9. Farrow, *Ascension and Ecclesia*, 43.

10. An "ecclesial version" of the answer to the Heidelberg Catechism's first question, "What is your only comfort in life and in death?"

tutional lives. Easter celebrations that focus on the empty tomb and the appearances of the risen Christ present a resurrection that appears restricted to an event of the past. The acclamation, "Christ is risen; he is risen indeed," may become "Christ *was* risen; he *was* risen indeed." Separated from the ascension, Pentecost is easily reduced to "the birthday of the church," a silly celebration of ourselves. A truncated Easter-[Ascension]-Pentecost narrative results in a diminished ecclesiology that fails to make sense of either Christ's presence or his absence.

Chrysostom's second homily on the book of Acts captures the pivotal significance of the ascension by noting of the disciples that "in the Resurrection they saw the end, but not the beginning, and in the Ascension they saw the beginning, but not the end."[11] Like the disciples, the church now sees the end of the risen Christ's localized presence. But, unlike the disciples, the church does not see clearly the ascension's inauguration of Christ's exalted presence and so lacks hope in "the fullness of time" when Christ will "gather up all things in him, things in heaven and things on earth" (Eph 1:10). The result is not only a diminished sense of Christ's presence but also a reduction of eschatological hope in the consummation of Christ's universal Lordship to personal hope in heavenly life after death.

The sequence of events in the Acts narrative directly following the ascension may give clues to the significance of Chrysostom's "in the Ascension they saw the beginning." Four events follow in suggestive order. First, the eleven fill out their number so that the twelfth becomes "a witness with us to his resurrection" (Acts 1:15–26). In their initial act of witness the twelve are "filled with the Holy Spirit and began to speak in other languages, as the Spirit gave them ability." Both Jews and proselytes from Persia to Judea to Egypt to Rome heard the witness to Christ (Acts 2:1–13). In the reconstitution of the Twelve and the proclamation to the nations, both the fullness of Israel and the fullness of the nations are now encompassed in everything that ensued.

Next, Peter addresses the crowd, proclaiming that God raised up the crucified Jesus. Now "exalted at the right hand of God" as Lord and Messiah, "he has poured out this that you both see and hear" (Acts 2:14–36). Peter proclaims a living and active Christ whose reign begins with the bestowal of the Holy Spirit on "all flesh." Christ's ascension is entrance into universal lordship inaugurated by the inclusion of Jew and gentile as the

---

11. Chrysostom, "Homily II on the Acts of the Apostles," in *Nicene and Post-Nicene Fathers,* vol. XI, ed. Philip Schaff (Grand Rapids: Eerdmans, 1969), 13.

ecclesia, the called ones. The Holy Spirit is not a surrogate for the departed Christ, then, but rather the divine presence who empowers disciples to proclaim Christ "as the Spirit gives them ability" and who gives multitudes ears to hear "in the native language of each." The first act of the reconstituted Twelve is proclamation, witness to the living and active Lord of all.

Following proclamation, "those who welcomed his message were baptized" (Acts 2:37–41). Those who embrace Peter's words are not reacting to the quality of his rhetoric, of course, but responding as those "whom the Lord our God calls to him." Baptism "in the name of Jesus Christ" is response to the present call of the exalted Lord. Baptism in the name of Christ is not simply formulaic, of course, but baptism into the fullness of the person and work of God-with-us/Messiah/Lord—baptism *into* Christ.

Finally, following baptism, "They persevered in the apostles' teaching and the communion [*koinōnia*], the breaking of bread and the prayers" (2:42). Whether *koinōnia* is understood as communion in the truth of the apostles' teaching, communion with Christ who is the subject of the teaching, communion with Christ and one another in the breaking of bread, or communion in all three, it is clear that believers quickly became a worshiping community and that Eucharist was central to their life together. Eucharist follows baptism which is generated by proclamation of "God's deeds of power," now addressed to the fullness of humankind.

Luke's narrative reveals the ascended Christ, no longer present in the localized mode of his life and resurrection, yet present as the exalted Lord. His presence is most clearly (although not exclusively) known in proclamation, baptism, and Eucharist. As the narrative of Acts 1–2 demonstrates, everything in the formation of the community of Christ's people is the act of the exalted Lord who pours out the Spirit, who authorizes witness to his life, death, and resurrection, who incorporates Jews and gentiles into his body through baptism, who gives himself in bread and wine. The *ecclesia*—the church—is called into being as the body of Christ by the exalted Christ. In the ascension, the church can see the beginning but not yet the end, for what was inaugurated in ascension will only be consummated in *parousia*. The church lives between beginning and end, "the ascension reminding us that the Church is other than Christ, while sanctified together with Him; the advent reminding us that the Church in its historical pilgrimage is under the judgment of the impending advent, while already justified in Him."[12]

12. Torrance, *Royal Priesthood*, 46.

And yet, while Scripture testifies to the enduring presence of the ascended Christ, it remains the case that the reality of this presence is "strangely elusive and haunting as well as difficult to describe."[13] The difficulty in describing Christ's presence in absence is apparent in three Acts narratives that follow Luke's account of the ascension, Pentecost, and the life of the early Christian community. First, Stephen's testimony in Acts 7 climaxes in the revealed "presence" of the ascended Christ when Stephen, "full of the Holy Spirit, gazed into heaven and saw the glory of God, and Jesus standing at the right hand of God" (Acts 7:55). The stark note following Stephen's martyrdom, "And Saul was consenting to his death," then points forward to the narrative of Paul's calling in Acts 9. On the road to Damascus, a light from heaven was accompanied by a voice. "And [Paul] said, 'Who are you, Lord?' And [the voice] said, 'I am Jesus, whom you are persecuting; but rise and enter the city, and you will be told what you are to do'" (Acts 9:5–6; 22:6–11). Stephen *saw* the ascended Christ in heaven; Paul *heard* the ascended Christ on earth. Finally, Paul's own martyrdom is foreshadowed as the ascended Lord "stood by him and said 'Take courage, for as you have testified about me at Jerusalem, so you must bear witness also at Rome'" (Acts 23:11).

To call these three instances "visions" is to displace the core of the narratives. Narrative attention is not on the experience of Stephen or Paul, but on the presence of the ascended Christ who ratifies Stephen's witness, commissions Paul's mission, and blesses Paul's apostleship. All of this is done from cloud and light, from the glory of God, from the ascended Christ's presence with his witnesses. And yet, these scriptural accounts of Christ's presence remain extraordinary, "strangely elusive and haunting as well as difficult to describe."

THE PROBLEM OF THE *CHRISTUS PRAESENS*

Perhaps the elusive and difficult nature of the undertaking accounts for "Western theology's embarrassment over the ongoing function and work of the risen Christ."[14] Classic liberal theology considers talk about the presence of the resurrected (not to mention ascended) Christ to be metaphysical at best and mythological in any case. More conservative theology is

---

13. Frei, *The Identity of Jesus Christ*, 153.
14. Dietrich Ritschl, *Memory and Hope* (New York: Macmillan, 1967), 10.

eager to maintain the historicity of Christ's resurrection, but only talks about its "meaning" in the present. The embarrassment is not confined to Western theology, however; it is also present in the everyday life of the church. Christians pray through Christ and bear witness to Christ in word and deed, but thinking and talking about Christ's presence here and now is most often restricted to moralisms that derive from the Gospels' accounts of Jesus's life and teaching. "Following Jesus" is less likely to mean going outside the camp to join the crucified and risen Christ than emulating Jesus's (synoptic Gospels) life and following his (synoptic Gospels) teaching. Wondering "What Would Jesus Do?" is different from asking "What is Christ doing?"

The ascended Christ is not lost in the mist of history or confined within the hearts of believers. In an ascension sermon on Ephesians 4:7–13, Calvin noted that although Christ is no longer present among us "after the fashion of men," we are not separated from him. "For however great the distance may be between our Lord Jesus Christ and us, as far as heaven and earth are concerned, yet nevertheless he does not cease to dwell among us. . . . This he shows by the gifts he bestows on us, so that we may be drawn to the union he has spoken of."[15]

Ascension marks the beginning of Christ's reign but not its *telos*: "Christ the first fruits, then at his coming those who belong to Christ. Then comes the end, when he hands over the kingdom to God the Father" (1 Cor 15:23–24). Between beginning and end, Christ's reign is known only in and by the church. Many people are "spiritual," but only in the church is spirituality intimately connected to the incarnation, life, death, and resurrection of the living and active Christ. Many people pray, but only in the church is prayer made "through Christ the Lord." Many people live out sacrificial service in the world, but only in the church is such service carried out in response to the call of Christ. None of this devalues the spirituality, prayer, and service of those outside of the Christian community. It simply states the evident reality that the shape of ecclesial existence is determined by theological convictions about the one God, Christological convictions about the person and work of Jesus Christ, and pneumatological convictions about the action of the Holy Spirit. "No one can say 'Jesus is Lord' except by the Holy Spirit" (1 Cor 12:3), but the question remains what we, the church, mean when we say that Jesus is the living, acting, present Lord.

---

15. John Calvin, *Sermons on the Epistle to the Ephesians* (Carlisle, PA: Banner of Truth Trust, 1973), 346.

CALL AND RESPONSE CHRISTOLOGY/ECCLESIOLOGY

Moltmann's axiom makes it necessary to sketch an account of the *Christus praesens* that can open its Christological implications for ecclesiology. Dietrich Ritschl's Christological approach is richly suggestive because it addresses directly the mode of Christ's presence. Ritschl notes with approval Bonhoeffer's critique of theologies that asks *what* is Jesus Christ rather than *who* is Jesus Christ?[16] Only by asking *who is?* can we avoid a separation between Christ's being and work, between his person and his benefits. "Indeed," says Ritschl, "we cannot speak of Christ without loving him and we cannot think of Christ without praying to him. . . . The function of Christology is that of clarifying what we can say about him *as well as* to him."[17] Thus, says Ritschl, the proper starting point for Christology is an understanding of the risen and ascended Christ, present in and with the church here and now. Christology begins with the presence of the one we love and pray to, all the while remembering his past and hoping in his future: Christ has died, Christ is risen, Christ will come again.

Hans Frei's discussion of the identity, the *who is?* of Jesus Christ, puts the matter plainly: "in Jesus Christ identity and presence are so completely one that they are given to us together: we cannot know *who* he is without having him present."[18] And we can only know who the present One is by knowing what he does. Thus, Ritschl bypasses Scripture's Christological "titles" in favor of a condensed view of New Testament passages that speak of Christ's actions, what Christ *does*, as a way of understanding who Christ *is*. Neither gospels nor epistles set out a self-contained Christ apart from his acts within Israel, with disciples, in the church, and for the world. Neither gospels nor epistles separate Christ's acts from his being. In the New Testament witness, Jesus acts as God to humans and as a human being to God. Ritschl's summary of these actions is displayed in a call and response schema: Jesus Christ is simultaneously:

YAHWEH'S	MAN'S
call	response
demand	fulfillment

16. Bonhoeffer, *Christ the Center*, 32.
17. Ritschl, *Memory and Hope*, 208.
18. Frei, *The Identity of Jesus Christ*, 20.

invitation	prayer
will	obedience
revelation	understanding
word	reply
command	following
anointed	servant
help	cry
etc.	etc.[19]

Ritschl's list is deliberately incomplete, and the specific terminology is not the main point. His basic contention is that "Jesus should not be described in terms of being, location, or relation of natures, but of functions."[20] He sets out a call and response Christology in terms of Christ's priestly actions as the One who does both the initiating works of God and the appositely responsive human works. In these priestly actions, the human response is no less astonishing and no less salvific than the divine call. In sum, how Jesus Christ acts reveals who Jesus Christ is, "for us and our salvation," the One who is both "the living and active Word of God" (Heb 4:12) and the One "who in every respect has been tempted as we are, yet without sinning" (Heb 4:15). In this view the creedal formula—"truly God and truly human"—is not a static description of substances but a dynamic condensation of God's faithful call and humanity's faithful response embodied in the one person, Jesus Christ, who is God to us and us to God.

Ritschl's aim is to inquire into the presence of Christ, so his call and response Christology is not restricted to long ago and far away Galilee and Jerusalem. The risen, living, ascended Christ remains present to us and with us as the mediator, as our "great high priest" (Heb 4:14) who continues to be God's call to us and who continues to be faithful human response on our behalf. Christ is the righteousness of God, whose call generates knowledge of God's covenantal will to be our God and to form us as his people. Christ is the righteousness of God whose call, once heard, elicits our response. Christ remains "the Speech of God made flesh," the One who now, as fully Human within the glory of God, voices the divine call to humans.

"The way one thinks about Christ is the way one thinks about the church."[21] Just as we ask who Christ is rather than what Christ is, and just

---

19. Ritschl, *Memory and Hope*, 208.
20. Ritschl, *Memory and Hope*, 215.
21. Moltmann, *Church in the Power of the Spirit*, 66.

as we answer who Christ is by what Christ does, so we can ask who the church is by observing what the church does. Like Christology, ecclesiology can be approached dynamically rather than statically by looking at the life of the church rather than distilling an abstract and static nature of the church. Looking theologically at the life of the church requires cutting through the myriad activities of countless congregations to perceive the actions that lie behind them. What we see in the life of churches is:

CHRIST'S	CHURCH'S
call	response and indifference
demand	fulfillment and obstinacy
invitation	prayer and curse
will	obedience and disobedience
revelation	understanding and ignorance
word	reply and silence
command	following and defiance
anointing	service and selfishness
help	cry and boast
etc.	etc.

A call and response Christology embodies dynamic movement rather than static categories, it focuses on actions rather than abstract natures, and it secures the humanness of the risen and ascended Christ against docetic distortions. Similarly, a call and response ecclesiology focuses on the church's actual life rather than an ideal nature, and it casts the relationship between the triune God and the church in dynamic reality within history. The way we think about Christ is the way we think about the church. But unlike its Lord, the church's response to God's call is always mixed, ambiguous, equivocal. *Ecclesia simul iustus et peccator*? Yes, not as static description of an ontological state, but as the dynamic reality of the church's ambivalent response to Christ's clear call.

Each gathered congregation consists of people who have responded to God's gracious call in Jesus Christ. Responses are never perfect; they may not even be intentional. The congregation gathered around pulpit, font, and table is a strange blend of faithfulness and faithlessness, ebbing and flowing in time. But the One who calls is the ever-faithful, ever-present, living Christ, whose invitation comes in a gracious multitude of ways. People are not gathered by virtue of their devotion but in their ambiguous yet actual response to the call—some in gratitude and others in hope, some in service and others in need, some in anticipation and others out of habit. The call of Christ cannot be limited, and the response cannot be divided into pure and tainted. God knows our hearts, but all we know is that the church is the *ecclesia*, the called ones whose responses remain mixed. The company of Christians is bound together, not by its faithfulness, but in the ambiguity of its life that it can least justify. The company of Christians is bound together by the faithfulness of God who alone justifies.

The thoroughly ambiguous church is not left on its own, however, reduced to self-deceptive marketing of its achievements or self-defeating despair over its failings. Response to Christ's call is always equivocal, but Christ's call remains his faithful call to communion with him, a call to be joined to him in doing the will of God on earth as it is in heaven. The church is the place where Christ's call is heard most clearly, even over the din of preaching that may be more about the preacher than the gospel, and even amid sacramental celebrations that may be more about congregational camaraderie than union with Christ. Through it all, Christ is present as God's word, invitation, revelation, command, and help. And, through it all, Christ is present as faithful human reply, prayer, understanding, obedience, and help while the church lives in both joyful response and casual indifference, obedience and defiance, service and selfishness. Present in and with the church, Christ's call is not a distant summons but an intimate disclosure that we are his friends, his sisters and brothers, his body. The church is most truly itself in grateful response and so in full communion with its Savior and Lord. But even when it lacks ears that hear, its Savior and Lord remains faithful and so the church remains the church.

In the beginning was the Word—the Speaking, the Speech, the Discourse. . . . And the Speaking became flesh and dwelt among us. . . . And lo, I am with you always, to the close of the age. Christ's localized presence in incarnation and resurrection appearances has concluded, but his ascended, vocalized presence endures. In three of the four Gospels, Jesus's first public act after his baptism was his calling of disciples. In Mark and Matthew, both the call and the response are startlingly abrupt. Encountering a group of fishermen, "Jesus said to [Simon and Andrew] 'Follow me' . . . and immediately they left their nets and followed him"; "Immediately he called [James and John] . . . and they followed him" (Mark 1:16–20; Matt 4:18–22). In John, the initiative lies with Andrew and an anonymous person who begin to follow Jesus after hearing John the Baptist identify him as the Lamb of God. "What are you looking for?" Jesus asks, to which they can only reply,

"Where are you staying?" "Come and see," Jesus replies, and so they do. The next day, Andrew goes to his brother Simon, saying, "We have found the Messiah" (John 1:35–42). Luke's Gospel places the calling of disciples after Jesus began to attract attention through his teaching and healing. Jesus encounters Peter by commandeering his boat as a platform for teaching a crowd that was eager "to hear the word of God." He then tells Peter to put out into deep water to fish, initially without result until Jesus effects a miraculous catch. Only then do Simon, James, and John become "fishers for people" (Luke 5:1–11).

Gospel accounts of disciples' calling are not paradigms for contemporary disciple-making and congregation-forming, but they do suggest that Christ's call comes in a variety of ways—surprisingly and slowly, dramatically and conventionally, with and without evidence, in trust and in hope. The Gospels' intensely honest accounts of disciples' ongoing responses to Jesus's continuing call range from dimness to acceptance, fidelity to betrayal, loyalty to abandonment. Christ's call is unqualified, while the response of disciples, congregations, denominations, and world communions is always equivocal.

The evident reality of the church is that God's "Yes" is met by the church's "Yes and No." It is not only individual disciples who respond to Christ's call with both glad obedience and diffident waywardness; the church—congregations, denominations, and world communions—also lives in a fickle mix of fidelity and duplicity. The church's history contains more than a measure of misjudgment, error, falsehood, and deceit. On a smaller scale, denominations and congregations, even at their best, are a blend of gospel truth and self-serving deception. The church in its congregations and denominations and communions—the only church we have—always responds to Christ's call ambivalently. There are moments when church sin is recognized, such as the World Alliance of Reformed Churches' expulsion of two South African Dutch Reformed Churches for their heresy in giving theological justification for the state's apartheid system. More often, church sin is evidenced in systemic ignoring of ecclesial racism, indifference to doctrine, sexual misconduct and abuse, liturgical negligence, and a host of other grand and petty transgressions.

The church's evident sin is unremarkable, except when churches ignore or deny its reality in ecclesial life. What is remarkable as well as hopeful is the presence of Christ who continues to call the church to faithful, joyful response. Christ's faithfulness is known in his constant, persistent call to the church. Thus, the church is continuously born of the Word of God and abides in the same. Christ's call is effective, not mechanistically, but as the powerful word of truth that will not return empty. Reformed churches express a central, sure conviction in the motto, *ecclesia reformata semper reformanda secundum verbum Dei*—"the church reformed always to be reformed in accord with the word of God."[22] The church cannot reform itself, but it is reformed by the *Speaking of God*, by the call of Christ that elicits the church's faith, hope, and love.

THE REAL PRESENCE OF CHRIST

Christ's faithful presence in and with the church is recognized most clearly (but not exclusively) in proclamation, baptism, and Eucharist. *Christus praesens* is known most distinctly in these events because word and sacrament are the central, repeated occasions in the church's life when explicit words and actions are focused on Emmanuel, God-with-us. Word, water, bread, and wine are theocentric because they are Christocentric, and they are Christocentric through the Holy Spirit as well as by their explicit referent. It is in *Christus praesens* that the church has audible and visible access to *Theos praesens* through *Pneuma praesens*. As the church comes to hear and know God-with-us in proclamation, baptism, and Eucharist, the church can hear and know itself as we-with-God. "This 'We with God,' enclosed in the 'God with us,' is Christian faith, Christian love and Christian hope," says Barth. "Our faith, love and hope and we ourselves—however strong may be our faith, love and hope—live only by that which we cannot create, posit, awaken or deserve."[23] It is in the call of Christ that the church hears again and again that which it cannot create or even imagine on its own and, in hearing, becomes able to respond in grateful understanding and obedient following.

The Word Proclaimed and Heard

As Scripture is read and proclaimed, God's speaking and acting are brought into focus. "Prayers for illumination" are a distinctive feature of Reformed

22. For more, see Harold Nebelsick, "Ecclesia Reformata Semper Reformanda," *Reformed Liturgy & Music* XVIII, no. 2 (Spring 1984): 59–63.

23. Barth, *Church Dogmatics* IV/1, 15.

liturgies. Before Scripture is read, the congregation prays for the Holy Spirit to make worshipers receptive to the life-giving Word. A typical prayer for illumination asks, "Lord, open our hearts and minds by the power of your Holy Spirit, that as the Scriptures are read, and your Word is proclaimed, we may hear with joy what you say to us today." Scripture and proclamation within worship are a primary occasion for the church to be opened to God's self-disclosure, to hear the call of Christ to the church and each of its members, and to respond faithfully. The word written and the word proclaimed are occasions for the Word revealed. Barth puts the matter nicely, for "in the form in which the Church knows God's Word— the one and only form which affects us at all necessarily because it affects us magisterially—in this form 'God's Word' means 'God speaks.' . . . We shall have to regard God's speech also as God's act, and God's act also as God's mystery."[24] In the speaking of the one triune God, the call of Christ is voiced.

It is also possible to say that Christ's call is seen. Calvin twice spoke of Scripture in the life of the church through the image of eyeglasses. "For just as eyes, when dimmed by age or by some other defect, unless aided by spectacles, discern nothing distinctly," Calvin wrote, "so Scripture, gathering up the otherwise confused knowledge of God in our minds, having dispersed our dullness, clearly shows us the true God."[25] Novelist Frederick Buechner provides an intriguing variation on Calvin's image: "If you look *at* a window, you see fly specks, dust, the crack where Junior's Frisbee hit it. If you look *through* a window, you see the world beyond. Something like this is the difference between those who see the Bible as a Holy Bore and those who see it as the Word of God which speaks out of the depths of an almost unimaginable past into the depths of ourselves."[26] Like Buechner's window and Calvin's eyeglasses, Scripture read and proclaimed is meant to be looked through, not examined for its own sake, so that what the church sees clearly is the one God whose "Speech" continues to call the church to respond. As the call of Christ is heard, the church can respond in the obedience that leads it beyond itself into the world where it lives out its witness in self-giving.

24. Barth, *Church Dogmatics* I/1, 150.
25. Calvin, *Institutes*, 1.14.1 and 1.1.2, conflated, 160 and 70.
26. Frederick Buechner, *Wishful Thinking: A Theological ABC* (New York: Harper & Row, 1973), 12.

The Sacraments Celebrated in Accord with Christ

Calvin cites with approval Augustine's teaching that sacraments are a visible form of an invisible grace, but he goes on to offer a more dynamic understanding. "I say that Christ is the matter or (if you prefer) the substance of all the sacraments," Calvin states, "for in him they have all their firmness, and they do not promise anything apart from him."[27] As Scripture is read and proclaimed, as baptism and Eucharist are celebrated, the church's awareness is drawn to Christ, and through Christ to the one God—Father, Son, and Holy Spirit. In baptism and Eucharist the church can "see" Jesus Christ, incarnate, crucified, resurrected, and ascended, and in "seeing" can hear his call, for "the sacraments have the same office as the Word of God: to offer and set forth Christ to us."[28] The call of the present Christ, who is the *Speaking of God*, comes to the church as Scripture's witness is read, preached, and taught and as baptism and Eucharist are celebrated in accord with Christ.

It would be a mistake to imagine that Christ's call is confined to Word and sacrament within the church's worship, however. It is true enough that worship is the gathering of the church rather than the province of individuals, and it is true enough that worship is the central setting in which the church can turn away from preoccupation with itself and turn toward its Lord. However, Word and sacraments lead the church beyond itself to faithful presence in the world. It may not be difficult to understand that hearing Christ's call impels the church into faithful participation in the mission of God. What may be less obvious is the missional significance of the sacraments.

Baptism is ordination to discipleship. The church is composed of those who have been made disciples, baptized in the name of the Father and of the Son and of the Holy Spirit and taught to obey everything that Christ commands by the Christ who is with us always (Matt 28:19–20). The church, composed of the baptized who have been called to discipleship, is the community that is sent into all the world. Baptism creates "disciples without borders," for baptism is not limited to private life, or to spiritual life, or to church life, or to denominational life, or to national life. As the community of the baptized, the congregation is sent into the whole world to join with the whole church in proclaiming the whole gospel.

27. Calvin, *Institutes*, 4.14.16, 1291.
28. Calvin, *Institutes*, 4.14.17, 1292.

Similarly, the Eucharist—the *Lord's* Supper—is not enclosed within the church. Fed at the table by Christ's body and blood, the church is sent out into the presence of "the thousands" who are still hungry, thirsty, homeless, naked, sick, and captive. The Lord still calls to the church, "You give them something to eat."

THE REAL PRESENCE OF CHRIST IN THE CHURCH

"Real presence" is an odd term, as if there could be an unreal presence of Christ. However, the modifier may be important as a way of insisting that the living Christ is present actually, not only in memory or influence. The church is always tempted to moderate its recognition of Christ's actual presence because the recognition comes with consequences. The presence of Christ is the presence of the church's Lord. The presence of the Lord means that Jesus Christ is no longer at our disposal, but that we are at his.

There is more to say, however. The title of a fine book by Michael Welker asks a crucial question: *What Happens in Holy Communion?*[29] The question can also be asked, "What happens in baptism?" and "What happens in proclamation?" The general answer is that proclamation, baptism, and Eucharist are the ordinary and primary means of our union with Christ. "Union with Christ" has long been a hallmark of Reformed ecclesiology. "Christ," says Calvin, "having been made ours, makes us sharers with him in the gifts with which he has been endowed. We do not, therefore, contemplate him outside ourselves from afar . . . but because we put on Christ and are engrafted into his body—in short, because he deigns to make us one with him . . . we glory that we have communion of righteousness with him."[30] Christ calls us to communion with him so that we are united to Christ as Christ has united himself to us, and in union with Christ we enter the communion of the one God—Father, Son, and Holy Spirit. Our union with Christ is not only a personal actuality, although it is that. Fundamentally, union with Christ is an ecclesial reality. Our Lord still prays, "As you, Father, are in me and I am in you, may they also be in us. . . I in them and you in me, that they may become completely one . . ."

29. Michael Welker, *What Happens in Holy Communion?* (Grand Rapids: Eerdmans, 2000).

30. Calvin, *Institutes*, 3.11.10, 737.

(John 17:21–23). Christ's call continues to beckon us to himself, and to encourage us, so that our reply may be growth as the body of Christ, loving the Lord our God with heart, soul, mind, and strength, and loving neighbors as ourselves.

Protestants have generally understood that union with Christ is, at the least, a hoped-for outcome of preaching. When the Word is set forth faithfully and clearly, persons are drawn to faith, united to Christ, and incorporated into Christ's body. Protestants, particularly preachers, may imagine that it is their call that elicits the response of faith, but it is the Speech of God, the call of the living Lord that is heard, and it is the ascended Christ who binds us to himself. To the degree that faithful preaching and teaching lend clarity to Christ's call, it is to be welcomed, but the word of God does not return empty because it is the Lord who speaks. Christ is active in human proclamation, and it is the action of Christ that draws us into union with him.

Baptism and Eucharist display and proclaim the gospel. Incarnation, life, crucifixion, resurrection, and ascension are all visibly present in water, bread, wine, and the actions surrounding them. The visible gospel is not mute, however, as it is accompanied by Scripture, prayers, and praise. Remember that Calvin, while critical of medieval Catholic sacramental practice, maintained with the whole Catholic tradition that Christ is the substance of baptism and Eucharist. "We have already seen how Jesus Christ is the only provision by which our souls are nourished," Calvin wrote. "But because it is distributed by the Word of the Lord, which he has appointed as instruments to this end, it is also called bread and water. Now what is said of the Word fitly belongs to the sacraments, by means of which our Lord leads us to communion with Christ."[31]

What happens in Holy Communion, Holy Baptism, and Holy Word? Christ happens! And when Christ happens, Christ calls the church to faithful response. The church's sacramental celebrations are less the church's acts than the occasions for the mighty acts of God. Those Protestant churches that are heirs of long-standing sacramental minimalism deprive themselves of clear presentations of the gospel, placing their trust in preachers and teachers alone. Moving from sacramental minimalism to sacramental fidelity requires that celebrants give the same time, preparation, conviction, and passion to baptism and Eucharist as to preaching and

---

31. Calvin, "Short Treatise on the Lord's Supper," in *Calvin: Theological Treatises*, ed. J. K. S. Reid (Philadelphia: Westminster, 1954), 143–44.

teaching. Only then will congregations be weaned from the infant formula of infrequent, mechanical rites.

When Church of the Word and sacrament becomes effectively church of the Word alone, it may benefit from novelist Frederick Buechner's observation that "Sermons are like dirty jokes; even the best ones are hard to remember. In both cases that may be just as well." They may also be encouraged by his assurance that "A sacrament is when something holy happens. It is transparent time, time in which you can see through to something deep inside time."[32]

32. Frederick Buechner, *Wishful Thinking*, 86, 82.

Chapter 7

PEOPLE OF GOD

For you are a people holy to the LORD your God; the LORD
your God has chosen you to be a people for his own possession,
out of all the people that are on the face of the earth. It was not
because you were more in number than any other people that
the LORD set his love upon you and chose you, for you were
the fewest of all peoples; but it is because the LORD loves you,
and is keeping the oath which he swore to your fathers, that the
LORD has brought you out with a mighty hand, and redeemed
you from the house of bondage.

Deuteronomy 7:6–8

Being among the elect is a theological notion that means: not as
a matter of merit but by a supernatural judgment, a free, even
capricious, determination of God, a people is chosen for something exceptional and extraordinary.

Milan Kundera, Slowness

People of God has become a favored image for the church in North American denominations. It is often paired with the image of *journey*, so that
churches describe themselves as *pilgrim people of God*, or *people of God on
a journey*. Neither the starting point nor the destination of the journey is
clear, but that is part of the image's appeal. *People of God* as a primary way
of understanding the church finds more substantive definition in *Lumen
gentium* (light of the nations), the Second Vatican Council's dogmatic constitution on the church. The title points, not to an amorphous collection

of persons on a trek with no goal, nor to a dangerous ideology of *Volk*, but to the One who addressed a particular people—"I will be your God and you shall be my people" (Lev 26:12)—and who spoke to that people—"I have given you as a covenant to the people, a light to the nations" (Isa 42:6; 49:6). *People of God* points us back to Israel. Only with Israel and the God of Israel can we avoid Cardinal Ratzinger's concern that "the enthusiasm for [*People of God*] far exceeded what the biblical foundations could support."[1]

Like *body of Christ, people of God* is a metaphor, not a sociological description. It brings two disparate elements—God the Creator and people the creatures—together in a way that creates new meaning. No longer god as generic deity, but God the Lord who relates to a particular people in their concrete, historical existence. No longer people as a contingent social-historical grouping, but a particular people who are bound to the God who made them who they are. *People of God* is not a malleable term that can be shaped at will, but a divine-human reality that exists only in accord with God's speaking.

People of God is a two-Testament reality. The term and its derivatives such as *laos* occur in both Old (LXX) and New Testaments, with New Testament usage shaped by Old Testament witness. Thus, *people of God* raises complex questions: Who are the people of God?—Jews? Christians? Christians instead of Jews? Both together? Who is Israel? Who is church? What is the relationship between Christians and Jews, church and synagogue? The questions are complex, and multiple answers are often incompatible. The way to approach these questions is to begin at the beginning.

It is impossible to understand Jesus and the early church—and impossible to understand the contemporary church—apart from an understanding of the history and faith of Israel and the continuing Jewish people. Jesus of Nazareth was born, matured, and lived as a Jew among Jews, and he understood his mission in terms of God's covenantal fidelity to Israel. His disciples and earliest followers were all Jews, and in the ensuing years many Christians continued to understand themselves as Jews "who have found the Messiah" (John 1:41). Yet tensions led to a gradual separation of "Christianity" from "Judaism." In time, the Christian church became an almost exclusively gentile phenomenon. The parting of the ways did not happen simply or quickly, and the exact causes and dynamics of separation

---

1. Joseph Cardinal Ratzinger, *Church, Ecumenism, and Politics: New Endeavors in Ecclesiology* (San Francisco: Ignatius Press, 1987), 29.

are the subject of scholarly debate. But what is not contested is the reality of the divergence and its consequences for both Christians and Jews.

One of the most significant consequences has been tendentious Christian readings of both Old and New Testaments, resulting in negative understandings of biblical Israel's history and faith, the character of second temple Judaism, the Pharisees, the Law, and the shape of continuing Jewish faith and life. The corollary of this consequence for Jews has been Christian theological abuse punctuated by intolerance, demonization, ghettos, pogroms, and, perhaps inevitably, Holocaust. The corollaries for Christians have been complicity in all aspects of anti-Jewish thought and action coupled with a diminished reception of the gospel and a distorted sense of the church's nature.

It is impossible to understand *church* apart from a conscientious understanding of Israel's history and faith or apart from a principled understanding of the enduring history and faith of the Jewish people. Thus, it is necessary to point out the ways contemporary Christian faith and life misconstrues its biblical, historical, and theological heritage. This chapter will deal, all too briefly, with the significance of two-Testament Scripture, while the following chapter will address the contemporary relationship of Judaism and Christianity, church and synagogue, Christians and Jews. It is not the purpose of these chapters to set out a comprehensive Christian theology of Jewish-Christian reality but rather to deepen theological and sociological comprehension of *church* by exploring the ecclesiological deficit that results from failing to know both Christians and Jews as *people of God*.

ALL SCRIPTURE IS INSPIRED AND PROFITABLE FOR TEACHING

An acute challenge to the faith of the early church came from Marcion of Sinope, writing in the mid-second century. Marcion believed that the teachings of Christ exposed "the God of the Hebrew Scriptures" as a deity different from and lower than the all-loving God and Father of the Christian Gospels and the letters of Paul. Marcion taught that although both are gods, YHWH, the God of Israel is a subordinate deity, merely the creator of the material world, the vengeful tribal God of the Jews. The God and Father of Jesus Christ, on the other hand, is the transcendent and spiritual Heavenly Father whose compassion embraced all of humanity. This loving

God sent his Son, a spiritual being who only appeared to be the human Jesus, for Marcion rejected accounts of Christ's bodily incarnation, crucifixion, and resurrection. He claimed that the spiritual Son of God beckons all people to a higher spiritual life that transcends the material world.

Marcion rejected the only writings known as Scripture at the time, what we now call the Old Testament. Furthermore, he confined his reception of the apostolic writings, what we now know as the New Testament, to bowdlerized versions of Luke's Gospel and the letters of Paul. He edited both to remove all mention of "Israel's God." Reaction against Marcion was swift, leading to condemnation of his views as heresy and to his excommunication from the church. Justin Martyr, Irenaeus, and Tertullian all wrote refutations of Marcion's thought, including his rejection of Scripture's wholeness. Irenaeus was particularly clear:

> He [Marcion] abolished the prophets and the law and all the works of God who made the world, whom he also styled the Word-Ruler. Besides this, he mutilated the Gospel according to Luke. . . . In like manner, he mutilated the Letters of Paul, removing whatever was clearly said by the Apostle about the God who made the world inasmuch as he is the Father of our Lord Jesus Christ.[2]

Tertullian also said:

> Marcion's special and principal work is the separation of the law and the gospel . . . committing the gospel to a variance with the law in order that the two documents which contain them may contend for a diversity of gods . . . it is this very opposition between the law and the gospel which has suggested that the God of the gospel is different from the God of the law . . . Marcion [is] the author of the breach of peace between the gospel and the law.[3]

The church responded to this early heresy by ensuring the preservation of Israel's Scripture as fully Christian, essential witness to the one God—Father, Son, and Holy Spirit. The church affirmed that there is but one God, who created the world, called Israel to be the people of God, was incarnate in Jesus of Nazareth, and raised the crucified Jesus from the dead.

2. Irenaeus, *Against the Heresies*, 1.27.
3. Tertullian, *Against Marcion*, I.19, www.newadvent.org/fathers/03124.htm.

But Marcion's heresy did not die; forms of it are alive and well in the Christian church today. Every pastor has heard parishioners contrast "the harsh judgmental God of the Old Testament" with "the loving merciful God of the New Testament." Among pastors and many theologians, categories of promise (Old Testament) and fulfillment (New Testament) have served to downgrade the life and faith of Israel to the status of a religious preface. Scholarly historical-critical biblical interpretation, for all its evident merits, has too often served to reduce the Old Testament to a historical artifact, a record of the religious life of an ancient people.

In the everyday life of the church, the Old Testament is most often treated as a repository of interesting stories, the best of which record God's mighty acts. But even these are usually coupled with notes of Israel's disobedience. Prophetic witness to Israel's unrighteousness is regularly used to express the need for Christian judgment of contemporary social injustice, seldom suspecting that the prophets' witness may be directed at the church just as it was directed at Israel. Prophetic texts that express hope in the coming of the Messiah are treasured as mere prelude to the church's celebration of the birth of Jesus. In popular Christian thought, ancient Israel is treated as an object lesson demonstrating the futility of trying to merit God's favor by fulfilling the law. In sum, the Old Testament is regularly treated as a record of legalism, disobedience, judgment, and hope, and its continuing significance for Christian faith and life is minimal.

Marginalization of the Old Testament can be seen in the emerging practice of referring to "Hebrew scripture." Clearly, the term does not identify the language in which most of the Old Testament is written (we would not say "Greek Scripture" for the New Testament). The use of "Hebrew scripture" implies several things, none of them appropriate to the church's proper understanding of the Old Testament's place in Christian faith and life. First, it lodges the writings firmly in the past, for "Hebrew" identifies an ancient people, no longer referring to contemporary Jews or to modern Israel. Study of "Hebrew scripture" then becomes textual archaeology, an exploration of the religious life of people long ago and far away. "Hebrew scripture" easily morphs into "the Hebrew's scripture," *their* scripture, not Christian Scripture, effectively excising it from the life of the church.

Retaining the shared designation "Testament" for both Old and New is essential in indicating the integral bond between the two. Some have suggested "First Testament" and "Second Testament" as a way of preserving fundamental interconnection without the implied denigration of "old." But whatever terms are used, language must not create or exacerbate disconnection between what is altogether Christian Scripture, from Genesis to Revelation, the unique and authoritative witness to God's way in the world.

RECLAIMING THE OLD TESTAMENT

Christian reading of the Old Testament is complicated. We come to the Old Testament from centuries of Christian interpretation that may obscure as well as illuminate understanding of the texts. Willie James Jennings places the complexity in bold relief:

1. we are Gentile readers reading the biblical narrative that is the story of Israel;
2. we are Gentile readers positioned to read the story of Israel as a result of the life of Jesus;
3. we are Gentile readers who should perceive living Israel through the lens provided by biblical Israel;
4. we are Gentile readers who should read our own existence by the lens provided by the Jewish Jesus.[4]

The church reads from within Israel's space. "And yet," says Jennings, "the election of Israel has never significantly entered into the social imagination of the church. Israel's election has not done any real theological work for Christian existence."[5] In contrast to its current marginalization, the Old Testament was Scripture for Jesus and for the early church. Christopher Seitz makes the point that "The 'New' Testament's scriptural authority was given its logic and its material form with reference to the Scriptures as first received by the church. 'Old' then referred not merely to something temporally precedent, but rather provided the signal point of reference by which to understand a second witness to the work of God in Christ."[6] Specifying theological deficits that result from marginalizing the Old Testament may open the way to an ecclesial reading of Israel's story.

---

4. Willie James Jennings, *The Christian Imagination: Theology and the Origins of Race* (New Haven: Yale University Press, 2010), 252.

5. Jennings, *The Christian Imagination*, 253.

6. Christopher Seitz, *The Character of Christian Scripture: The Significance of a Two-Testament Bible* (Grand Rapids: Baker Academic, 2011), 17.

Covenant

The Old Testament is the Scripture of covenants. It all begins with the creation saga in Genesis 1–11, Israel's testimony to how things stand between God and creation. The "very good" of Genesis 1 and 2 is soon stained by human estrangement from the Creator, from one another, and from nature (Gen 3), leading to violence and death (Gen 4), and to collective wickedness and evil (Gen 6). Does the Creator then give chaos free rein in the waters of the Flood? Or does God wash the world clean? Or both? In any event, the receding waters not only restore the world, but also reveal God's covenant with all of humankind and all creatures: "never again shall there be a flood to destroy the earth" (Gen 8:11). "The LORD said in his heart, 'I will never again curse the ground because of humankind . . . nor will I ever again destroy every living creature as I have done. As long as the earth endures, seedtime and harvest, summer and winter, day and night, shall not cease'" (Gen 8:21–22). The Lord's covenant through Noah is universal, encompassing all of creation, then and now, in the mercy and enduring love of the Creator.

Biblical history then begins with a particular person—Abram. Called away from everything he had known, called to journey to an undisclosed place, Abram is at the beginning of God's dealings with a particular people. "I will make of you a great nation, and I will bless you," the Lord says to Abram, "so that you will be a blessing" (Gen 12:2). God's call and promise is then sealed in a covenant with renamed Abraham, a covenant that stretches beyond what will become Israel. Through Sarah, Abraham will also be "the ancestor of a multitude of nations": "I will bless her, and she shall give rise to nations; kings of peoples shall come from her" (Gen 17:5, 16). From the outset of Israel's life, God's covenant promise to a people is encompassed within the horizon of all people, so that Abraham's "great nation" will live within the "multitude of nations." Moreover, the great nation is to be a blessing to the multitude of nations. God's righteousness is revealed as eternal faithfulness to his covenant promise. Abraham's righteousness is shown as trust in God's covenant faithfulness. The righteousness of God and the righteousness of Abraham are not reciprocal, however; God's righteousness, his covenant faithfulness, does not depend on Abraham's trust.

The covenant of Sinai follows from God's covenants with Abraham, Isaac (Gen 26:2–5), and Jacob (Gen 28:13–17; 35:9–13), for it was at Sinai that Israel was constituted as a great nation. God spoke to Moses, "I have heard the groaning of the Israelites whom the Egyptians are holding as slaves, and I have remembered my covenant. Say therefore to the Israelites, 'I am the LORD, and I will free you. . . . I will take you as my people, and I will be your God. You shall know that I am the LORD your God'" (Exod 6:5, 7). The Decalogue was then given as a mark of the covenant, not its condition. As that defining covenant was recalled again and again, generations of Israel confessed that "the LORD our God made a covenant with us in Horeb. Not with our ancestors did the LORD make this covenant, but with us, who are all of us here alive today" (Deut 5:2–3).

Obeying the commandments, living the Torah, is the shape of Israel's faithfulness to the covenant but not the condition for God's faithfulness. "Now therefore, if you obey my voice and keep my covenant," says the Lord, "you shall be my treasured possession out of all the peoples. Indeed, the whole earth is mine, but you shall be a priestly kingdom and a holy nation" (Exod 19:5–6). Keeping covenant is the requirement for Israel's living its vocation as a priestly kingdom and a holy nation, but it is not the requirement for God's covenantal fidelity. Israel witnesses to the total claim on its life, answering, "Everything that the LORD has spoken we will do" (Exod 19:8). Everything—not to merit God's faithfulness but to live in correspondence to God's faithfulness. Isadore Epstein explains that "while the Ten Commandments indicated the substance and the scope of Israel's universal 'priestly mission,' the other Commandments were designed to train Israel for the holiness which they were to follow as a nation called upon to become 'holy unto God.'"[7] Living the Torah is not confined to ancient Israel, for living Israel—the Jewish people—is called to know itself both in God's eternal fidelity and in its own faithful response. Israel, then and now, is called to be a holy people.

It is unfortunate that much Christian thinking about Israel's covenants has been reduced to "law" in opposition to "gospel." Neither the Hebrew word *torah* nor its Greek equivalent *nomos* refers primarily to a legal code. Yet both Old Testament *torah* and its corresponding New Testament *nomos* have come into English via Jerome's translation by the Latin *lex*—"law"—with its formal forensic overtones. Better English translations of *torah* are *instruction, teaching, guidance, direction*. Torah is the divinely ordered way of life for a redeemed people living within the Lord's covenant. The first five books of the Old Testament are Torah, with narrative as well as cov-

---

7. Isadore Epstein, *Judaism: A Historical Presentation* (Harmondsworth: Penguin, 1959), 23.

enant stipulations serving as "instruction/guidance" to Israel about the Lord's way and the way of a covenant people. John Calvin understood that "the principal use [of the Law], which pertains more closely to the proper purpose of the law, finds its place among believers in whose hearts the Spirit of God already lives and reigns. . . . Here is the best instrument for them to learn more thoroughly each day the nature of the Lord's will to which they aspire, and to confirm them in their understanding of it."[8]

In the Old Testament, *mitzvot* (commandments) are not legal requirements, but communal obligations that follow from the Lord's covenant of redemption. The "Ten *Mitzvot*" emerge from the foundational preamble, "I am the LORD your God, who brought you out of the land of Egypt, out of the house of bondage" (Exod 20:2, Deut 5:6). Observing *mitzvot* is not simply obeying commands, much less an effort to merit God's favor, but rather the way of life that reveres God, follows in God's Way, loves and serves God. *Mitzvot* are responses of gratitude to the grace of God. Calvin had it right. In his Strasbourg and Geneva liturgies, the Ten Commandments come after prayers of confession and assurance of forgiveness, not before; they were not employed to convict people of their sin but as a response to grace, sung joyfully by the congregation![9] Torah is not opposed to gospel, but rather sets out the shape of life for a redeemed people, Christians as well as Jews.

Subsequent covenants—with Israel at Shechem, with David, even the "new covenant" announced through Jeremiah—are not replacement covenants but rather further expressions of the Sinai covenant. Did Israel always keep covenant? No. Do contemporary Jews always keep covenant? No. Has the church always kept covenant, and do contemporary Christians always keep covenant? No again. Did God judge Israel for its failures to keep covenant? Yes. Does God continue to hold the Jewish people to account? Yes. Has God judged the church for its failures to keep covenant, and does God continue to hold the churches to account? Yes again. The Book of Judges opens with a narrative of Israel's disobedience, proceeds to catalogue its waywardness, and concludes with the sober summary, "all the people did what was right in their own eyes" (Judg 21:25). Yet the entire narrative is framed by the Lord's word, "I brought you up from Egypt, and brought you into the land that I had promised to your ancestors. I said, 'I

8. John Calvin, *Institutes*, 2.10.2, 429.

9. See Bard Thompson, *Liturgies of the Western Church* (Philadelphia: Fortress, 1961), 197–98.

will never break my covenant with you'" (Judg 2:2). Little wonder that the apostle Paul wrote regarding the Jews, "the gifts and the calling of God are irrevocable" (Rom 11:29).

God chose a particular people to live God's way in the world. The Lord says to Israel, "I have called you in righteousness, I have taken you by the hand and kept you; I have given you as a covenant to the people, a light to the nations" (Isa 42:6). As Paul van Buren makes clear, "The *people* are this light, not just their Scriptures; their life, not just some of their words."[10] Israel's call to be a holy people means that this people shall be different, distinctive, not like the other nations. Israel's distinctiveness is not intrinsic, however, but God-given: "For you are a people holy to the Lord your God; the Lord has chosen you to be a people for his own possession, out of all the peoples that are on the face of the earth" (Deut 7:6). Israel's call, then, is not to speak to the nations so that they will become Israel but to be a light to the nations so that they can see the way of the one God in the world.

Old Testament as Christian Scripture

Reading the Old Testament as a history of Israel's failed striving to merit God's favor by obedience to the Law is not only erroneous, but leads to Christian supersessionism, the belief that the church has now replaced Israel as the people of God. This idea fosters unrelentingly negative assessments of Israel's history and faith, and persistently hostile assessments of the continuing Jewish people. It is not necessary to catalogue the indignities, damage, and suffering this has caused Jews throughout the world. Anti-Jewish thought and action has spread beyond the church to become "A Convenient Hatred," characterized by demonizing stereotypes, accusations of "racism," attacks on Jews and synagogues, and Holocaust denial.[11]

Tendentious readings of the Old Testament have led not only to Christian complicity in anti-Semitism but also to a diminished understanding of the gospel and misguided views of the church. The fundamental corrective is recovery of the Old Testament as Christian Scripture as well as Jewish

---

10. Paul M. van Buren, *A Theology of the Jewish-Christian Reality, Part 2: A Christian Theology of the People Israel* (New York: Harper & Row, 1983), 166.

11. See Phyllis Goldstein, *A Convenient Hatred: The History of Anti-Semitism* (Brookline, MA: Facing History and Ourselves National Foundation, 2012).

Scripture. How do pre-Christ writings provide witness that is essential to the Christian church? The first thing to be said is that, unlike Marcion and his heirs, the church must understand that the God of Israel, YHWH, the great I AM, is the one God—Father, Son, and Holy Spirit. It is Christian dogma that the one triune God is the God of creation, the God of Abraham, Isaac, and Jacob, the God of Exodus, the God of the Covenant, the God of Exile and Return. It is not as if God the Father was the lone actor in the Old Testament, with the Son appearing in the incarnation, and the Holy Spirit at Pentecost. The same God is the God of both Old and New Testaments. In Robert Jenson's memorable formulation, "God is whoever raised Jesus from the dead, having before raised Israel from Egypt."[12]

All the acts and words of the Lord, from Genesis to Malachi, are the acts and words of the only God. New and Old Testaments together bear witness to the one covenant-making Lord. But Christians have too often divided the purpose and will of the one God, separating the "covenant of grace" in Christ from the "covenant of law and works" with Israel, thereby making God's acts in Israel incompatible with God's acts in the church. In contrast to deceptive theories of disjunction, John Calvin went to great lengths to confirm that "all men adopted by God into the company of his people since the beginning of the world were covenanted to him by the same law and by the bond of the same doctrine as obtains among us. . . . The covenant made with the patriarchs is so much like ours in substance and reality that the two are actually one and the same."[13] God called Israel into being and God called the church into being, both callings of grace. In what sense, then, is the Old Testament Christian Scripture? Or, to put the question more starkly, is Christological interpretation of the Old Testament appropriate? Is it responsible to "read Christ in the Old Testament" or is that an anachronistic appropriation of someone else's story?

It is obvious that Jesus understood himself in Old Testament terms and that the earliest Christian witnesses—all of them Jews—did as well. The letters of Paul, the four Gospels, indeed the whole New Testament is incomprehensible apart from the Old Testament, which provides all the significant language by which Jesus Christ is understood. The Old Testament teaches us how to read the New Testament. But does the New Testament teach us how to read the Old Testament? Do Trinitarian or Christological

---

12. Robert W. Jenson, *The Triune God*, vol. 1 of *Systematic Theology* (New York: Oxford University Press, 1997), 63.

13. Calvin, *Institutes*, 2.10.1, 428; 2.10.2, 429.

readings of the Old Testament undermine the integrity of Israel's witness? They can. For instance, naïve readings of the "suffering servant" texts as Isaiah's conscious predictions of Jesus Christ do colonize and destabilize the text. However, the New Testament's own use of the Old Testament provides the church with more responsible interpretive guidance.

Richard Hays, Christopher Seitz, Ephraim Radner, and others explore the New Testament pattern of figural interpretation as the way to engage in Trinitarian, Christological reading while respecting the integrity of the Old Testament. Hays cites Erich Auerbach's classic definition of figural reading:

> Figural interpretation establishes a connection between two events or persons in such a way that the first signifies not only itself but also the second, while the second involves or fulfills the first. The two poles of a figure are separated in time, but both, being real events or persons, are within temporality. They are both contained in the flowing stream which is historical life, and only the comprehension, the *intellectus spiritualis*, of their interdependence is a spiritual act.[14]

Hays emphasizes that figuration is not prediction. "Figural reading need not presume that the OT authors—or the characters they narrate—were conscious of predicting or anticipating Christ. Rather, the discernment of a figural correspondence is necessarily retrospective rather than prospective."[15]

Figural readings of the Old Testament do not annihilate the integrity of the text. "To the contrary," says Hays, "they affirm its reality and find in it a significance beyond that which anyone could previously have grasped."[16] So, for instance, it is not at all necessary to imagine that Isaiah predicted or envisioned Christ in the suffering servant song of 52:13–53:13. Isaiah may well have understood Israel itself or idealized Israel as the servant. But when the earliest Christian witnesses—themselves Jews thoroughly familiar with Scripture—construed what they had seen and heard in Jesus, crucified and raised to new life, they saw one who was despised and rejected, a man of sorrows and acquainted with grief. They knew that the crucified one had borne our griefs and carried our sorrows, that he was

---

14. Erich Auerbach, *Mimesis* (Princeton: Princeton University Press, 1968), 73.

15. Richard B. Hays, *Reading Backwards: Figural Christology and the Fourfold Gospel Witness* (Waco, TX: Baylor University Press, 2014), 2.

16. Hays, *Reading Backwards*, xv.

wounded for our transgressions, and that we are healed by his wounds. They affirmed that he was exalted and lifted up. Knowing the reality of God's presence in the faith and life of Israel, the early church assumed correspondence between what God had done and what God was continuing to do. The *Speaking of God* in the life of Israel and the *Speaking of God* in Jesus Christ are the continuous discourse of the one God.

"The Gospels teach us to read the OT for figuration," says Hays. "The literal historical sense of the OT is not denied or negated; rather, it becomes the vehicle for latent figural meanings unsuspected by the original author and readers."[17] Figural interpretations of the Old Testament are not fanciful projections, but recognitions that the God made known to Israel is the same God made known in Christ. Figural readings have never been limited to Christological interpretation, however. Ecclesial readings of the Old Testament are also apposite, so that what we see in Israel makes clear what we see in the church. Conversely, failure to see the Christian community through Israel diminishes our understanding of the life to which the church is called. To paraphrase Auerbach, figural interpretation of the Old Testament establishes connection between Israel and the church in a way that Israel signifies not only itself but also the church, while the church involves or fulfills Israel. Israel and the church are separated in time, but both are within temporality. They are both contained in the flowing stream which is God-shaped life; it is the *understanding* of their interdependence that is a spiritual act.

The interdependence of Israel and the church—now as well as then—is real. Recognizing that reality requires the church's spiritual perception, its comprehension, its understanding. It should go without saying that just as the contemporary church sees itself through the lens of the New Testament so it must also see itself through the lens of the Old Testament, for the same God has called both Israel and the church.

It should also go without saying that the church must see the contemporary Jewish people as living out Torah just as the church sees itself living out gospel. Failing to see itself through the lens of God's way with covenant people Israel—both ancient Israel and the contemporary Jewish people—and imagining that it has replaced Israel, the church becomes susceptible to distorted, idealized images of itself. Seeing itself through the lens of God's consistent way with his people opens the church to a more faithful understanding of its life and a more faithful understanding of the Lord of its life. When the church looks, what can it see?

17. Hays, *Reading Backwards*, 15.

People of God: Although it is currently fashionable to apply "people of God" to the church, the term is often understood as applying individually to many churches, each of which understands itself as a distinct people of God. What is lost is the scriptural sense of a people called to be God's people in the world. What is lost is the knowledge that God has chosen us, not we who have chosen God. What is lost is the church as a light to the nations by virtue of its life, not just its words. What is lost is knowing the church as "a chosen race, a royal priesthood, a holy nation, God's own people" (1 Pet 2:10). All of these titles are, of course, designations of Israel. They are now applied also to the (gentile) church of whom Peter says, "Once you were not a people, but now you are God's people" (1 Pet 2:10). The twelve tribes of Israel were together the people of God. The thousands upon thousands of Christian denominations do not understand themselves together as the one people of God. Sadly, the church's attenuated sense of its peoplehood has too often been accompanied by denial that living Israel, the ongoing Jewish people, continues to be God's people.

Keeping Covenant: Because the churches do not see themselves together as the people of God, they fail to understand their faith and life as communal response to God's covenantal faithfulness. The earliest church received from the Lord what it has handed on to us: "This [bread] is my body that is for you (*plural*). Do this in remembrance of me. . . . This cup is the new covenant in my blood. Do this, as often as you (*plural*) drink it, in remembrance of me." Too often, "as often" is reduced to occasionally, and to what is done personally. What does the church do when it "does this"? What does the church remember when it remembers Jesus Christ? The Great Thanksgiving in the eucharistic liturgy remembers God's work in creation, election, and providential care; it remembers the acts of salvation in Christ; and it remembers promised renewal in the Holy Spirit. As the church prays at the table, it re-members—it knows again—the faithful presence of the one triune God in Israel and the church. What does the church do in bread and wine? It confirms its covenantal faithfulness to the faithful God of the covenant. And, just as in Israel's covenant "renewal" at Shechem, the church is called to "choose this day whom it will serve," keeping covenant as the people of God.

The Church Sins: The Old Testament understands clearly that Israel sins. From Solomon's prayer—"your people Israel, having sinned against you . . . forgive the sin of your people Israel" (1 Kgs 8:34–35)—through Hosea's accusation—"Since the days of Gibeah you have sinned, O Israel" (Hos 10:9)—to Jeremiah's decree—"The sin of Judah is written with an iron pen; with a diamond point it is engraved on the tablet of their hearts" (Jer 17:1)—and beyond, the sin of the covenant people of God is laid bare. Israel's sin is not simply the sin of some Israelites but the corporate sin of the nation. The church's failure to see its life as people of God through the lens of Israel's life as people of God, imaging itself as better than Israel, has reduced its understanding of sin to individual sins. Whether explicitly, as in Catholic understanding, or implicitly, as in most Protestant understanding, a clear sense of ever-possible and ever-present ecclesial sin is absent. Apart from awareness of ecclesial disobedience, the church's confession and repentance become impossible. Apart from knowing itself through Israel, the church endows itself with a false sense of its sanctity, even if only for its invisible self.

God's Judgment: The Lord was not indifferent to Israel's sin. "Thus says the LORD, 'For three transgressions of Judah and for four, I will not revoke the punishment. . . . For three transgressions of Israel and for four, I will not revoke the punishment'" (Amos 2:4, 6). It seldom occurs to the church that it is being judged for its transgressions. Mainline Protestant churches in North America often use *exile* as a biblical figure to characterize their weakened situation in contemporary culture. In a time of declining membership, diminished resources, and waning influence, the church imagines itself in "Babylonian exile," living in anticipation of return to "Jerusalem." What the church fails even to imagine is that the Lord may be judging the church now, just as he judged Judah then, and that God may have driven the church into its "exile" as consequential chastisement for its sin. Free from God's judgment, the churches free themselves for a life of goals, strategies, plans, and programs of their own devising.

God's Fidelity: Karl Barth captures in one sentence the Christian necessity of confidence in Israel's eternal election as God's covenant people: "God's faithfulness in the reality of Israel is in fact the guarantee of His faithfulness to us too, and so to all men."[18] If God breaks his covenant promise to Israel, how can the church be confident in God's promises in Christ? The church can be confident in God's enduring fidelity because it can see, here and now, the Jewish people of God.

Christian denial of God's continuing fidelity to the Jews, people of the covenant, not only calls God's faithfulness into question; it implies that everything hinges on our faithfulness to God. We are the ones who must have sufficient faith to merit God's approval. We are the ones who must

---

18. Karl Barth, *Dogmatics in Outline*, trans. G. T. Thompson (London: SCM, 1949), 80.

fulfill our promise to God in order to avoid divine judgment and rejection. The implicit insecurity hidden within all forms of supersession can easily morph into the ecclesial pretention that individual Christians must demonstrate their faithfulness to God by living out faithfulness to the church!

RECLAIMING THE NEW TESTAMENT

Failure to see the church through the lens of biblical Israel and the contemporary Jewish people produces theological and ecclesiological deficits that are exacerbated by malformed readings of the New Testament. The New Testament is marked by multiple issues surrounding interpretation of the relationship between Jesus and the Pharisees, Paul and Israel, the Gospel writers and the Jews, the Jewish/gentile makeup of the earliest churches, and more. Although none of these issues lends itself to easy resolution, most are popularly understood as strongly or mildly anti-Judaic. Amy-Jill Levine, a Jewish New Testament scholar, has concluded that "neither historical nor literary nor any other critical method can resolve the question of whether the Synoptic Gospels and Acts were written with an anti-Jewish agenda and/or whether they were read as anti-Jewish by their original audiences. At best, we can, and should, seek to expose anti-Jewish traditional readings as well as those passages that lend themselves to such readings."[19] It may be helpful to point out several matters that have made possible popular misconceptions of the New Testament's treatment of Jews. This, in turn, may encourage more careful, and more faithful, reading of the church's Scripture.

Translation

The original Preface to the King James Bible warns that "the same things uttered in Hebrew, and translated into another tongue, have not the same force in them: and not only those things, but the law itself, and the prophets, and the rest of the books, have no small difference, when they are spoken in their own language." The same is true of New Testament Greek.

---

19. Amy-Jill Levine, "Matthew, Mark, and Luke: Good News or Bad?" in *Jesus, Judaism, and Christian Anti-Judaism*, ed. Paula Fredriksen and Adele Reinhartz (Louisville: Westminster John Knox, 2002), 97–98.

Translation is as much an art as a science, and the consciousness of the translator plays a role in rendering one language into another. English-speaking readers of the Bible should be aware that English renderings of Hebrew or Greek may distort as well as enlighten.

Romans 11:28—The Revised Standard Version (RSV), the New Revised Standard Version (NRSV), the Revised English Bible (REB), and the English Standard Version (ESV) all read (with minor variations), "As regards the gospel they [the Jews] are enemies of God for your sake; but as regards election they are beloved, for the sake of their ancestors." "Enemies of God" is a serious charge, but the charge should be dismissed because Paul did not write "of God." The words simply do not appear in Paul's Greek! The NRSV is honest enough to include in some editions the footnote, "Gk lacks *of God*." But if the Greek lacks the words, why include them? The King James Version (KJV), Today's New International Version (TNIV), and the Common English Bible (CEB) follow the Greek and do not add words that are absent from Paul's letter. Following Paul, then, we read in rhetorical parallel:

> with respect to the *gospel* they are *enemies* for the sake of *you;*
> with respect to the *election* they are *beloved* for the sake of *the fathers.*
> (Rom 11:28)

Jewish opposition to the gospel opens redemption to the gentiles. Election of Israel and the covenants through Abraham, Moses, David, and beyond confirm the Jewish people as beloved. It is the hardening of Israel that makes possible the inclusion of the gentiles so that, at the end, the "full number of the Gentiles" and "all Israel" will be saved.

Romans 10:4—The RSV, the NRSV, the REB, and the ESV read, "Christ is the *end* of the law. . . ." In contrast, the TNIV reads, "Christ is the *culmination* of the law so that there may be righteousness for everyone who believes," and the CEB reads, "Christ is the *goal* of the law, which leads to righteousness for all who have faith in God." Paul's meaning hinges on translation of the Greek *telos* (from which we get the English word "teleology," referring to direction toward/shaped by a purpose). *Telos* does not suggest simple termination (Christ is the cessation, the shutdown, the rejection of the law), but rather purpose/goal/completion/accomplishment. Paul is not saying that Torah is now finished and done, replaced by faith, but rather is being consistent with Jesus's own words—"Do not think that I have come to abolish the law or the prophets; I have come not to abolish but to fulfill" (Matt 5:17). Christ has fulfilled Torah so that in him righteousness is no longer restricted to Israel but is now open in faith to the gentiles.

John 19:14–16—The text reads in the NRSV, "[Pilate] said to the Jews, 'Here is your King!' They cried out, 'Away with him! Away with him! Crucify him!'" This is only one of the many passages in the Gospels in which "the Jews" are antagonists who seek and then collude in Jesus's death. New Testament use of "the Jews" (Greek *ioudaios*) is not monovalent; it is used with reference to Jesus, and to Jesus's disciples, followers, and friends as well as to his adversaries. Even in instances when it is used to describe Jesus's opponents, it refers only to some Jews, not all Jews. Moreover, in hostile, death-dealing contexts, it is possible that *ioudaios* is used as an epithet referring to Jews who are the Jerusalem Temple establishment. That seems to be the case in John 19:14–16, where "Jews" is synonymous with "chief priests." That is the judgment made by the translators of the CEB: "Pilate said to the Jewish leaders, 'Here's your king.' The Jewish leaders cried out, 'Take him away! Take him away! Crucify him!'" In any case, it should be noted that the ones calling for Jesus's crucifixion are not the leaders of all Jews but rather leaders of the Jerusalem Temple establishment.[20]

Because the same name "Jews" refers to both a first-century and a contemporary people, special care should be taken in the interpretation of *"the Jews"* every time the word is used in the New Testament. Throughout Christian history it has been all too easy to equate some biblical Jews with all biblical Jews, and then with all contemporary Jews: the opposition of some Jewish leaders in early first-century Judea is imputed to all Jews in every age. The New Testament should never be misread as giving support to virulent or mild forms of anti-Semitism, in the church or in society.

Pharisees

When the Gospels are read as the drama of Jesus's conflict with the Jews, Pharisees play the role of chief villains. Whatever we make of Jesus's relationship to the Pharisees, the disputes were an intra-Jewish controversy. Disagreements centered on what the Law required; they were not con-

---

20. John's Gospel may reflect intra-Jewish antagonism between Hellenistic Jews and Jerusalem's Temple institution. This might explain John's placing of the Temple cleansing at the beginning of Jesus's ministry.

flicts between observing Torah or disregarding it. Jesus's "formula" in the Sermon on the Mount—"You have heard that it was said. . . . But I say to you"—does not eradicate what was said but rather intensifies it: righteousness must now exceed that of the Pharisees. First-century Judaism was pluralistic; Pharisees were but one of a number of groups—Sadducees, Essenes, Zealots, followers of John the Baptizer, Hellenistic Jews living outside of Judea, collaborators with Rome, and probably other Jewish groups whose names have been lost to history. The Judaism of the day was not as fragmented as contemporary Christianity, but it exhibited diverse understandings of Jewish faith and life.

Jacob Neusner,[21] E. P. Sanders,[22] and others have demonstrated that traditional Christian stereotypes of the Pharisees do not fit the evidence, even when the evidence is restricted to the Gospels. Far from being self-assured legalists who imagined they could earn salvation by the merit of their good works, Pharisees were devout "laity" who strove to sanctify all of life through obedience to the Torah and its interpretations. In Neusner's view, the Pharisees dealt with the reality of foreign occupation by concentrating on what they believed was crucial to the maintenance of Jewish identity: "fulfillment of all the laws of the Torah, even ritual purity and tithing, to achieve elevation of the life of all the people, at home and in the streets, to what Torah had commanded: *You shall be a kingdom of priests and a holy people.*"[23] Among other things, this meant that Pharisees (who were not priests) attempted to live as if they were always in Jerusalem's Temple sanctuary. Even complicated and inconvenient purity laws were extended to social life. Their concern was "to preserve, maintain, and defend Israel's status as the people of the covenant and the righteousness of the law."[24]

Jesus's disagreement and conflict with the Pharisees occurred within ongoing intra-Jewish disputes about what it meant to be the people of God. James D. G. Dunn notes that "the issue as it came to be at the time of Jesus . . . was not merely about points of law, or of ethical decision, but

---

21. Jacob Neusner, *From Politics to Piety: The Emergence of Pharisaic Judaism* (Englewood Cliffs, NJ: Prentice Hall, 1973); Neusner, *Judaism in the Beginning of Christianity* (Philadelphia: Fortress, 1984).

22. E. P. Sanders, *Paul, the Law, and the Jewish People* (Philadelphia: Fortress, 1983); Sanders, *Jesus and Judaism* (Philadelphia: Fortress, 1985).

23. Neusner, *From Politics to Piety*, 146.

24. James D. G. Dunn, *Jesus, Paul and the Law* (Louisville: Westminster John Knox, 1990), 71.

about how Jews should live as being the people of God, about what walking (*halakah*) according to God's statutes actually involved."[25] The issue was not Torah as such, but whether all Jews must observe all laws and traditions as the essential mark of God's gracious election. Thus, works of the law were constraining, "*not* because they constituted impossible merit-earning demands, but because they were so firmly identified as marks of the Jewish nation and so in effect confined the grace of God to members of that nation."[26]

Jesus's difference with the Pharisees was more than a demonstration that human need justifies an occasional breach of otherwise valid laws. The dispute concerned the scope of God's covenant, the shape of covenant faithfulness, and the purpose of Torah. Three vignettes in Mark 2:13–28 dramatize the difference. These controversy narratives suggest that the difference between Jesus and the Pharisees concerned openness to those on the outside rather than the purity of those on the inside: "I have come not to call the righteous but sinners" (2:17); joy rather than rigor: "As long as they have the bridegroom with them, they cannot fast" (2:19); and God's covenant as a gift rather than a compulsion: "The sabbath was made for humankind, and not humankind for the sabbath" (2:27).

The Pharisees may have come up with limited answers, but they asked the right questions: What is the scope of the covenant? What is the character of God's people? How can God's people live faithfully in the midst of a culture that may overwhelm them? What does it take for God's people to remain *God's* people? Jesus was not indifferent to these questions, which is why the Pharisees were worth arguing with.

The New Testament as Christian Scripture

The few examples discussed above suggest the need for Christian reexamination of the New Testament's understanding of Israel and the Jews—both Jewish followers of Jesus and Jews who did not find the Messiah in Jesus. Christian Scripture—Old and New Testament together—witness to the one God's way in the world, from creation to redemption in the hope of consummation. If the New Testament is severed from the Old Testament

---

25. James D. G. Dunn, *The Partings of the Ways Between Christianity and Judaism* (London: SCM, 1991), 102.

26. Dunn, *Jesus, Paul and the Law*, 11–12.

in crude Marcionite fashion, or if the New Testament is read in ways that denigrate Israel and the Jewish people, Christian understanding of who God is and how God acts in the world is diminished. A half century ago, J. B. Phillips wrote an enduring classic, *Your God Is Too Small*.[27] Christian dismissal of God's way with Israel and God's continuing way with the Jewish people can turn the Lord who is "the hope of all the ends of the earth" (Ps 65:6) into a too-small god whose care is focused on individual Christians, fulfilling their personal needs and wishes.

The God and Father of the Lord Jesus Christ is the God of Abraham, Isaac, and Jacob. "A wandering Aramean was *our* father" (Deut 26:5). And so, together with the Jewish people, the church is called to "ask now about former ages, long before our own, ever since the day that God created human beings on the earth; ask from one end of heaven to the other: has anything so great as this ever happened or has its like ever been heard of?" (Deut 4:32)

---

27. J. B. Phillips, *Your God Is Too Small* (New York: Touchstone, 1952).

Chapter 8

IN OUR TIME

Remember that at one time you Gentiles in the flesh . . . remember that you were at that time separated from Christ, alienated from the commonwealth of Israel, and strangers to the covenants of promise, having no hope and without God in the world. But now in Christ Jesus you who were once far off have been brought near in the blood of Christ. For he is our peace, who has made us both one, and has broken down the dividing wall of hostility.

Ephesians 2:11–14 (RSV)

It went without saying that Mr. Mawhinney was a Christian, a long-standing member of the great overpowering majority that fought the Revolution and founded the nation and conquered the wilderness and subjugated the Indian and enslaved the Negro and emancipated the Negro and segregated the Negro, one of the good, clean, hard-working Christian millions who settled the frontier, tilled the farms, built the cities, governed the states, sat in Congress, occupied the White House, amassed the wealth, possessed the land, owned the steel mills and the ball clubs and the railroads and the banks, even owned and oversaw the language, one of those unassailable Nordic and Anglo-Saxon Protestants who ran America and always would run it—generals, dignitaries, magnates, tycoons, the men who laid down the law and called the shots and read the riot act when they chose to—while my father, of course, was only a Jew.

Philip Roth, *The Plot Against America*

Two mid-twentieth-century events occasioned a major shift in relationships between Christians and Jews. The first was full comprehension of the horrors of *Shoah*, Holocaust. Nazi Germany's systematic attempt to exterminate the Jewish people, coupled with Allied failures to acknowledge the disaster and curtail its effects, laid bare the consequences of centuries-long contempt of Jews. Much of "Christian Europe" participated willingly in the Third Reich's systematic procedures of separation, deportation, and annihilation. There were too few Righteous Gentiles, and Le Chambons were too rare. The second event, perhaps made possible by the first, was the establishment of the modern state of Israel, providing a land of haven for the Jewish people. Both events led to a diminution of overt anti-Jewish social and political discrimination, and both necessitated theological and moral self-examination by the churches.

IN OUR TIME

The Catholic Church led the way. Prior to the opening of the Second Vatican Council, Pope John XXIII instructed the Secretariat for Promoting Christian Unity to prepare a statement on the Jews. The five-year development process shaped a series of draft documents, each one building on and strengthening its predecessor. The result was a groundbreaking advance in the church's understanding of the relationship between Christians and Jews. The Council approved the final draft, resulting in the adoption of a rich biblical and theological text.[1]

Nostra Aetate—Vatican II's "Declaration on the Relation of the Church to Non-Christian Religions"—is a consideration of "what men have in common and what draws them to fellowship."[2] It begins with some vague thoughts about religion in general before mentioning Hinduism, Buddhism, and Islam. A few generous words are said about each of the three, together with a call for mutual understanding and cooperation. If *Nostra Aetate* had ended there it would soon have been forgotten. If it had gone

---

1. For a more thorough treatment of the process, *Nostra Aetate* itself, and the response of American Protestant churches, see Joseph D. Small, "In Our Time," in *A Jubilee for All Time: The Copernican Revolution in Jewish-Christian Relations*, ed. Gilbert S. Rosenthal (Eugene, OR: Pickwick Publications, 2014). Some of the material in this chapter is drawn from that essay.

2. All citations of *Nostra Aetate* are from http://www.vatican.va/archive/hist_councils/iivatican_council/documents./

on to treat Judaism in as cursory a manner as it had other world religions, it would have been filed away and ignored.

The Declaration is remembered primarily for its lengthy section on "the bond that spiritually ties the people of the New Covenant to Abraham's stock." Unlike its brief references to other religions, the eight paragraphs on Judaism are deeply theological affirmations of the enduring link between God's chosen peoples. *Nostra Aetate* does not treat the relationship of Christianity to Judaism as one instance of "various religions," but as the embodiment of "shared patrimony." *Nostra Aetate* soon proved to be more than a Roman Catholic statement, for it prompted other Christian churches to undertake their own examinations of the relationship between Christianity and Judaism.

Nostra Aetate advanced Christian understanding in five important ways. First, it forcefully affirms Christianity's continuing debt to the faith of Israel, acknowledging that "the beginnings of [the church's] faith and her election are found already in the Patriarchs, Moses and the prophets," and that "the Apostles, the Church's main-stay and pillars, as well as most of the early disciples who proclaimed Christ's Gospel to the world, sprang from the Jewish people." The Decree moves beyond historical acknowledgment to affirm that the contemporary church "draws sustenance from the root of that well-cultivated olive tree onto which have been grafted the wild shoots, the Gentiles." *Nostra Aetate* affirms that Christian faith and life continuously spring from Israel's faith and life. The relationship of Christians and Jews is enduring.

This profession leads to a second generative affirmation: God's fidelity to the Jewish people is permanent. Far from rejecting them, "God holds the Jews most dear for the sake of their Fathers; He does not repent of the gifts He makes or of the calls He issues—such is the witness of the Apostle." A corollary to this fundamental declaration is that the Jews are not to be held responsible for the crucifixion of Christ. Although Jerusalem authorities pressed for Christ's death, "what happened in His passion cannot be charged against all the Jews, without distinction, then alive, nor against the Jews of today." *Nostra Aetate* underlines this statement by giving forceful instruction to all bishops, priests, and teachers: "All should see to it, then, that in catechetical work or in the preaching of the word of God they shall not teach anything that does not conform to the truth of the Gospel and the spirit of Christ."

A third creative element is *Nostra Aetate*'s forceful rejection of the long history and present reality of discrimination, hostility, and persecution of

Jews. While rejecting persecution of any people, it emphasizes that, "the Church, mindful of the patrimony she shares with the Jews and moved not by political reasons but by the Gospel's spiritual love, decries hatred, persecutions, displays of anti-Semitism, directed against Jews at any time and by anyone." This statement was essential in 1965, when Shoah was a living horror, but the Declaration's ongoing importance lies in its even more comprehensive rejection of centuries of persecution, and its proleptic denunciation of the virulent anti-Semitism that has reemerged in subsequent decades.

Fourth, while *Nostra Aetate* expresses the Christian hope in "that day, known to God alone, on which all peoples will address the Lord in a single voice," it disavows evangelization of Jews. Instead, it holds that, "since the spiritual patrimony common to Christians and Jews is thus so great, this sacred synod wants to foster and recommend that mutual understanding and respect which is the fruit, above all, of biblical and theological studies as well as of fraternal dialogues."

Finally, all elements of *Nostra Aetate*'s decree on the Jews grow from its introductory affirmation of "the bond that spiritually ties the people of the New Covenant to Abraham's stock." The Decree proclaims that the relationship between the church and the Jewish people is fundamental, enduring, and contemporary. Judaism is not just one of the other religions, and the relationship between Christians and Jews is not merely one case of interfaith liaison. The church's connection to both historic Israel and contemporary Judaism is intrinsic to Christian faith and the life of the church.

Nostra Aetate's paragraphs are brief, but they contain dramatic reversals of centuries-old misrepresentations that resulted in physical and emotional harm for generations of Jews and spiritual harm for the church. The paragraphs are also highly suggestive, giving substance to the call for further biblical and theological studies. The Catholic Church has heeded its own call, resulting in a series of statements that culminated fifty years later in "The Gifts and Calling of God Are Irrevocable," issued by the Commission for Religious Relations with Jews of the Pontifical Council for Promoting Christian Unity.[3]

---

3. "The Gifts and Calling of God Are Irrevocable," www.vatican.va/roman_curia/pon tifical_councils/chrstuni/relations-jews-docs/rc_pc_chrstuni_doc_20151210. Accessed December 11, 2015.

THE FRUIT OF BIBLICAL AND THEOLOGICAL STUDIES

Prior to Vatican II, American Protestant churches gave scant attention to Catholic theology, ethics, and church structures except to criticize them. But the Council fulfilled Pope John XXIII's desire for Catholic *aggiornamento*, and Protestant churches took notice. The Council prompted deeper academic and ecclesial biblical inquiry that, in turn, inspired Protestant liturgical renewal, ecclesiological understanding, ecumenical openness, and ethical development. Notably, *Nostra Aetate* moved Protestant churches beyond customary censure of anti-Semitism toward sustained consideration of the relationship between Christians and Jews.

The movement toward deeper understanding coincided with a complicating factor, however. The 1967 Six-Day War led to Israel's occupation of Sinai, the Golan Heights, the Gaza Strip, and the West Bank. The establishment of military outposts in the occupied territories led to a policy of Israeli settlements that was commenced in earnest following the 1973 "Yom Kippur war." Previous Catholic concern about the reaction of Arab states to positive conciliar statements about the Jews now became Protestant concern about Israeli state policy in the West Bank and Gaza. Religious opposition to Israel's occupation policies increased in subsequent years, producing boycotts and divestment actions. Condemnation of Israel was not confined to geopolitical policy, however, for all too often critique of "the Jewish state" slid into denunciation of "the Jews."

Nevertheless, *Nostra Aetate* raised the fundamental issue of the Jewish-Christian link, and Protestant churches understood that they too had to address the issue. Many American churches issued studies and statements that exhibited common approaches to the major themes introduced in *Nostra Aetate*.[4] The most ambitious of the attempts to address Jewish-Christian relations was the 1986 Presbyterian Church (USA)'s extensive treatment—"A Theological Understanding of the Relationship between Christians and Jews." Prepared as a pastoral and teaching document to facilitate discussion within the PCUSA and to guide conversation, cooperation, and dialogue between Presbyterians and Jews, it addresses the basic theological question: "What is the relationship which God intends between Christians and Jews, between Christianity and Judaism?" The

---

4. A collection of statements by the World Council of Churches and its member churches, some pre-dating *Nostra Aetate*, is found in *The Theology of the Churches and the Jewish People* (Geneva: WCC Publications, 1988).

document is organized around careful explication of seven theological affirmations.[5]

> We affirm that the living God whom Christians worship is the same God who is worshiped and served by Jews. We bear witness that the God revealed in Jesus, a Jew, to be the Triune Lord of all, is the same one disclosed in the life and worship of Israel. (514)

The affirmation goes beyond recognition of common history and shared concepts to affirm that an enduring bond between Christians and Jews is established by the faith of both in the one true God. Despite the "partings of the ways" between synagogue and church, the statement affirms that "there are ties which remain between Christians and Jews: the faith of both in the one God whose loving and just will is for the redemption of all humankind, and the Jewishness of Jesus whom we confess to be the Christ of God." These ties are affirmed to be God-given and so must be lived out by Christians and Jews.

> We affirm that the church, elected in Jesus Christ, has been engrafted into the people of God established by the covenant with Abraham, Isaac, and Jacob. Therefore, Christians have not replaced Jews. (515)

Supersessionism is firmly rejected by stating that "God's covenants are not broken" and "the church has not 'replaced' the Jewish people." The affirmation goes beyond rejection, however, to affirm that "the church, being made up primarily of those who were once aliens and strangers to the covenants of promise, has been engrafted into the people of God."

> We affirm that both the church and the Jewish people are elected by God for witness to the world and that the relationship of the church to contemporary Jews is based on that gracious and irrevocable election of both. (517)

The relationship between Christians and Jews is not formed by shared history or contemporary choice. God establishes shared witness to the

---

5. All citations of "A Theological Understanding of the Relationship between Christians and Jews" are from *Selected Theological Statements of the Presbyterian Church (U.S.A.) General Assemblies (1956–1998)* (Louisville: Office of Theology and Worship, 1998), 510–23. References are noted in the text by page numbers in parentheses.

world. The affirmation explicates the common calling of Christians and Jews: "God chose a particular people, Israel, as a sign and foretaste of God's grace toward all people. It is for the sake of God's redemption of the world that Israel was elected. . . . God continues that purpose through Christians and Jews. The church, like the Jews, is called to be a light to the nations."

> We affirm that the reign of God is attested both by the continuing exis-tence of the Jewish people and by the church's proclamation of the gospel of Jesus Christ. Hence, when speaking with Jews about matters of faith, we must always acknowledge that Jews are already in a covenantal rela-tionship with God. (517)

The affirmation goes beyond condemnation of proselytism to affirm that God's covenant with Jews is inviolable and that the Jewish people con-tinue to bear witness to God's gracious purposes. While acknowledging the commission to bear witness to Christ, the affirmation also acknowl-edges God's covenant fidelity to the Jews. Therefore, dialogue, not targeted evangelism, is affirmed as the appropriate form of conversation about faith between Christians and Jews, stipulating that "dialogue is not a cover for proselytism. Rather, as trust is established, not only questions and con-cerns can be shared but faith and commitments as well."

> We acknowledge in repentance the church's long and deep complicity in the proliferation of anti-Jewish attitudes and actions through its "teaching of contempt" for the Jews. Such teaching we now repudiate, together with the acts and attitudes which it generates. (519)

The affirmation goes beyond general contrition to catalogue past and present instances of the "teaching of contempt." Recognizing the reality of mutual hostility in the early centuries, the church admits that, "in subse-quent centuries, after the occasions for the original hostility had long since passed, the church misused portions of the New Testament as proof texts to justify a heightened animosity toward Jews." The lengthy explication concludes with the church's oath, "We pledge, God helping us, never again to participate in, to contribute to, or (insofar as we are able) to allow the persecution or denigration of Jews or the belittling of Judaism."

> We affirm the continuity of God's promise of land along with the obliga-tions of that promise to the people of Israel. (520)

The issue of the land, absent from *Nostra Aetate* and mentioned only as a political issue in other Protestant statements, is recognized as a theological matter. The document acknowledges that a faithful explication of the biblical material relating to the covenant with Abraham cannot avoid or dismiss the reality of God's promise of land. "The question with which we must wrestle is how this promise is to be understood in the light of the existence of the modern political state of Israel which has taken its place among the nations of the world." The draft document encountered opposition, leading to negotiation and revision of the text . Eugene March notes that "what emerged was more 'compromised' and less coherent. The theological significance of the modern state of Israel was not addressed and remains a debatable subject for many Presbyterians. A degree of 'spiritualizing' the land and seeing it too much as a metaphor was introduced."[6]

> We affirm that Jews and Christians are partners in waiting. Christians see in Christ the redemption not yet fully visible in the world, and Jews await the messianic redemption. Christians and Jews together await the final manifestation of God's promise of the peaceable kingdom. (522)

Christians and Jews are bound in hope as well as in memory and present life. Shared hope has a deep theological significance because "Christian hope is contiguous with Israel's hope and is unintelligible apart from it." Jewish and Christian partners in hope are "called to the service of God in the world." Forms of service may differ, but the vocation of each shares these elements: a striving to realize the word of the prophets, an attempt to remain sensitive to the dimensions of the holy, an effort to encourage the life of the mind, and a ceaseless activity in the cause of justice and peace.

AN ECCLESIOLOGICAL UNDERSTANDING OF THE RELATIONSHIP BETWEEN CHRISTIANS AND JEWS

Nostra Aetate's call for biblical and theological studies has borne fruit. In addition to denominational statements, numerous journal articles and books have probed aspects of the link between Judaism and Christianity.[7]

---

6. W. Eugene March, "Presbyterians and Jews: A Theological Turning Point" (unpublished paper, cited with permission).

7. Significant Jewish contributions to the dialogue include: Tikva Frymer-Kensky et

Of particular interest are statements produced by Jewish and Christian scholars. *Dabru Emet: A Jewish Statement on Christians and Christianity* and the Christian Scholars Group's *A Sacred Obligation: Rethinking Christian Faith in Relation to Judaism and the Jewish People* are primary examples of an emerging consensus.[8] The scholarly consensus has yet to fully permeate the consciousness of congregations and their members, however, and deeper relations continue to be blocked by differences concerning contemporary realities in Israel and Palestine.

Extensive literature and official statements hold promise, although they are marked by a significant lacuna. Most are concerned with aspects of the relationship between Christianity and Judaism or relationships between Jews and Christians. Less explored territory is the significance of those relationships for understanding the faith and life of the church itself. The relationship between Judaism and Christianity has implications for the church's self-understanding that must be addressed if the church is to know fully who it is.

In reducing biblical Israel to preparation for the coming of Christ, in confining the Old Testament to a record of the faith and life of an ancient people, and in failing to understand the God-graced reality of the Jews through the centuries, the church becomes a stranger to itself. Willie James Jennings notes that Christian failure to recognize the continuing importance of Israel to Christian existence makes it impossible for the church to answer the basic questions, "How did we get here in the first place? Where is here?" Jennings goes on to say, "The here is outside Israel, outside the conversation between biblical Israel and its God, outside the continuing conversations Israel has with that same God."[9] Apart from understanding both biblical Israel and the ongoing life of the Jews, the church cannot fully understand itself. Comprehension of God's way in the world is attenuated apart from comprehension of God's way with the Jews. Throughout the centuries, Christian distance from the Jews has made the church "aliens

---

al., eds., *Christianity in Jewish Terms* (Boulder, CO: Westview Press, 2000); David Novak, *Talking with Christians: Musings of a Jewish Theologian* (Grand Rapids: Eerdmans, 2005); and Peter Ochs, *Another Reformation: Postliberal Christianity and the Jews* (Grand Rapids: Baker Academic, 2011).

8. Both documents, together with other historical and contemporary material, are available in *Christians and Jews: People of God* (Office of Theology and Worship: "Church Issues Series No. 7"), www.pcusa.org/resources/christians-and-jews-people-god-church-issues-series/.

9. Willie James Jennings, *The Christian Imagination: Theology and the Origins of Race* (New Haven: Yale University Press, 2010), 252.

from the commonwealth of Israel, and strangers to the covenants of promise" (Eph 2:12).

The apostle Paul, himself a Jew, "of the people of Israel, of the tribe of Benjamin, a Hebrew born of Hebrews; as to the law a Pharisee" (Phil 3:5), agonized over the reality that most of his fellow Jews did not find the Messiah in Jesus the Christ. Although interpretation of his thought is complex and varied, attention to several features in his letter to the Romans will provide an angle of vision on the continuing reality of the Jewish people apart from Christ and on the faith and life of the church.

What Advantage Has the Jew?

Romans 9–11 is Paul's extended discourse on the Jewish people apart from Christ, but it is not the only place in the letter where he addresses the matter. Paul's letter to the church in Rome opens with a condemnation of gentile sinfulness followed by a critique of Jewish sinfulness. He makes it clear that "all who have sinned apart from the law will also perish apart from the law, and all who have sinned under the law will be judged by the law" (2:12). This raises the obvious question, "Then what advantage has the Jew?" (3:1). The advantage, says Paul, is that they were entrusted with the oracles of God—the sayings, the teaching, Torah. But how is this an advantage if the oracles only serve to judge? Remarkably, Paul says, "What if some were unfaithful? Will their faithlessness nullify the faithfulness of God? By no means! Although everyone is a liar, let God be proved true" (3:3–4).

What is at stake in Romans is the faithfulness of God. In a real sense, the theme of Romans 9–11 is not the Jews but the righteousness of God. "They are Israelites, and to them belong the adoption, the glory, the covenants, the giving of the law, the worship, and the promises; to them belong the patriarchs, and from them, according to the flesh, comes the Messiah, who is over all, God blessed forever" (9:4–5). But, of course, most of the Jews do not acknowledge Jesus as Messiah. Although this causes "great sorrow and unceasing anguish" in Paul's heart, and though he will probe the mystery of Israel's unbelief, he is certain of one thing: "it is not as though the word of God had failed" (9:6). Paul's discourse on the Jews apart from Christ is punctuated by three rhetorical questions with declarative answers.

What then are we to say? Is there injustice on God's part?
> By no means! (9:14)
I ask, then, has God rejected his people?
> By no means! (11:1)
So I ask, have they stumbled so as to fall?
> By no means! (11:11)

The first question follows Paul's discussion of Israel's election and its status as "children of the promise." The certainty of Israel's election leads to a declaration of the freedom of the electing God who calls a people "not from the Jews only but also from the Gentiles." But the calling of the gentiles leads to another question: "What then are we to say? Gentiles, who did not strive for righteousness, have attained it . . . but Israel, who did strive for the righteousness that is based on the law, did not succeed in fulfilling that law." Paul goes on to say that Israel's failings result from genuine zeal for God that nonetheless failed to comprehend the righteousness of God by seeking to establish their own righteousness. God's righteousness is revealed in Christ who is the fulfillment of the law.

Israel's failure leads to the second question, "I ask, then, has God rejected his people?" Paul's answer is an emphatic "No!" "God has not rejected his people whom he foreknew." Israel failed to obtain what it sought, but by God's grace now as then, a remnant always remains. But what of the rest? What of those who continue to live as Jews apart from Christ? That leads to the third question: "So I ask, have they stumbled so as to fall?" "By no means," says Paul, for "through their stumbling salvation has come to the Gentiles." Furthermore, says Paul, "if their stumbling means riches for the world, and if their defeat means riches for Gentiles, how much more will their full inclusion mean!"

Interlude

There is more to be said about Romans 9–11, but before proceeding it should be stressed that the central element in Paul's letter is the righteousness of God, not the unrighteousness of Israel or gentiles. Comprehensive human unrighteousness is evident in the simple observation that "all have sinned and fall short of the glory of God" (3:23). What is not clear by simple observation is that "the righteousness of God has been disclosed, and is attested by the law and the prophets, the righteousness of God through the faithfulness of Jesus Christ for all who have faith" (3:22, altered). So, "*since all have sinned and fall short of the glory of God, they are now justified by his grace as a gift*" (3:23). God's righteousness, sinners' justification, grace and faith are all complex matters in Romans, but one thing is clear: the righteousness of God is not dependent on the righteousness of humans. To the contrary, human unrighteousness—the unrighteousness of Jews and gentiles alike—serves to confirm the righteousness of God (3:5). Romans 9–11 is confirmation that the word of God has not failed, that there is no unrighteousness on God's part, because God has not rejected his people and God's people have not fallen.

N. T. Wright makes the point forcefully that when Paul speaks of the righteousness of God in Romans he means "God's faithfulness to the covenant with Abraham, to the single-plan-through-Israel-for-the-world and to the whole of creation."[10] God's covenant faithfulness to a particular people will be a blessing to the "many nations." God's righteousness is even apparent in Israel's stumbling, for through it salvation has come to the gentiles. Yet, says Paul, if a particular people's stumbling "means riches for the world, and if their defeat means riches for Gentiles, *how much more will their full inclusion mean!*" (11:11–12). Again, "If their rejection is the reconciliation of the world, *what will their acceptance be but life from the dead!*" (11:15). Again, "A hardening has come upon part of Israel until the full number of the Gentiles has come in. *And all Israel will be saved*" (11:25–26). In the redemption of the world—all Israel and the full number of the gentiles—God is proved true and God's righteousness is confirmed.

First Fruits and Trees

The church has been almost exclusively gentile for centuries. Although some Jews continue to find the Messiah in Jesus Christ, the vast majority of Jews have remained Jews. Those few Jews who have professed faith in Christ have been quickly assimilated into a church that is gentile in character, ethos, and practice. Therefore, when Paul speaks across the centuries to the contemporary church about Jews and gentiles he is speaking about Jews and Christians. New Testament letters are always from someone to someone about something. The book of Romans was a letter from Paul to

---

10. N. T. Wright, *Justification: God's Plan and Paul's Vision* (Downers Grove, IL: IVP Academic, 2009), 179.

the Christians in Rome about the righteousness of God, including God's righteousness regarding Jews and gentiles. As Romans is read by twenty-first-century Christians, it is a letter from Paul, through the Spirit, to the church about the righteousness of God, including God's righteousness regarding Jews and Christians, synagogue and church.

Two striking images in Romans 11:16 are particularly important to a theological understanding of the relationship between Jews and Christians, synagogue and church: "If the part of the dough offered as first fruits is holy, then the whole batch is holy; and if the root is holy, then the branches also are holy." The first image is an allusion to one of Torah's regulations regarding offerings: "whenever you eat of the bread of the land, you shall present a donation to the LORD. From your first batch of dough you shall present a loaf as a donation" (Num 15:19–20). If Israel, the first fruit of God's way in the world, is a holy nation, then the many nations are now holy in Christ. If the Jewish people of God are holy, then the gentile people of God are now holy; if the synagogue is holy, then the church is now holy. Jesus said, "Salvation is from the Jews" (John 4:22), and so the holiness of the church flows from the holiness of the Jews. The Jews are the first fruits through which blessing has come to the (gentile) church.

The second image—"and if the root is holy, then the branches are holy"—is more easily understood. The root nourishes the branches; branches separated from the tree wither away. Paul elaborates this image by picturing the pruning of the tree and the grafting of new branches onto the tree. Pruning is a familiar image for the Lord's judgment of both Israel and the nations. In Paul's use of the image, the tree is Israel. Some branches have been pruned, but the tree is not cut down; its roots remain deep in the soil. Gentiles—wild shoots—are grafted on "to share the rich root of the olive tree." The righteous God now gives gentiles a share in the life of the strong tree that he cultivated while the gentiles were growing wild. "Remember," Paul says to the gentiles, "it is not you who support the root, but the root that supports you." James D. G. Dunn comments that "God has not abandoned the tree as a whole. He has not reversed the roles, lavishing his horticultural care on the Gentiles while leaving Israel to run wild."[11]

Everything goes back to God's promise to Abraham, the Lord's enduring choice of Israel. It is as true now as then that "they [the Jews] are Israelites, and to them belong the adoption, the glory, the covenants, the

---

11. James D. G. Dunn, *Romans 9–16*, vol. 38 of *Word Biblical Commentary* (Waco, TX: Word, 1988), 673.

giving of the law, the worship, and the promises." Paul regrets that most Jews have not found the Messiah in Jesus, but he knows that "through their stumbling salvation has come to the Gentiles." He also knows that "by no means has God rejected his people" because "the gifts and the calling of God are irrevocable." Paul's grappling with the "riches and wisdom and knowledge of God" is not merely an interesting glimpse into the life of the early church; it serves to prompt the contemporary church's grappling with God's judgments and the Lord's ways with Jew and gentile, synagogue and church. As the church faces the matter, it must acknowledge at the outset it cannot boast, as if it has now become the tree while Jews are only lopped-off branches.

Paul's understanding of the relationship between Jews and gentiles within the Christian community, and between the church and Jews, means that the church, by and of itself, cannot claim that it is *the* people of God. The church is called to remember that at one time we gentiles were "without Christ, being aliens from the commonwealth of Israel, and strangers to the covenants of promise" (Eph 2:12). The gentile church is the newcomer in the kingdom of God, the younger sibling to the Jews who remain "a royal priesthood, a holy nation" (1 Pet 2:9). Markus Barth writes of the letter to the Ephesians that "the Jews formed the people of God long before Gentiles joined in. He who would want to have peace on earth apart from the Jewish Messiah, and without community with the people of which Jesus is a native son, would separate himself from salvation. . . . It is not enough to say that salvation *came* from the Jews; for salvation *comes* from the Jews."[12] Gentile Christians and the gentile church lack biblical warrant to deny that Jews continue to be God's people. Christians and Jews, synagogue and church, are bound together irreversibly, precisely as the peoples of God.

That Christians and Jews are, together, the people of God is a conviction of Christian theology. This conviction does not presume agreement by the Jewish people. Jews are certainly not dependent on Christians to justify or define their existence. In fact, Jews have every reason to be wary of Christian definitions of Jewish faith and life. Yet, neither is Christian understanding dependent on Jewish approval. It is vital that both church and synagogue pursue self-awareness that leads to deepened self-understanding. The preface to *Christianity in Jewish Terms*, a collection of Jewish reflections on Christianity, notes that, "as a minority in a still largely Christian America—and Christian West—Jews need to learn the

---

12. Markus Barth, *The People of God* (Eugene, OR: Wipf & Stock, 1983), 47–48.

languages and beliefs of their neighbors."[13] Similarly, the religious majority, the church, needs to learn the faith and life of the other covenant people, the Jews. Then the church can know more fully who it is as the Christian people of God together with the Jewish people of God.

ECCLESIOLOGY AND THE PEOPLE OF GOD

The church knows that God has revealed himself in the Word made flesh, knows God's presence in the grace and truth of Jesus Christ. The church also knows the advent of Christ as both climax and inauguration: "In many and various ways God spoke of old to our fathers by the prophets; but in these last days he has spoken to us by a Son, whom he appointed the heir of all things" (Heb 1:1–2, RSV). Yet, in both overt and subtle ways, the church acts as if God's speaking through the prophets has been overridden, rendered obsolete, silenced, replaced by God's speaking through the Son. Even when Christian replacement of Judaism is forcefully denied, the church fails to recognize the ways in which it ignores the abiding significance of God's way with biblical Israel and with contemporary Jewish faith and life. Not only does this denigrate Judaism; it also diminishes the church's understanding of its own faith and life.

People of God

The creation saga in Genesis ends with the Tower of Babel. There the presumption of human hegemony is met by the Lord who confuses human language and scatters them over the face of the earth. Biblical history then begins with the Lord's covenant with Abraham, with the gathering of the people of God. Gerhard Lohfink has shown that the "gathering of the people of God" is a fundamental element of Israel's faith. The account of covenant renewal in Deuteronomy is typical: "the LORD your God will restore your fortunes and have compassion on you, gathering you again from all the peoples among whom the LORD your God has scattered you . . . the LORD your God will gather you, and from there he will bring you back" (Deut 30:3–4). Lohfink's examination of multiple Old Testament references to the gathering of the scattered leads to a dual conclusion: "The

---

13. Frymer-Kensky et al., *Christianity in Jewish Terms*, ix.

one who gathers the people is always God. It is never said that Israel will gather itself," and, "The gathering of the people of God of course means more than an external bringing together. It always means, in addition, that Israel achieves an internal unity."[14]

No Christian church would deny that God gathers the church. Yet implicit in each church's affirmation is the assumption that God has gathered *it*, not that it remains but one of the scattered people. God's Pentecostal gathering of scattered peoples is ongoing, yet scattered Christian churches overlook God's will to gather them into one cohesive people of God. Israel's evident judgment and dispersion was the occasion for Isaiah's prophecy of the Lord's will to regather the scattered ones:

> [The LORD] will raise a signal for the nations
> > and will assemble the outcasts of Israel,
> and gather the dispersed of Judah
> > from the four corners of the earth.
> The jealousy of Ephraim shall depart,
> > the hostility of Judah shall be cut off;
> Ephraim shall not be jealous of Judah,
> > and Judah shall not be hostile towards Ephraim. (Isa 11:12–13)

Unlike Israel, the church's sense of itself as the people of God has devolved into satisfaction with the existence of multiple peoples of God scattered across the ecclesial landscape.

Renewed attention to Old Testament witness can deepen ecclesiology in two significant ways. First, it can suggest to the churches a perception of what it could mean to be, together, the people of God. Even in our scattered existence it is possible to know that jealousy and hostility (and their siblings, indifference and competition) are not our ecclesiastical fate. Instead, the churches can know that they are called to live out common peoplehood in an atomized world.

Second, the churches' theological/sociological ecclesiology will be deepened when they begin to learn what it means to be a people, not just a group of individual persons. Individual congregations might come to understand themselves as a people called by God, not a mere assortment of persons who have chosen to "join" a church. Congregations may then

---

14. Gerhard Lohfink, *Does God Need the Church?* (Collegeville, MN: The Liturgical Press, 1999), 52–53.

discover their life as participation in God's mission, not merely as a self-determined array of programs and services. Congregations might go on to recognize their relationship with other congregations in denominations as a sharing in the common life of God's people, not as an affiliation of convenience. Denominations might then learn that autonomy is not a mark of the people of God. They could begin to comprehend their mutual participation in God's single purpose in the world. God does not call scattered churches to form an institutional union but to be God's people gathered into multiple patterns of deep, abiding ecclesial communion.

Covenant Fidelity

The apostolic church's first recorded decision confirmed that gentiles were included in the people of God without having to observe the Law that marked the Jews as the people of God. The presenting issue was circumcision, but the larger question was whether gentiles had to observe all the obligations of Torah. The answer was announced by James: "I have reached the decision that we should not trouble those Gentiles who are turning to God" (Acts 15:19). However, inclusion of gentiles *as gentiles* in the people of God did not mean the exclusion of Jews from the people of God. Rather, gentiles were included in the Christian community by faith together with Jews who continued to live Torah faithfully. Covenant fidelity was not restricted to one form.

The depth and breadth of gentile inclusion is expressed by their sharing Israel's identity as "a chosen race, a royal priesthood, a holy nation, God's own people" (1 Pet 2:9). Like Israel, gentiles were elected "in order that you may proclaim the mighty acts of him who called you out of darkness into his marvelous light" (1 Pet 2:9). And, together with Jews, gentiles were called to live out their election by walking in a new Way. The originating word of the Lord came to first-century gentiles—and comes now to the twenty-first-century gentile church—"Now therefore, if you obey my voice and keep my covenant, you shall be my treasured possession out of all the peoples. Indeed, the whole earth is mine, but you shall be a priestly kingdom and a holy nation" (Exod 19:5–6). Keeping covenant is the church's requirement for living out its vocation as a priestly kingdom and a holy nation.

The apostolic witness is clear that gentile believers are not subject to the complete range of Torah and its elaborations. But freedom from the law is not freedom for lawlessness. John gives voice to New Testament witness when he writes, "Now by this we may be sure that we know him, if we obey his commandments" (1 John 1:3). The law and the prophets may be summed up in love of God and neighbor, but this affirmation is only the foundation for discerning what love of God and neighbor entails in specific cases and changing circumstances. The church remains subject to the Decalogue and, like Israel, must struggle to understand what covenant fidelity requires. The church's covenant obligations are different from Israel's, but they are obligations nonetheless.

The church fails to understand that covenant obligations are those of the people of God as community and only derivatively those of individuals within the community. Coupled with a reflexive aversion to "legalism," this misunderstanding produces an individualistic, laissez-faire understanding of morality. Ethical behavior is the personal obligation of Christians, of course, but only within the covenant obligations of corporate life does the "chosen race, royal priesthood, holy nation, God's own people" proclaim the mighty act of God in Christ.

Jews understand themselves as a people whose Jewishness entails certain obligations and practices. Even non-observant Jews continue to understand themselves as part of a people marked by distinctive ways of being in the world. While some Christian denominations understand themselves as people marked by communal obligations, these practices are generally restricted to denominational distinctives, rather than covenantal obligations that mark the whole Christian people of God. In many churches, enduring aversion to "legalism" has contributed to the weakening and abandonment of corporate disciplines. Christian behavior becomes indistinguishable from average American behavior. Robert Wilken notes that the early Christian movement was revolutionary "because it created a social group that promoted its own laws and patterns of behavior. . . . Like the Jews, Christians held profane what the Romans held sacred, and permitted what others thought reprehensible."[15] The church may need to learn again what it could mean to live in this time as the Christian people of God.

Place

People of God is not an abstraction, but a substantive community of actual persons existing in specific places. The history of the people of God

---

15. Robert Louis Wilken, *The Christians as the Romans Saw Them*, 2nd ed. (New Haven: Yale University Press, 2003), 119.

began when the Lord called Abram to go from one place to another, a God-provided land. The formation of the great nation began with movement from a place of slavery to a land of promise. Throughout the Old Testament narrative, Israel's life as the people of God takes place in places, whether the land of promise or regions of exile and diaspora. By the rivers of Babylon, a captive people ask, "How could we sing the LORD's song in a foreign land?" (Ps 137:4). How indeed, for the people of God are not an ethereal assemblage, existing outside of time and space, but people who weep and laugh in distinct places. God's people are not transported out of earthly places; rather, God dwells in the places of his people. From Eden's garden to the new Jerusalem of Revelation, place is central to God's way with his people.

In an interconnected world of mass migrations, some voluntary but many forced, land becomes a simple geographic designation for many, one land exchanged for another. But land often becomes the focus of a people, leading to proposals for geographic separation from large nation states. Scots in the United Kingdom, Quebecois in Canada, Basques and Catalans in Spain, and Kurds scattered throughout the Middle East assert distinct peoplehood in a distinct place that may require distinct nationhood. In the Middle East, the Jewish people now dwell in a land that is also a nation state, a land also claimed by Palestinians who demand autonomy and statehood.

To many in this world land is merely a parcel of earth, but to many others land is sacred. Gilbert Rosenthal gives voice to the significance of land for contemporary Jews: "For the Jew, there is a land, a country that is special and holy; its very soil is sacred. . . . It is the homeland, the fatherland, the center of the Jew's universe and of humanity's as well. That land is the Land of Eretz Yisrael."[16] Whatever Christians may think about current Israeli state policy in Palestine, it is essential to take considerate account of the connection of Jews to the land. The church relativizes the biblical understanding by reducing land to a placeless metaphor, however, keeping consistent with a long-standing Christian tendency to "spiritualize" the Old Testament, transforming the Old Testament's earthy terrain into timeless truths.

Abstracting place is not limited to land, however. For Israel and for contemporary Jews, holy ground and holy things are found in holy land. From

16. Gilbert S. Rosenthal, *What Can a Modern Jew Believe?* (Eugene, OR: Wipf & Stock, 2007), 131.

the Western Wall to the Torah Scroll to Yom Kippur, God's holiness infuses quotidian reality, transforming place and thing and time into encounter with the LORD. Churches such as my own, however, transform holiness into a generic concept by asserting that "Christians may worship at any time, for all time has been hallowed by God. . . . Christians may worship in any place, for the God who created time also created and ordered space" and by warning against "offering the material as a substitute for offering the self to God."[17] While these directives may be true in their own way, their elaboration in the church's "Directory for Worship" makes clear their intent to desanctify place, time, and things.

In classic Orthodox liturgy, the priest holds bread and wine, chanting to the assembly, "Holy things for holy people." Many contemporary American churches have "translated" this as "The gifts of God for the people of God."[18] Eucharistic bread and wine are certainly God's gifts for God's people, but the Americanized version loses a sense of the holiness of ordinary bread and wine and the holiness of ordinary people made holy by God in ordinary time and space. Christian distance from the Jewish people of God severs the intimate connection between God's people and God's things in God's place and time.

Sin and Repentance

Prayers of confession in Christian liturgy tend to enumerate personal shortcomings—increasingly focused on interior dispositions—while rarely addressing the sin of the congregation, the denomination, the church. Even corporate petitions are generally understood individualistically. The church seldom acknowledges its sin and therefore makes it impossible to repent and trust the gospel. Sixteenth-century reformers had no difficulty recognizing and condemning the sins of the Catholic Church but confined their deep insights concerning sin and repentance within the evangelical churches to individual persons. Contemporary critics of the church have no difficulty in identifying the real and imagined sins of the church, but the church itself replaces confession with planning and repentance with reorganization.

17. Presbyterian Church (USA), "Directory for Worship" (Louisville: Office of the General Assembly, 2015), W-1.3011; 1.3021; 1.3031.

18. Gordon Lathrop, *Holy Things: A Liturgical Theology* (Minneapolis: Fortress, 1993), 117.

The church can know about itself what Israel knew—that the people of God are called to covenant faithfulness but are not inoculated against infidelity. It has become commonplace for Christians to read the Old Testament as enduring witness to Israel's sin without recognizing itself in the long history of the Lord's way with his people. The Word of the Lord continues to call the church to account for its faith and life; the words of the prophets, from Amos to Zephaniah, are addressed to the whole people of God, from Israel to the church.

CHRISTIANS AND JEWS: PEOPLE OF GOD

When the churches begin to understand themselves within the whole people of God, they can embrace the God-given reality that Christians and Jews are, together, the people of God. It will then become possible for the church to know that God is now gathering his scattered Jewish and gentile people, calling them to covenantal companionship in shared peoplehood, confessing that God's righteousness—the Lord's covenant fidelity—endures for and with Israel, and for and with the church, so that both Jewish and Christian witness to the one God endure. Such a confession is not a form of polite syncretism. Israel's covenantal identity in Torah is Israel's, and the church's covenantal identity in Christ is the church's.

Church and synagogue understanding themselves as covenantal partners does not mean that Jews must become Christians or that Christians must moderate the foundational belief that God was in Christ reconciling the world to himself. As Israel receives and lives God's covenant, respecting Christian witness, and the church receives and lives God's covenant, respecting Jewish witness, they receive and live their mutual calling as the people of the only God. Then, as the people of God together, Jews and Christians "will raise a signal to the nations"—a signal to those who remain "strangers to the covenants of promise" (Isa 11:12; Eph 2:2).

The church can recover the fullness of its peoplehood as it rediscovers its roots in biblical Israel and its continuing connection to the Jews by its ingrafting into "the tree of life with its twelve kinds of fruit . . . and the leaves of the tree are for the healing of the nations" (Rev 22:2). Many Protestants decry the corrosive effects of individualism on the faith and life of the churches, yet they neglect, or are unaware of, the foundational realities of Israel's comprehension of its role in God's way with the world as people of God. The apostolic witness says of the gentile church, "Once we were not a people, but now we are God's people" (1 Pet 2:10). We "are no longer strangers and aliens, but we are citizens with the saints and members of the household of God" (Eph 2:19). Because the church is "built upon the foundation of the apostles and the prophets" (Eph 2:20), it can fully comprehend its vocation only in light of the two-Testament witness.

The Jewish prayer book, *Gates of Prayer*, contains this supplication:

> O God of Israel, teach us to be worthy of the name of Jew. May we do nothing to disgrace it. May our every act bring honor to our faith and glory to Your name. May we understand our responsibility as Jews, to continue the task begun by earlier generations of our people who achieved greatness by their faith in the mission to which You had called them: to serve in Your name, to bring light and blessing to all the families of the earth.[19]

With appropriate alterations—"O God of Israel, teach us to be worthy of the name of Christian"—it is a prayer that Christians can pray, side by side with Jews who continue to pray, each understanding themselves and recognizing the others as, together, the people of God.

---

19. Chaim Stern, ed., *Gates of Prayer: The New Union Prayerbook* (New York: Central Conference of American Rabbis Press, 1975), 705.

Chapter 9

PROFESSING THE FAITH

But how are they to call on one in whom they have not believed? And how are they to believe in one of whom they have never heard? And how are they to hear without someone to proclaim him? And how are they to proclaim him unless they are sent?

Romans 10:14–15

"The first Christians he met as a boy in Korea were Adventist missionaries, very simple people. They had no power and wanted no power. They told us Bible stories, it is true. But they gave us food and shelter and medicine first, and told us jokes and played with us and loved us. So we *begged* them for the stories." He laughed again. "This is what Joon thought Christianity meant! Food and medicine for the body, and stories for the heart if you begged for them. Then he came here, found a country full of people begging *not* to hear the stories, went to seminary, and found out why. No food. No medicine. No doing unto others. Just a bunch of men learning how to bellow the stories at others whether they wanted to hear them or not!"

David James Duncan, *The Brothers K*

"The ecclesiastical situation in North America today is confusing in many ways," says Douglas John Hall, "but in no area of ecclesiology are the churches of our continent more bewildered than in what has formally been called their missiology."[1] The two decades since Hall's assessment have seen a profusion of books on "missional theology," epitomized by the work of Darrell Guder and the Gospel and Our Culture Network. Yet, while there is an emerging consensus that the church is, by its very nature "missional," there is no clear answer to the question, "What, precisely, *is* the Christian mission?" Too often, whatever churches do is arbitrarily identified as mission. Denominations, judicatories, and congregations are tempted to designate more and more of their programs as "mission" as a way of demonstrating their missional *bona fides*. The old rule applies: if everything is mission, then nothing is mission.

The name of the Gospel and Our Culture Network suggests that the church's mission is to be found at the intersection of the gospel and culture. Not culture in the abstract, of course, but the specific culture in which the church resides at a given time. Not an indistinct gospel, of course, but the good news of God's way in the world that is known through Israel and in Christ. What, then, can be said about North American culture in the early twenty-first century? What can be said about the shape of the gospel? And what can be said about how the gospel is to be proclaimed here and now?

PUBLIC SQUARE AND PRIVATE FAITH

In the early 1980s Richard John Neuhaus published an influential book with a provocative title—*The Naked Public Square*. At the time Neuhaus was an activist Lutheran pastor, but it was *The Naked Public Square* that struck a responsive chord in both church and society and that made Neuhaus a widely recognized public figure. In his book, Neuhaus lamented the retreat of religion into private life and the exclusion of religion and religiously grounded values from the conduct of public business. He asserted that prevailing "political doctrine and practice" had resulted in public space emptied of the positive presence of religious values and social critique. He attributed the religious absence from public life to a dominant political doctrine—"America is a secular society." This doctrine, he maintained, found dogmatic expression in "the ideology of

---

1. Douglas John Hall, *Confessing the Faith: Christian Theology in a North American Context* (Minneapolis: Fortress, 1996), 143.

secularism," which assumed a high wall of separation between church and state.[2]

Reading *The Naked Public Square* more than three decades after its publication provides a salient perspective on the current state of American political doctrine and practice and on the population of the public square. In the 1980s, Neuhaus asserted that "we are witnessing today a contention between religious groups—evangelical, fundamentalist, Catholic—to succeed mainline Protestantism as the culture-shaping force that provides moral legitimacy for democracy in America."[3] He was right that mainline Protestantism no longer provides moral legitimacy for democracy, but what he did not envision is the rapid expansion of religious (and nonreligious) pluralism in America. Increased religious and moral diversity has expanded far beyond Christian options, intensifying contention for moral legitimacy. This has accelerated religion's retreat into the private sphere, consigning it to an even smaller space in a remote corner of the public square.

It is true enough that evangelicals remain a public presence but primarily as an amorphous electoral bloc of "Christian conservatives" rather than a culture-shaping force. Media evaluations of electoral influence, characterized by what evangelicals oppose, does not translate into a moral force, let alone a moral majority. It is also true enough that Catholic moral teaching retains a measure of political currency, although it is overshadowed in the media by accounts of the moral failings of some priests and bishops. It is even true enough that mainline Protestant churches continue to issue policy papers and make pronouncements on a wide range of social issues, but their statements are disregarded by the *polis* and ignored within the churches. Public life is totally denuded of religious presence, but the church's occupancy has contracted since *The Naked Public Square*.

More than two decades ago, historian Mark Noll also published an influential book with a provocative title—*The Scandal of the Evangelical Mind*. The book's first sentence was even more provocative: "The scandal of the evangelical mind is that there is not much of an evangelical mind."[4] Noll's critique came from within evangelicalism, but it was consistent with broader assessments about the shallowness of Christian thought in Amer-

---

2. Richard John Neuhaus, *The Naked Public Square: Religion and Democracy in America* (Grand Rapids: Eerdmans, 1984), vii.

3. Neuhaus, *The Naked Public Square*, vii.

4. Mark Noll, *The Scandal of the Evangelical Mind* (Grand Rapids: Eerdmans, 1994), 3.

ica's churches. Douglas John Hall, taking note of the statistical symptoms of Christendom's waning, asserts that grim numbers provide only superficial accounts of the situation. "No doubt, certain statistical and other aspects of that deeper malaise are made visible through the activities of pollsters and popular sociologists," Hall states, "but the crisis behind the crisis cannot be submitted to computer programming. For that rudimentary crisis is *a crisis of thinking*."[5]

Noll and Hall represent a consistent, decades-long identification of diminishing ecclesial attention to the theological and ethical core of Christian faith and life. Their criticism of churchly inattention to the profound truths of the gospel, resulting in such thin beliefs as Moralistic Therapeutic Deism and prosperity gospel, may be nothing new. Perhaps every generation echoes Luther's lament that church members and their pastors "know absolutely nothing about the Christian faith,"[6] but traditional lament about thin faith within the church is now coupled with diminished cultural interest in the faith and moral values of the churches. Noll's observation remains true: "The general impact of Christian thinking on the evangelicals of America, much less on learned culture as a whole, is slight."[7] Noll might have added that it is not only evangelicals and learned culture that feel no impact.

A SECULAR AGE

None of this comes as news to us. We see contracted public presence and thinned-out faith as symptomatic of secularity—the marginalization of Christian churches as they, along with other religious institutions, are pushed to the periphery of the public square coupled with an evident decline in Christian belief and practice. It is true enough that Christmas has given way to "the Holidays," that Easter is now marked by "Spring break," and that the churches are no longer influential actors in political and societal arenas. It is also true enough that the religious faith of American Christian teenagers and the churches that shape their faith is marked by a generic deity's therapeutic support for conventional morality. But these signs of secularity—public spaces emptied of signif-

---

5. Douglas John Hall, *Thinking the Faith: Christian Theology in a North American Context* (Minneapolis: Augsburg, 1989), 12.

6. Martin Luther, "Preface to the Small Catechism," in *Martin Luther's Basic Theological Writings*, ed. Timothy F. Lull, 2nd ed (Minneapolis: Fortress, 2005), 318.

7. Noll, *Scandal of the Evangelical Mind*, 5.

icant religious presence and the thinning out of fully Christian belief and practice—are themselves only symptoms of a deeper problem for the church.

Charles Taylor's monumental study, *A Secular Age*, focuses on the cultural conditions that affect religious belief. He characterizes the shift to secularity in the West as "a move from a society where belief in God is unchallenged and, indeed, unproblematic, to one in which it is understood to be one option among others, and frequently not the easiest to embrace."[8] Taylor tells the story of this shift in a tour de force that ranges over five hundred years and takes nearly eight hundred pages to narrate. While some of the details in Taylor's story may be arguable, his depiction of the pervasive experience of our secular age is all too recognizable.

What does it mean to say that we live in a secular age? Taylor is not interested in demonizing secularism, but rather in describing "our contemporary lived understanding; that is, the way we naïvely take things to be." Not naïve in the sense of simple, credulous belief but more precisely as "the construal we just live in, without ever being aware of it as a construal, or—for most of us—without ever formulating it."[9] Taylor wants to uncover our straightforward, embedded experience of the way things are. This naïve experience can be discerned in our everyday engagement in commercial, political, cultural, educational, professional, and recreational activities. The way we function in each of these areas of life—the norms we follow and the deliberations we engage in—are commonly shaped by prevailing societal assumptions and practices. The ordinary, everyday choices we make do not typically refer to God or to religious beliefs but to the commonplace, widely shared understanding of life in twenty-first-century America. The "we" Taylor speaks of in all of this does not include every single person, of course, but "we" encompasses religious as well as nonreligious persons. The "we" also encompasses much of the life of American churches. Churches make decisions and engage in economic planning, marketing, and political activities that are shaped by prevailing social rationalities with only habitual, de rigueur reference to the gospel.

Taylor gives needed nuance to the standard narrative of secularity. "Everyone can see that there have been declines in practice and declared belief

---

8. Charles Taylor, *A Secular Age* (Cambridge: Belknap Press/Harvard University Press, 2007), 3.

9. Taylor, *A Secular Age*, 30.

in many countries, particularly in recent decades, that God is not present in public space as in past centuries, and so on for a host of other changes," he notes. "But how to understand and interpret these changes may not be evident."[10] Taylor moves beyond what everyone can see to explore the resulting vulnerabilities of religion and religious faith. What does it mean that in our time and place belief in God is understood to be one option among others, and frequently not the easiest to embrace?

In our secular age, moral aspirations and worthy lives do not necessarily originate from God or intend toward God. Rather, we live in a time when it is widely understood that moral goals can be related to many different motivations, only some of which may be religious. Furthermore, commendable moral aims are most often dedicated solely to human flourishing, requiring no god to inspire them and no god to give them purpose. What is true of noble moral aspirations is also true of more commonplace, day-to-day ambitions and plans. In neither honorable goals nor quotidian aims is obligation or gratitude to God a natural or necessary component in the choices we make daily.

In this secular age, believers in a transcendent God experience a social setting in which many others live quite contentedly with negligible or no religious faith. Most are ordinary people who live conventional lives, some are virtuous people who live honorable lives, others are self-serving people whose lives are disreputable, but all of them manage their lives without reference to the transcendent. "A secular age," says Taylor, "is one in which the eclipse of all goals beyond human flourishing becomes conceivable; or better, it falls within the range of an imaginable life for masses of people."[11] Whether it is the flourishing of the self alone or the flourishing of a community, a nation, or the planet, the unquestioned focus is on the immanent, the here and now, and what we humans can bring about.

While there is an increase in aggressive atheism and explicit agnosticism in our secular age, more typical is the growing number of people who simply experience no need for religious faith. A recent novel narrates the unexpected, unconventional conversion to Christian faith of a young woman, Sophie Wilder. Sophie's new-found Catholicism is a puzzle to her friends, even to Sophie herself. An acquaintance responds to Sophie's new faith with sarcasm:

10. Taylor, *A Secular Age*, 426.
11. Taylor, *A Secular Age*, 19–20.

"It's funny," he says. "After all this time, people still can't do without God. I never would have guessed that He'd survive to your generation. Even the atheists are militant. They can't quite get over Him."

"Most of my friends don't think one way or another about it," Sophie told him. "They're not for or against it; they're just beyond it."[12]

In our secular age, religious belief in general, and Christian belief in particular, are only options within myriad possibilities for arranging life—options that many have just moved beyond. Nonreligious possibilities reflect what Taylor calls "exclusive humanism"—living a meaningful human life within a closed, self-sufficient universe. Taylor's "exclusive humanism" is not the demonic "secular humanism" of popular Christian mythology but simply ordinary life that may be decent, even virtuous, without reference to God or to any transcendent reality, and certainly without the church. Exclusive humanism is not one thing but many things "which leave no place for the 'vertical' or 'transcendent,' but which in one way or another close these off, render them inaccessible, or even unthinkable."[13] Christian faith, then, is simply one option within a broad range of religious beliefs that, in turn, comprise but one possibility within an all-encompassing world that has no apparent need for anything beyond the human.

A secular age is not one in which religious people experience their lives as fully derived from God and directed to God in contrast to secular people who arrange their lives without reference to the transcendent. Religious people, and the subset of committed Christian people, are immersed in a secular age characterized by the assumption of human self-sufficiency. In this secularized society, belief itself becomes more challenging. Stripped of what Peter Berger calls "plausibility structures"—the social and cultural supports for transcendent faith—churches can no longer assume that faith will be supported by strong cultural norms.

"The tight normative link between a certain religious identity, the belief in certain theological propositions, and a standard practice, no longer holds for a great number of [Christian] people," says Taylor. "Many of these are engaged in assembling their own personal outlook, through a kind of

---

12. Christopher R. Beha, *What Happened to Sophie Wilder* (Portland, OR: Tin House Books, 2012), 85.

13. Taylor, *A Secular Age*, 556.

bricolage."[14] And so, while believing without belonging may characterize some outside of the church, it may be that within the church belonging without believing is a consequence of our secular age.

PROCLAIMING THE GOSPEL IN A SECULAR AGE

All of this has obvious implications for proclaiming the gospel and shaping life within Christian communities of faith. Churches are no longer culturally sanctioned and can no longer rely on attractional strategies to draw people through their doors. Positioning themselves as alluring religious options is less and less likely to appeal to people who see no need for the multiple programs and service opportunities the churches offer. As challenging as this reality is for the church, the other side of the condition obtaining in a secular age is more fundamental: the extent to which the churches themselves and their members have come to share the assumptions and practices of the secular setting in which we all live and move and have our being.

Nonreligious descriptions of reality are the underlying assumptions shared throughout modern, Western societies. These taken-for-granted secular notions of "the way things are" find themselves at home in the churches, although they are partially concealed under a patina of religious rhetoric. Denominational divisions in America, as well as progressive-evangelical divides, are tempered by common allegiance to the values, motivations, and aims that characterize a secular age. There is a sense in which this is understandable, perhaps even inevitable. Christians and their churches are not only in the world but also—in substantial measure—of the world as well. We pray to God, "thy kingdom come," but we live in a world and a church characterized by reliance on human action to bring about desired ecclesial and social ends.

Marginalized American churches find the very shape of their Christian faith and life affected by the secular age in which they live. This is "natural" in the sense that church people—priests and ministers as well as members—breathe the same cultural air that everyone else breathes. But it is also "intentional" in the sense that churches appeal to our secular age's increasingly disinterested populace by seeking to demonstrate their correspondence to secular rationality. Worship, programming, evangelism,

14. Taylor, *A Secular Age*, 514.

mission, morality, and even church governance assume an understanding of reality that all people share—religious and nonreligious alike—and to which the church can and should appeal. But this comes with a cost.

In his incisive studies of American denominations in the twentieth century, social historian David Hollinger notes liberal Protestantism's emergent conviction that Christian faith was not essential to social and political improvement: "Christianity became one of a number of useful vehicles for values that transcended that ancestral faith. . . . Christianity of any variety became a strategic and personal option rather than a presumed imperative." One result, says Hollinger, has been that children of mainline Protestant churches "found that Christianity was not so indispensable to the advancement of the values most energetically taught to them" by their churches.[15] To the extent that the churches speak and act merely as a religious version of aims pursued by numerous nonreligious organizations and institutions (usually more effectively), loyalty to the church becomes optional, even extraneous. Liberal Protestantism, says Hollinger, "enabled its community of faith to serve, among its other roles, as a commodious halfway house to what for lack of a better term we can call post-Protestant secularism."[16]

THE CHURCH'S PROCLAMATION OF THE GOSPEL IN A PREVIOUS AGE

How is the church to proclaim the gospel in a secular age? The answer begins with a negation. The church is called to turn away from its characteristic proclamation of itself—marketing its attractive suite of religious goods and services—and turn toward God's new way in the world in and through Jesus Christ, crucified, risen, and ascended. But how is this to be done in an age when fewer people are interested in what the church has to say? Even a strengthened, clarified, unified proclamation of the gospel is easily muffled by the cacophony of conflicting messages proclaiming alternate "salvations," from hedonism through self-improvement to narcissistic mysticism, from expanding rights through genetic engineering to saving the planet. Even at its best, the church is but one voice in a world inun-

---

15. David A. Hollinger, *After Cloven Tongues of Fire: Protestant Liberalism in Modern American History* (Princeton: Princeton University Press, 2013), 44.

16. Hollinger, *After Cloven Tongues of Fire*, 46.

Any curiosity about why?

dated with words. In an age when religious faith in general, and Christian faith in particular, is but one option among many, how is the gospel to be heard, and how will hearing lead to faith?

It is often said that the religious and secular pluralism of twenty-first-century America resembles the Greco-Roman religious and philosophical pluralism in which the early church grew. It is then proposed that the solution to the church's current proclamation dilemma is to emulate the early church so that the contemporary church will be strengthened in faith and increase in numbers daily (cf. Acts 6:7; 9:31; 12:24; 16:5; 19:20; 28:30–31). Recourse to the Book of Acts encourages bold proclamation, persuasive apologetics, and heroic missionary endeavors. Peter and Paul are the models—their *kerygma*, their *didachē*, their travels and church planting provide the prototype for twenty-first-century church growth.[17] However, using Acts as the sole model does not provide a complete or even typical picture of the church's three centuries of growth from a tiny Jewish sect to the favored religion of the empire. Something more than heroic apostolic action was at work.

Robert Wilken, Rodney Stark, Robin Lane Fox, and others would agree with Alan Kreider's assessment that, "according to the evidence at our disposal, the expansion of the church was not organized, the product of a mission program; it simply happened."[18] Perhaps not "simply," but the history of the expansion of Christianity is not the continuation of the Acts of the apostles, and it certainly does not provide a blueprint for church-wide evangelism programs. It is post-apostolic Christian growth that is suggestive for the life of the church in our secular, pluralistic age. Latourette asks, "Why, among all the many cults and philosophies which competed in the Graeco-Roman world and in spite of more severe opposition than was encountered by any other, did the faith outstrip them all?"[19]

The early church lived and spoke the gospel in the context of the Roman Empire. The "glories" of Rome, evident in the remains of centuries-old structures and the pristine re-creations of modern movies, should be viewed together with the underside of life in the totalizing imperial state:

17. See, e.g., Eddie Gibbs, *The Rebirth of the Church: Applying Paul's Vision for Ministry in Our Post-Christian World* (Grand Rapids: Baker Academic, 2013).

18. Alan Kreider, *The Patient Ferment of the Early Church* (Grand Rapids: Baker Academic, 2016), 9.

19. Kenneth Scott Latourette, *The First Five Centuries*, vol. 1 of *A History of the Expansion of Christianity* (London: Eyre and Spottiswoode, 1952), 162.

social dislocation, ethnic antagonisms, crushing poverty for the masses, urban disorder, and cultural chaos. All of this was accompanied by acute depopulation, frequent natural disasters, plague, and other deadly epidemics. The effect was pervasive social distress that neither the empire nor its religions could alleviate.

Christians lived in the same circumstances, of course, but Christians responded to social dislocation and natural disaster in ways that set them apart. Christians lived distinctive lives shaped by cohesive communal convictions. The Christian difference was twofold. First, Christians faced adversity with confident hope that God's purpose in Christ was being fulfilled in their new life. One of the two most frequently cited texts in early Christian writing gave assurance that their eternal destiny and the world's future were in God's hands:

> It shall come to pass in the latter days
>> that the mountain of the house of the LORD
> shall be established as the highest of the mountains,
>> and shall be lifted up above the hills;
> and all the nations shall flow to it,
>> and many peoples shall come, and say:
> "Come, let us go up to the mountain of the LORD,
>> to the house of the God of Jacob;
> that he may teach us his ways
>> and that we may walk in his paths." . . .
> He shall judge between the nations,
>> and shall decide disputes for many peoples. . . . (Isa 2:2–4 [ESV])

The promise of this text produced assurance that the tribulations of this world were not a fate that could only be endured, but transitory realities in the arena of God's providence. Confident that the Lord of all would establish his reign, Christians could love God fully and love others boldly, certain that the Lord would "judge between the nations and decide for many peoples."

Hope led to the second, more visible difference. Christians responded to social dislocation by living as a distinctive, cohesive community. The second-century apology, "Epistle to Diognetus," testified that "Christians cannot be distinguished from the rest of the human race by country or language or customs. . . . Yet at the same time they give proof of the remarkable and admittedly extraordinary constitution of their own com-

Inclusion

monwealth."[20] Their unusual commonwealth was immediately evident in its composition. In the mid-second century the Greek philosopher Celsus derided Christians for appealing to "illiterate and bucolic yokels, children, and stupid women." He was astonished that "they themselves admit that these people are worthy of their God."[21] The social inclusion of Christian communities incorporated a wide range of class, education, sex, and age. Especially notable was the mixing of slaves and masters and the full inclusion of women, not only as members, but as leaders—patrons and *diakonoi.*

Christian faith and life was formed in closely knit communities that were joined with sister communities across the empire in a new, universal family. "The Christian assembly was not one of a palette of social commitments of an urban Roman," says Kreider, "it was the center of the Christians' lives. . . . The Christians were creating an alternative community that had nonconformist approaches to common social problems and that imparted to its participants a powerful sense of individual and group identity."[22] "They busy themselves on earth, but their citizenship is in heaven," says the letter to Diognetus. "They obey the established laws but in their own lives they go far beyond what the law requires. They love all men."[23]

Rodney Stark applies contemporary sociological categories in interesting ways to his examination of Christianity's growth in the first three centuries. He views the early church's organization through the lenses of exclusive commitment and nonexclusive commitment. A central factor distinguishing one from the other is that nonexclusive religious organizations specialize in "*privately produced* religious goods," while exclusive religious organizations specialize in "the *collective production* of religion." Stark follows with two propositions: First, when religious organizations function by providing private religious goods, they find themselves in competition with other providers of private goods, leading religious "consumers" to patronize multiple providers in order to satisfy their personal taste. Alternatively, when religious organizations exist to facilitate com-

20. "Epistle to Diognetus," in *Early Christian Fathers*, ed. Cyril C. Richardson (Philadelphia: Westminster, 1953), 216–17.

21. Origen, "Against Celsus," in *A New Eusebius*, ed. J. Stevenson (London: SPCK, 1965), 142.

22. Kreider, *Patient Ferment of the Early Church*, 60.

23. "Epistle to Diognetus," 217.

prehensive collective goods, they necessitate communal commitment that diminishes religious dabbling.[24]

The language of Stark's categories—production, religious goods, providers, patronize—may be jarring, but it helps to clarify the difference between the profusion of pagan cults offering diverse, private, temporary religious promise, and the early church's witness to a comprehensive, communal, God-given way of life in this world. Rather than seeking out one or many of the pagan cults to provide temporary personal benefit, persons were drawn to the church, which guided them in shaping a shared life distinguished by community practices centered in the one God. Tertullian gives expression to "the peculiarities of the Christian society. . . . We are a body knit together as such to a common religious profession, by unity of discipline, and by the bond of a common hope."[25] The church was organized around common faith, a unified way of life, and shared confidence, giving it a cohesion that contributed to its endurance in times of opposition and persecution as well as its distinctive attractiveness in the midst of capricious "old gods and new."

A central element among "the peculiarities of the Christian society" was its life of loving care for pagans as well as for one another. Christians understood themselves as a people guided by Jesus's Sermon on the Mount, so they went "far beyond what the law requires. They love all men." Justin's mid-second-century *Apology* explains Christian care for all: "This is what [Jesus] taught on affection for all men: 'If you love those who love you, what new thing do you do? for even the harlots do this. But I say to you, Pray for your enemies and love those who hate you and bless those who curse you and pray for those who treat you despitefully.'"[26] Christian care was not confined to members of their communities but expanded to embrace those outside of the church who were in need.

At the close of the third century, Tertullian's *Apology* included a revealing description of the church's care for both Christians and pagans. In explaining the nature of Christian associations and communal gatherings, he contrasted the church's response to social misery to that of pagan cults. How did the church live its faith in the use of its resources?

---

24. Rodney Stark, *The Rise of Christianity* (New York: HarperOne, 1997), 203–4.

25. Tertullian, "Apology," in *Ante-Nicene Fathers*, vol. 3, ed. Philip Schaff (Grand Rapids: Eerdmans), ch. XXXIX, 46.

26. "The First Apology of Justin, the Martyr," in *Early Christian Fathers*, ed. Cyril C. Richardson (Philadelphia: Westminster, 1953), 251.

There is no buying or selling of any sort in the things of God. Though we have our treasure-chest, it is not made up of purchase-money, as of a religion that has its price. On the monthly day, if he likes, each puts in a small donation, but only if it be his pleasure, and only if he be able: for all is voluntary. These gifts are, as it were, piety's deposit funds. For they are not taken thence and spent on feasts, and drinking-bouts, and eating-houses, but to support and bury poor people, to supply the wants of boys and girls destitute of means and parents, and of old persons confined now to the house; such, too, as have suffered shipwreck; and if there happen to be any in the mines, or banished to the islands, or shut up in the prisons, for nothing but their fidelity to the cause of God's Church, they become the nurslings of their confession. But it is mainly the deeds of love so noble that lead many to put a brand upon us, *See*, they say, *how they love one another.*[27]

Not just "one another," but also pagans in need. Tertullian went on to say, "We call one another brothers, but we also consider you [Romans] brothers as well, because we all share a common human nature." Christians provided food and clothing for the poor and burials for the indigent; they opened their homes to orphans, including infants abandoned on trash heaps; they cared for discarded slaves; they rescued sailors; and they provided for prisoners in Roman gulags. All of these were thrown-away people in Greco-Roman society, thrown away by all except Christian communities.

Especially notable was Christian care for the sick and dying. In the mid-third century, the North African city of Carthage experienced a severe outbreak of plague. Those who became ill were avoided and the many who died were simply piled up in the streets. Cyprian, bishop in Carthage, assembled the church, urging the excellence of mercy toward the sick and dying. His biographer relates that "he subjoined that there was nothing wonderful in cherishing our own with the fitting dutiful-ness of charity," invoking the example of Jesus, who loved all, even his enemies. "Accordingly [the Christians] did good in the profusion of ex-uberant works to all, and not only to the household of faith."[28] Christian concern for all people did not go unnoticed by pagan society. Even Emperor Julian (the Apostate) complained that "the impious Galileans

27. Tertullian, "Apology," 46.
28. Pontius, "Life of Cyprian," in *A New Eusebius*, ed. J. Stevenson, 245–46.

support not only their poor, but ours as well; everyone can see that our people lack aid from us."[29]

The cohesive life of its communities also strengthened Christianity in its refusal to compromise with social customs and moral practices of the day. It took far more than a sudden decision to believe; it took a radical change in the way one lived; it was not simply mental assent to God's truth but living in God's way. Christians condemned and would not tolerate in the church common practices of the day: infanticide, abortion, incest, marital infidelity, polygamy, and divorce. Christianity was not easy for people to adopt. Protracted catechetical instruction was required to induct converts into the demanding *habitus* of Christian life. They not only had a new narrative of God and humankind to learn; they had to adopt the new ways the narrative required people to live. It is not going too far to say that people found it more difficult to live as Christians lived than to believe as Christians believed. The demands of initiation into the Christian community discouraged some but attracted others who understood that they were embarking on a deeply meaningful journey together with others into a world-shattering way of new life.

The distinctive life of individual Christians and their churches was at odds with the norms of Roman society. The puzzling life of Christians appalled some and appealed to others, but there was increasing curiosity about why they lived as they did. Although Justin, Tertullian, and others wrote *apologia*, appealing to the intelligentsia, the normal way of communicating the faith was through natural networks of family, friends, neighbors, and contacts made through work. There was no organized mission of the church and no mass evangelism programs. Christians did not invite outsiders to "worship with us," and there is no evidence that individual Christians saw it their duty to convert others to the faith. Christians kept a low profile. The faith was spread organically, through direct, intimate, interpersonal association in existing social networks. "Above all," says Robin Fox, "we should give weight to the presence and influence of friends. It is a force which so often escapes the record. . . . One friend might bring another to the faith; a group of friends might exclude others and cause them to look elsewhere for esteem. When a person turned to God, he found others, 'new brethren,' who were sharing the same path."[30]

Christians were not made in a hurry. "New birth" meant entrance into a new life, and the church's protracted catechesis aimed to shape new life

29. Rodney Stark, *The Rise of Christianity*, 84.

30. Robin Lane Fox, *Pagans and Christians* (San Francisco: Harper & Row, 1986), 316.

before new Christians were invited to hear the fullness of the gospel. In Alan Kreider's nice formulation, outsiders "said '*Vide*, look! How they love one another.' They did not say, '*Aude*, listen to the Christians' message'; they did not say, '*Lege*, read what they write.' . . . Christianity's truth was visible; it was embodied and enacted by members."[31]

However, none of this by itself answers Larry Hurtado's question, *Why on earth did anyone become a Christian in the first three centuries?*[32] Hurtado focuses his brief inquiry not on the rise of Christianity but on the phenomenon of individuals becoming Christians in spite of considerable familial, social, commercial, political, and legal costs involved in becoming a Christian. The answer has to do with Christian *faith*, faith in the one powerfully transcendent God who relates to the world in love, who comes to persons in deep, abiding, eternal relationship with Jesus Christ, who calls persons into community, who requires people to love others, even enemies. These distinctive Christian beliefs were not simply intellectual propositions but affective personal and interpersonal realities that outweighed impediments to embracing Christian life.

Kenneth Scott Latourette rounds off his summary of factors accounting for the expansion of Christianity in the early centuries by identifying the foundational element that gave substance to everything in the life of the church. "It is clear that at the very beginning of Christianity there must have occurred a vast release of energy," he wrote. "Without it the future course of the faith is inexplicable. . . . Something happened to the men who associated with Jesus. In his contact with them, in his crucifixion and in their assurance of his resurrection and of the continued living presence with his disciples of his spirit, is to be found the major cause of the success of Christianity."[33] This release of energy, radiating from the risen Christ through the Holy Spirit, resulted in a distinctive way of life in the church, a way of life that attracted increasing numbers of people to the faith.

THE EMERGING CHRISTIAN MINORITY

The difference between the church's first three centuries and the continuing effects of developed Constantinian establishment may be characterized

---

31. Kreider, *Patient Ferment of the Early Church*, 61.

32. Larry W. Hurtado, *Why on Earth Did Anyone Become a Christian in the First Three Centuries?* (Milwaukee: Marquette University Press, 2016).

33. Hurtado, *Why on Earth Did Anyone Become a Christian*, 167–68.

by Alan Kreider's formulation: "Conversion, which had made Christians into distinctive people—resident aliens—now was something that made people ordinary, not resident aliens but simply residents."[34] For most of its history, the church has resided as the religious reality of Europe and later of the Americas. For most of these centuries Judaism was viewed as a continuing irritation, Islam as a periodic threat, and other world religions as exotica; Christianity was the taken-for-granted religious norm. All of that has ended now, although many in the church have not yet come to terms with the change; the church is now "the emerging Christian minority."

How does an emerging minority church proclaim the gospel in a secular age? Direct parallels with the church of the first three or four centuries are unsatisfactory, but certain realities press upon us. Whether *secularity* or *pluralism* is one's preferred term for the current social reality of the West, the church can no longer rely on a range of cultural props to sustain its implicit prominence in American consciousness. Cultural supports made proclamation of the gospel easier, for it was possible to assume public familiarity with the Exodus, parables of the prodigal son and the good Samaritan, the Gospels' passion narrative, justification by faith, and other features of Christian faith. Cultural awareness made belief itself more natural because the plausibility of faith's claims is woven into the social fabric. But in a secular, pluralistic age, when belief in the Christian gospel is "only one option among many," and an increasing number of persons "are just beyond it," the words we are accustomed to speaking find difficulty in being heard.

Proclamation of the gospel in a secular age may find its initial grounding, not in words, but in the character of the church's communal life—the *church's* life, not just the witness of exemplary Christians. The disciples of John the Baptist asked Jesus, "Are you the one who is to come, or shall we look for another?" Jesus responded, "Go and tell John what you have seen and heard." What there was to see and hear was remarkable: blind seeing, lame walking, lepers healed, deaf hearing, the dead living, and poor people hearing good news" (Luke 7:18–23). What does the church have to say when people ask, "Are you the real thing, or shall we look elsewhere?"

Remember how Tertullian characterizes the peculiarities of the Christian society: "We are a body knit together as such to a common

---

34. Kreider, *The Change of Conversion and the Origin of Christendom* (Harrisburg, PA: Trinity Press International, 1999), 91.

religious profession, by unity of discipline, and by the bond of a common hope." Tertullian's words are not a mere sociological description, let alone a prescription for churchly success. However, they do give voice to the fundamental qualities of a church that is capable of professing the gospel, equipped to be a "missional church." Is it possible to echo Tertullian by construing the contemporary church in America as a body knit together in common religious profession, unity of discipline, and common hope?

A Body Knit Together

Tertullian's allusion to Ephesians 4:15–16 is obvious—"we are to grow up in every way into him who is the head, into Christ, from whom the whole body, joined and knit together by every joint with which it is supplied, when each part is working properly, makes bodily growth and upbuilds itself in love." The body is knit together in Christ, by Christ. The church is not a natural body, knit together by affinities of race, economic class, gender, age, or other shared features. Its "peculiarities" are found in its unnatural composition. The astonishing inclusivity of the early church was itself a proclamation of the gospel, for it displayed a new life in Christ where there was no longer distinction between Jew and Greek, slave and free, male and female, rich and poor, sick and well, learned and uneducated, young and old; no longer were there divisions among races and ethnicities. It was as the body birthed *by* Christ, the body *in* Christ, and the body *of* Christ, that the church proclaimed Christ by displaying the birth of a new community in and for the world.

Churches in contemporary America are not the church of the first three centuries. Too often, churches exhibit the same tired partitions of race, class, ethnicity, and gender that are so apparent in the nation. The church has become a typical society known by its conformity to prevailing social norms, not by its peculiarities. Some church growth gurus even advocate planned homogeneity as a prerequisite for effective outreach that will attract new members. The early church's inclusivity certainly attracted new members, but this was not a growth strategy or an evangelism methodology. Ecclesial catholicity was a mark of the gospel. But catholicity was not an isolated characteristic of the early church. Rather than a laissez-faire assemblage, the Christian society was knit together in Christ by clear, nonnegotiable theological, organizational, and ethical norms.

Common Religious Profession

The early church's rule of faith is a précis of its common religious profession. As we have seen, the rule of faith was not the imposed product of a centralized ecclesiastical authority but an organic outgrowth of the need to teach the gospel to new Christians. Bishops throughout the church imparted central elements of the faith after it had been determined that catechumens were able to live as Christians lived. Hippolytus's *Apostolic Tradition* describes the ancient practice:

> And when they are chosen who are set apart to receive baptism let their life be examined, whether they lived piously while catechumens, whether they "honored the widows," whether they visited the sick, whether they have fulfilled every good work. If those who bring them bear witness to them that they have done thus, let them hear the gospel.[35]

New Christians were not ignorant of the church's faith, of course, for they worshiped with the community, listening to Scripture and its interpretation, learning the language of faith. But it was at the climax of their incorporation into the body of Christ that they were taught the deep mysteries of the faith and called to affirm the core of the church's common religious profession. It was then that they were baptized and welcomed to the Lord's Table. Reshaped praxis preceded full theological articulation, but shared theological articulation was necessary to knit the body together as a community of faith.

American churches are characterized, not by common religious profession, but by the inviolability of personal conviction and the celebration of theological diversity. The wholesale approval of multiplicity in faith and life is so pervasive that calls for commonly held faith are accused of demanding oppressive orthodoxy. Common faith is not uniform faith, however, requiring detailed doctrinal conformance. But a church that does not share common profession of the gospel will find it difficult to live the gospel and impossible to proclaim the gospel publicly. The church cannot live faithfully without ecclesial clarity about the faith.

35. Hippolytus, *The Apostolic Tradition*, ed. Gregory Dix and Henry Chadwick (London: Alban Press, 1937/1991), 23.

Unity of Discipline

The early church lived in patterns of mutual responsibility and account-ability. People were born again into a new communal life in which all were brothers and sisters in faith and in life. Their love for one another showed itself in frequent gatherings for worship, meals together, clothes closets and food pantries, praying for one another, welcoming travelers, caring for the sick and those in prison, solidarity with martyrs—in short, sharing new life in Christ. New communal life reached beyond the church, for loving care was given to all people, even to enemies, just as the Lord's love encompassed all. None of this was dependent on personal inclina-tion, interest, or convenience; the church understood itself as obligated by the gospel.

Churches in contemporary America are voluntary societies in which many step forward not to serve but to be served. This should not be taken as evidence of members' moral deficiency, for the churches present them-selves as religious providers, catering to perceived needs. Churches are not devoid of persons whose service within and beyond the community of faith is evident in everything from taking flowers to shut-ins, teaching Sun-day School, and sponsoring refugee families to sheltering homeless people, building Habitat houses, installing water purification systems in Haiti, and working to combat racism in church and society. But all of these and more remain optional activities for those who are so inclined rather than the ecclesial norm. Devoid of the requirement of common faith and common life, the easy path of contemporary church membership announces, not the gospel, but the church's dispensability.

Common Hope

The early church's hope was placed in the mercy of God. Christians hoped in their own eternal salvation, yet their shared hope was not limited to life beyond death. The church was confident that God was working his purpose out in the world, for the world. Because the church knew that it would come to pass that the nations would flow to the mountain of the house of the Lord and that many peoples would learn God's way and walk in his path (Isa 2:2–4), the church remained hopeful in the face of harass-ment, persecution, and martyrdom. Common hope in God and God's way meant that the church did not have to plan its own future, devise its own strategies, or create its own programs. The church was not passive, but it was confident, trusting in God, not seeking to control events.

Churches in America today are anxious, not hopeful. The prospect of institutional decline leads to a frantic succession of vision statements, strategic plans, measurable objectives, and the displacement of "outputs" by "outcomes," all dependent on the latest management trends. Hope in God's way is replaced by reliance on the latest fads in management techniques accompanied by official expressions of optimism that sound eerily like whistles in the dark.

Call and Response

"When the church faces the prospect of its own demise," writes Michael Jinkins, "it faces a critical moment when its vocation is called into question, when it has unparalleled opportunity to comprehend and to render its life."[36] The church in America has not yet faced the prospect of its own demise, even though the trajectory of its decline is evident. If reality is faced, the church may find fresh angles of vision in openness to the life of our early ecclesial forebears and the life of our recent offspring. The early church and the church of the global South may provide us with perspective on our ecclesial life by removing the scales of this time and place from our eyes. But necessary awareness of the church's past and attention to the growing churches in the global South are not sufficient to comprehend and render our ecclesial life. What is required is what has always been required—awareness of and attention to the call of the present Christ, who calls us to be one, to be holy, to be catholic, to be apostolic, to be the church.

36. Michael Jinkins, *The Church Faces Death: Ecclesiology in a Post-Modern Context* (New York: Oxford University Press, 1999), 13–14.

Chapter 10

ONE, HOLY, CATHOLIC, AND APOSTOLIC CHURCH

... to preach to the Gentiles the unsearchable riches of Christ, and to make all people see what is the plan of the mystery hidden for ages in God who created all things; that through the church the manifold wisdom of God might now be made known to the principalities and powers in the heavenly places.

Ephesians 3:9–10, RSV

Putting together the Monthly Bulletin was the drawing of a short short straw. She'd never paid much attention to the little magazine, but now that she did, she was appalled. "Senior Spotlight." Look, the seniors are going to Concord Mills outdoor mall on a field trip. God be praised. "Calling all young adults!" Hoops4Him.

"Basketball for Jesus, really?"

"That's an interchurch activity. We've been doing Hoops-4Him for years. You don't approve?"

"Don't recall the twelve disciples playing one-on-one."

The Book Group was reading some piece of Christian fiction with a serial killer in it. The Covenant Class was renting and discussing Mel Gibson's *The Passion of the Christ.* It's time for the Young Men's Retreat. *Between bouts of sock wrestling, log throwing, skeet shooting and paintball war, fifteen young men of the faith will grow closer to each other and to God. Participation fee $45.00.*

"I don't suppose any slight hint of working toward Christ's

kingdom could trickle into our scheduled activities for our congregation."

"Hey, the church is getting along again. Bonding. All this is good."

"No, it is not good. What are we? Cruise directors?"

Wilton Barnhardt, *Lookaway, Lookaway*

The church's foundational creed announces the church as "one, holy, catholic, and apostolic." Since the churches we can see are not visibly or categorically any of those things, what do we mean when we make our creedal confession that we believe in, trust, and are loyal to a church that is one, holy, catholic, and apostolic? Are we affirming an actual entity? An immaterial phenomenon? A transcendent archetype? An ecumenical myth? An ideal to pursue? A hoped-for future? Although we may have questions or doubts about other elements in the creed, their intention is relatively clear. But it is difficult to know what the creed expects of us when it asks us to believe in the one church, the holy church, the catholic church, the apostolic church.

Whatever judgments we may make about the character of oneness, holiness, catholicity, and apostolicity, it is evident that they are not intended as a list of discrete items. The creed does not assume that the church could be one but not catholic, or holy but not apostolic. Neither does the creed assume that the elements of the church are linearly progressive, so that first the church must be one to be holy, one and holy to be catholic, and one holy and catholic to be apostolic. None of the creedal elements of church is privileged, and none is contingent on another. The elements are an interrelated whole, each informing the other and all together informing church.

HEAR, O ISRAEL: THE LORD IS OUR GOD, THE LORD ALONE

The church's creedal marks are derivative. The church is one, holy, catholic, and apostolic because the church is the people of *God*, the body of *Christ*, the communion of the *Holy Spirit*. The church's character is dependent upon God, who alone is one, who alone is holy, who alone is complete, who alone creates, redeems, and sustains the world. Oneness, holiness, catholicity, and apostolicity are not ontological attributes, as if the church possesses them in and of itself. Nor are they existential, as if the church itself can bring them into being. The church's oneness, holiness, catholicity, and apostolicity is derivative, dependent, and contingent.

God is the source and ground of the church. Thus, the way toward understanding the Nicene confession concerning the church begins with understanding who God is. Barth asks, "What does it mean to say that 'God is'? What or who 'is' God?" He then responds, "If we want to answer this question legitimately and thoughtfully, we cannot for a moment turn our thoughts anywhere else than to God's act in His revelation."[1] Among other things, this means that we cannot know what oneness, holiness, catholicity, and apostolicity are by crafting generic definitions that we then apply to God. We only know one, holy, catholic, and apostolic by knowing who God is as he shows himself to be through Israel and in Christ. The one God, the holy God, the catholic God, the apostolic God is the source and ground of the church.

God Is One: Our Father in Heaven

Singularity and *simplicity* are classical theological terms for the oneness of God. *Singularity* seems straightforward: only God is God; there are no gods beside this One God. *Simplicity*, on the other hand, seems an odd way to signify the oneness of God. God does not appear to be simple, at least not in the everyday meaning of the word. Simplicity's theological meaning, from the Latin *simplicitas*, indicates God's absolute self-sufficiency, complete integrity, and perfect freedom. Barth expresses this succinctly: "God is simple. This signifies that in all that He is and does, He is wholly and undividedly Himself. At no time or place is He composed out of what is distinct from Himself. At no time or place, then, is He divided or divisible."[2]

The simplicity of God is God's oneness in unqualified integrity. Dividing God, as in distinguishing the "judgmental God of the Old Testament" from the "loving God of the New Testament," or differentiating God, as in "creator, redeemer, and sustainer" are mistaken and dangerous. If God were one thing in one time and place, and another thing in another time and place, God would be a thing, and therefore unpredictably changeable. If

---

1. Karl Barth, *Church Dogmatics* II/1, trans G. W. Bromiley and T. F. Torrance (Edinburgh: T&T Clark, 1957), 261.

2. Barth, *Church Dogmatics* II/1, 445.

God's acts are separated, the relationship of world, redemption, and hope is fractured. The simplicity of God is the unqualified unity of God's being, purpose, and acts. God is trustworthy because God is *simplicitas*. God's people are called to be trustworthy, whole and undivided in integrity of faith and life.

God Is Holy: Hallowed Be Your Name

Holy does not define God; God defines *holy*. God's holiness is known in distinction from all creation and in intimate relation to creation: "I am God and not human, the Holy One in your midst, and I will not come to destroy" (Hos 11:9). God, the "wholly other," is the Holy One who cares for the creation, and who establishes and maintains communion with the people he calls to be his own. In John Webster's formulation, "God's holiness is the undeflected purposiveness with which God ensures that his will for humankind will not be spoiled."[3]

The Holy God is known in the creation, preservation, and purification of Israel, a people called to be "a kingdom of priests and a holy nation" (Exod 19:6), to be saints [*hagioi* = holy ones]. "You shall be holy," God declares, "for I the LORD your God am holy" (Lev 19:2). God alone is holy, but holiness is not God's private possession, for the Lord calls a people to reflect his holiness as a testimony to the nations. Yet the distinction remains: "The attribution of holiness is not a matter of the straightforward ascription of a property," says Webster. "God's holiness is proper to him; indeed, it *is* him. . . . The holiness of the Church, by contrast, is not a natural or cultural condition."[4]

God Is Catholic: Your Kingdom Come

Catholic derives from the Greek *katholikos*, a compound word formed from *kat' holos*, "in accordance with/corresponding to the whole." In this sense, only God is catholic, for God alone shapes the whole, from creation to consummation. The Nicene Creed confesses that God alone is "creator of heaven and earth, of all that is, seen and unseen;" God alone is "for

---

3. John Webster, *Holiness* (Grand Rapids: Eerdmans, 2003), 49.

4. Webster, *Holiness*, 63.

us and our salvation;" God alone is "the Lord, the giver of life." Only the one God—Father, Son, and Holy Spirit—is universal, comprehending the whole.

The One, Catholic God relates to the world and all that is in it in love. God's love is not fully known in the catholicity of geographic reach or numerical inclusivity, but as comprehensive, consistent, steadfast wholeness in word and act. "God is love" can easily become a catchphrase in which God is defined by our notions of what love is. But this reverses the biblical testimony that love is defined by God's actions with Israel and in Christ, God's saving way of *chesed* and *agapē* for the world. Only God comprehends and embraces the whole world and all that is in it. Because God is love, the people of God are called to wholeness in love.

God Is Apostolic: Your Will Be Done on Earth as in Heaven

It has become a commonplace in missional church circles to speak of the *missio Dei*, the mission of God, from which the apostolic mission of the church is to be understood. The classical understanding of *missio Dei* encompasses the sending of the Son by God the Father and the sending of the Holy Spirit by God the Father and the Son. It is of this sending that David Bosch can say that "God is a missionary God."[5] In the one *missio Dei* the Father's sending of the Son (Luke 4:18–19, 43), the Father and Son's sending of the Spirit (John 15:26), and the risen Lord's sending of the church (John 20:21) are the active work of God in the world to gather wandering, lost, and willful humanity.

The *missio Dei* is the active work of God in the world to gather scattered, wandering humanity. This does not simply describe something that God does, however, but also reveals who God is—the One who is with and for the human. What God does in and for the world is the outpouring of who God is. "Peace be with you," says the risen Christ to his disciples. "As the Father has sent me, so I send you" (John 20:21). The church is now called to show who it is in faithfulness in God's mission.

---

5. David Bosch, *Transforming Mission: Paradigm Shifts in Theology of Mission* (Maryknoll, NY: Orbis Books, 1991), 390.

LET ANYONE WHO HAS AN EAR LISTEN TO WHAT
THE SPIRIT IS SAYING TO THE CHURCHES

God alone is fully one, holy, catholic, and apostolic, so it is only as God's people that the creed attributes these qualities to the church. And yet, the churches we see before us are not fully one, holy, catholic, and apostolic. Just as Israel was not purely "a kingdom of priests and a holy nation," so with the church. The creedal notes do not exalt the church. To the contrary, their first function is to stand over against the church as reproach, even as God's judgment upon the church. Ephesus, Smyrna, Pergamum, Thyatira, Sardis, Philadelphia, and Laodicea are not the only churches judged by God to be visibly ambiguous demonstrations of what God intends for the world.

Karl Barth's theological commentary on the epistle to the Romans contains many surprising twists on familiar themes. Nowhere is the surprise greater than his treatment of Paul's extended struggle with the reality that the majority of Israel had not received the gospel of Christ. Barth does not deal with the Jews in Romans 9–11, however, but with the church! Because Romans is now a letter read by the church, Barth turns the problem of "Israel's unbelief" into the problem of the church's unbelief. Like Israel, the church has "the sonship, the covenants, the giving of the law, the worship, and the promises" (9:4). And yet, like Israel, "To a greater or lesser extent, the Church is a vigorous and extensive attempt to humanize the divine, to bring it within the sphere of the world of time and things, and to make it a practical 'something', for the benefit of those who cannot live with the Living God, and yet who cannot live without God."[6] Barth contends that in Romans we can see clearly the inadequacy of the church, inadequacy "not because of its weakness and lack of influence, not because it is out of touch with the world; but, on the contrary, because of the pluck and force of its wholly utilitarian and hedonistic illusions, because of its very great success, and because of the skill with which it trims its sails to the changing fashions of the world."[7] As with Israel, so with the church.

One may take exception to Barth's theological table turning, but it is difficult to escape his searing honesty about the church. The church endeavors to justify itself by presenting itself as the grand religious option—as

---

6. Karl Barth, *The Epistle to the Romans*, 6th ed. (London: Oxford University Press, 1968), 332.

7. Barth, *Epistle to the Romans*, 335.

one, as holy, as catholic, as apostolic. Yet when the church is observed from the outside—whether from the vantage point of opposition, abandonment, indifference, or forgetfulness—it is visibly divided and divisive, wordly and flawed, partial and restrictive, self-absorbed and unresponsive to the world. *Una, sancta, catholica, apostolica* stand over the church not as affirmation, but as judgment.

The contemporary church is uncomfortable with talk about God's judgment. It is even more uncomfortable with mention of God's wrath. The church reserves judgment and wrath for God's relationship with ancient Israel, imagining that previous unpleasantness is now replaced by God's mercy and love for the church. But ecclesial contentment comes with a price, for avoiding the possibility of its own sinfulness and God's judgment leads to cheap grace and a domesticated God. If God can be counted on to tolerate the church's every shortcoming, overlook its every failing, and forgive its every disobedience, then God becomes essentially irrelevant to the church's life, present only as a vaguely supportive guide toward a bright ecclesiastical future.

God's withdrawal is a characteristic form of the judgment of God. "The time is surely coming, says the Lord GOD, when I will send a famine on the land; not a famine of bread, or a thirst for water, but of hearing the words of the LORD" (Amos 8:11). "Because you are lukewarm, I am about to spit you out of my mouth" (Rev 3:16). The possibility that God judges the church by letting the church have its own way, suffering the consequences, is terrifying. We will not understand God's withdrawal for what it is but will mistake God's judgment for mere misfortune, or place the blame for our troubles elsewhere, or even assume that God approves and blesses whatever we do. Can churches face the possibility that our un-one, un-holy, un-catholic, un-apostolic ecclesial existence encounters the wrath of God in divine acquiescence to our choices and their consequences?

The Divided Church

The church is not one, but divided. The church's division is not only characterized by the partition of Orthodox, Catholic, Protestant, and Pentecostal, or by the profusion of thousands of denominations. Variety in forms of faithfulness does not necessarily negate the church's unity. What does deny the church's oneness is the absence of ecclesial *simplicitas*. Only God is one, yet God's people are called to mirror, however dimly, and echo, however faintly, the integrity and consistent purpose of the one God who calls the church into being. But rather than rich human variety living the one faith in communion, "standing firm in one spirit, striving side by side with one mind for the faith of the gospel" (Phil 1:27), the churches wander about in self-chosen isolation, each admiring its own way in autonomy from other ways.

Inevitably, the atomized disunity among the churches leads to painless disunity within denominations. God-given diversities such as gender, race, culture, talents, and more frequently harden into enclaves of privileged experience. God-blessed latitudes in piety, interpretation, worship, and mission are intersected by longitudes that segment and detach. Diversity too easily leads to difference, then to separateness, sequestration, opposition, and ultimately schism. The endless proliferation of denominations that live at a distance from one another grows from the absence of diversity's common faith and shared purpose within each denomination and its congregations. The church is not one.

The Conformed Church

The church is worldly, not holy. The church does belong in the world, but it does not belong to the world. And yet, as many have noted, the church regularly becomes of, but not in the world! Rather than salt of the earth and light of the world, the church conforms itself to prevailing patterns of institutional life. Rather than a city built on a hill, the church settles for being a religious emporium. As it camouflages itself in society's clothing, the church focuses its gaze inward, serving the real and imagined needs of its members with only occasional, episodic forays into its neighborhoods.

English translations of the New Testament render the Greek adjective *hagios* as "holy," but translate the noun *hagioi* as "saints" rather than the more literal "holy ones." Either way, we are quick to say modestly that we are not saints, and certainly not any more holy than thou. Yet most of Paul's letters to churches are addressed to the *hagioi*, and it is precisely in his salutations that the tension is felt. Clearly, communities of Christians are called holy, yet their actions seem to belie the honorific. How can the Corinthians be *hagioi* when their life together is characterized by quarreling, boasting, sexual immorality, lawsuits, class distinctions, and a host of other behaviors all too parallel to Roman society?

It is even more difficult for the contemporary church to identify itself as holy than to assert its (invisible) oneness, (restrictive) catholicity, and (inward) apostolicity. Its conformity to the world's values is evident in its social divisions, internal confusion, and factional struggles. The church's life refracts the "undeflected purposiveness" of holiness, spoiling its life in and for the world by grand and petty compliance with the world's ways.

The Fractional Church

The church's catholicity is not a mere geographic designation—worldwide or universal—but even if it were, most churches would fall short. Many churches even identify themselves by their geopolitical location, but cartographic confinement is only a graphic display of churches' deeper limitations. Orthodox-Lutheran-Presbyterian confines are further constricted by their Russian-American-East African differences in language, history, culture, and more. The church is composed of churches, each of which is constituted in accordance with its part, not in accord with the whole. Orthodox have little to do with Reformed, Lutherans and Presbyterians remain distant cousins, and all view Pentecostals as strangers. Even the Catholic Church, not bound by national borders, remains apart from the whole as a self-contained ecclesia.

The church's catholicity is not only a matter of inclusivity but, even if it were, most churches would fall short. The church, together with the world of which it is a part, constructs categories of people, distinguishing persons by race, culture, gender, economics, and politics, each with multiple subsets. These sociological groupings serve as separators that are even perpetuated in the rhetoric of inclusion and the regulation of representation. The separated churches are internally separated by their congregations' racial, economic, and social apartness from one another. The church is not constituted in accord with the human whole.

Churches, each constituted in accordance with its part within the whole, are also characterized by limited perceptions of the whole gospel of God's way in the world. Ecclesial traditions and denominations can be characterized by distinctive emphases—sacraments, spiritual gifts, justification, episcopacy, holiness, scriptural authority, polity, service, personal decision, and more. No one denomination can know and live the faith in accord with the whole faith, of course, but the pervasive deficiency of catholicity lies in each denomination's contentment with its particular emphases, unaware or uninterested in the perception of others. The faith of the gospel is fractionated, separated into different portions. The church becomes *kat' meroi*, in accordance to its parts, rather than *kat' holos.*

The Domesticated Church

A striking instance of the church's catholicity deficit lies in its fragmented understanding of apostolicity. Does apostolicity mean the apostolic succession of bishops, fidelity to the apostolic tradition, or engagement in mission? These ways of understanding apostolicity are not mutually exclusive, yet unrelated articulations domesticate office, tradition, and mission. Episcopal office, when detached from apostolic faith and mission, becomes mechanistically institutional. Commitment to apostolic faith without ecclesially ordered mission turns into an abstract intellectual pastime. Mission apart from grounding in ecclesially ordered apostolic faith becomes haphazard and aimless. In each case, the dynamic of apostolicity is lost.

Without the coherence of apostolic faith, ministry, and mission, the church occupies itself with institutional functioning, settles for incoherent religious opinions, and mistakes mere activities for mission, thus taming the pneumatic force of the gospel. Apostolic faith, known in Scripture and tradition, is relegated to a supporting role in the church's self-determined life. Office, whether episcopal, conciliar, or ministerial, is yoked to institutional maintenance. Mission is reduced to the episodic exercise of selective commitments.

The result is that even the churches' institutions are not strengthened. The authority of ministerial offices erodes in a torrent of multiple personal preferences. Scripture and tradition give way to new "constructive" theologies. Mission becomes an optional service opportunity for the few. "What is originally apostolic," says Wolfhart Pannenberg, "is sending to bear witness to the universal and definitive truth of the revelation of God in Jesus Christ. Primarily, then, the church's apostolicity means that the sending out of the apostles to all humanity is continued by the church."[8] Is continued? The segmentation of Pannenberg's "original" apostolicity diminishes the church's capacity to be sent out to bear witness to the revelation of God in Christ.

---

8. Wolfhart Pannenberg, *Systematic Theology*, vol. 3 (Grand Rapids: Eerdmans, 1998), 406.

OVERLY ZEALOUS PROSECUTION?

Are the preceding indictments too harsh? Surely the church seeks unity; its divisions are not the only reality. The church is not wholly accommodated and completely devoid of consistent purpose; it formalizes plans and takes new initiatives. The church is conscious of its partitioned faith and exclusive practices; it strives for wholeness in faith and life. We acknowledge that the church may become theologically forgetful, bureaucratically constituted, and missionally trivial, but it also becomes aware of its need for reform and renovation. We object that the indictment is not the whole truth. While the church is not fully unified, sanctified, all-encompassing, and other-oriented, the church is not wholly devoid of the creedal marks. But defense of the church's failure to be fully one, holy, catholic, and apostolic only serves to demonstrate the church's proclivity to justify itself, to display its ecumenical *bona fides*, its opposition to the world's evils, its commitments to inclusivity, and its mission programs.

Self-justification in the face of critique invariably leads to programmatic action. Ecumenical agreements are sought and cooperative ministries established. Statements are released deploring social and political evils. Mandated diversity and inclusivity measures are put in place. Work plans are developed to include more and more church activities under the umbrella of mission. The Gospel and Our Culture Network, for instance, follows its extensive critique of the Church's Constantinian captivity with the declaration that "this is a time for a dramatically new vision. The current predicament of churches in North America requires more than a mere tinkering with long-assumed notions about the identity and mission of the church. Instead . . . there is a need for reinventing or rediscovering the church in this new kind of world."[9] The Network's appeal for reinvention is repeated in constant, widespread denominational calls for reconfiguring or transforming the church. The common thread in such statements is the conviction that it is the church's task to reinvent, reconfigure, transform itself.

"A diseased institution cannot reform itself," according to C. Northcote Parkinson, the mid-twentieth-century satirist of business organizations. "The cure," he wrote, "whatever its nature, must come from outside."[10]

---

9. Darrell L. Guder, ed., *Missional Church: A Vision for the Sending of the Church in North America* (Grand Rapids: Eerdmans, 1998), 77.

10. C. Northcote Parkinson, *Parkinson's Law and Other Studies in Administration* (New York: Ballantine Books, 1957), 110.

The church may be able to reinvent its missionary training, reconfigure its bureaucratic structure, and transform its communications strategy, but it cannot make itself one, holy, catholic, and apostolic. The cure for its divisions, conformities, exclusions, and domestication must come from outside. It must come from the One, Holy, Wholly, Sending God, for the *notae ecclesiae* are fundamentally and always derivative from the One who gives life to the people of God. The church is continually tempted to imagine, on the one hand, that it actually is one, holy, catholic, and apostolic, and on the other, that it can accomplish the task of making itself more unified, sanctified, inclusive, and missional. Comfortable assurance and confident exertion are not shields against creedal reproach but rather eye patches that blind us to the source of our hope.

CALL AND RESPONSE

The charge against the church is not the last word. When the people of God acknowledge the judgment leveled upon them, they know that it is not an abstract indictment, but the judgment of the one God, the holy God, the God who reigns over the whole, the God who seeks to gather the wandering and the lost. Repentance, then, grows out of the knowledge of God, not the fear of punishment. Repentance is response to the gospel. "Return, faithless Israel, says the LORD. I will not look on you in anger, for I am merciful, says the LORD: I will not be angry forever. . . . Return, O faithless children, says the LORD" (Jer 3:12, 14). "Indeed, God did not send the Son into the world to condemn the world, but in order that the world might be saved through him" (John 3:17). The church's failings are known in light of the overflowing grace of the Lord Jesus Christ, the steadfast love of God, and the all-embracing communion of the Holy Spirit. It is grace that points the way to honest recognition of judgment and repentance, not judgment that leads to repentance that, in turn, produces grace. The church's remorse and repentance flow from the church's recognition of its gracious Lord.

The entrée to the dynamic circle of the one, holy, catholic church is by way of Jesus's inaugural proclamation: "The time is fulfilled, and the kingdom of God is at hand; repent, and believe the gospel" (Mark 1:15). The church's current time is troubled, yet because God's time flows into our time, and because God's way in the world is near us, on our lips and in our hearts, the church is not left to its own devices. The call of the *Christus praesens* comes to the church: *turn around, reorient your life, trust the good news and follow me.* The gracious Lord of the church always calls his people to oneness, holiness, catholicity, and apostolicity, and the gracious Lord of the church always shows the way. The church's all-too-evident reality of division, accommodation, exclusion, and forgetfulness is judged, but it is only known fully in light of the grace of the Lord Jesus Christ, whose call to repentance is his invitation to hope that does not lie in human capacity but in the capacity and purpose of God.

Called to Be One—"The Good News of God"

Christ's call to unity among the various congregations, denominations, and world communions into which the church is divided is clear and audible. Nowhere in Scripture is there a hint of satisfaction with the disunity of the people of God. From Abraham, in Christ, and on to consummation, God's way in the world is to gather the scattered people so that all will be his people and he will be the God of all. Gathering happens within the scattering, of course, so that the evident reality of human diffusion is confronted by the call of the risen Lord to a new community of Jew and gentile, which is to say, of all. The call is heard most poignantly in a plea, Jesus's own prayer for those given to him by the Father, a prayer for all of those gathered by him from then to now, a prayer for the church:

> I am no longer in the world, but they are in the world, and I am coming to you. Holy Father, protect them in your name that you have given me, so that they may be one, as we are one. . . . I am not asking you to take them out of the world, but I ask you to protect them from evil. . . . I ask not only on behalf of these, but also on behalf of those who will believe in me through their word, that they may all be one. As you, Father, are in me and I am in you, may they also be in us, so that the world may believe that you have sent me. The glory that you have given me I have given them, so that they may be one, as we are one. I in them and you in me, that they may become completely one, so that the world may know that you have sent me and have loved them even as you have loved me. (John 17:11–23, altered)

Jesus prayed "when the hour had come" (17:1), timing that underlines the urgency of his petitions. The "high priestly prayer" embraces themes that are prominent throughout John's Gospel. In the beginning the evangelist proclaimed, "the Word became flesh and dwelt among us, full of grace and truth; we have beheld his glory, glory as of the only Son from the Father" (1:14, RSV). At the end, Jesus prayed, "Father . . . glorify your Son so that the Son may glorify you" (17:1). In the beginning the evangelist proclaimed, "No one has ever seen God; the only Son, who is in the bosom of the Father, he has made him known" (1:18, RSV). At the end, Jesus prayed, "that they may know you, the only true God, and Jesus Christ whom you have sent" (John 17:1–3). The intimate oneness of the Father and the Son, stressed throughout the Gospel, has been manifested to those who know and believe the truth— not as abstract, conceptual truth, but as the truth of the gospel, the truth of lived communion with God. The unity of God's people is thus grounded in the very nature of the One to whom they are bound; Jesus prays, "that they may be one, as we are one." As the Father and Son are one, so those who know the only true God and Jesus whom he has sent are to be one.

But those who are to be one have not been one and are not one. If the unity of the people of God were inherent, there would have been no need for Jesus to pray for our oneness. Yet Jesus did and does pray for our unity. The Lord of the church prayed for our protection from evil because he knew that the church's unity was imperiled at the outset. Jesus prays for our protection from the forces of disunity, for only then can our unity cohere with the oneness of the Father and the Son. From the outset, Christian unity has been at risk, dependent on protection from the danger posed by the world and by evil. Yet, though the church prays daily, "lead us not into temptation, but deliver us from evil," we remain insufficiently aware that among our temptations is easy acquiescence to the evil of our indifferent separation.

Jesus Christ, risen and ascended as the living Lord of the church, continues to call the people of God to the unity of communion, a call that is heard again and again in the words of Paul, James, and Peter. Christ's call to unity is not a minor theme in Scripture but a strong current throughout. The question posed to the church is whether Christ's call can be heard amid the cacophony of assertive denominational self-sufficiency and implicit congregational competition. Can the churches know and follow the way that bears visible witness to the one church?

Called to Be Holy—"The Kingdom of God Is at Hand"

Christ's call to holiness in the church and its people is clear and audible. The church prays daily, "Our Father in heaven, holy be your name," and the church's Lord prays, "Holy Father, protect them in your name." Paul sings out, "Blessed be the God and Father of our Lord Jesus Christ, who has blessed us in Christ with every spiritual blessing . . . to be holy and blameless before him in love" (Eph 1:3–4). The church is called to be holy, not only in the sanctity of its own life, but for the sanctification of the world. "The LORD will establish you as his holy people, as he has sworn to you, if you keep the commandments of the LORD your God and walk in his ways. All the people of the earth shall see that you are called by the name of the LORD" (Deut 28:9–10).

The church is called to be the church, not to be the world. Christ does not call the church out of the world but to be the body of Christ, the communion of the Holy Spirt, the people of God in the world. The character of the church's life is to be discernably different from that of the world's associations, organizations, and institutions, many of which are admirable in their own way. The call to holiness does not assume that other social and political institutions are evil; It only recognizes a difference between their ways and the way of the church. The church's calling to holiness places it in the world as the people that so walk in God's way that social and political institutions will see that the church is "called by the name of the LORD."

The Sermon on the Mount is more than a collection of sayings addressed to the crowds and his disciples; it voices Christ's call to a way of living that is dramatically different from the way things are in the world. Christ calls the church to be holy because the church's abiding temptation is to be comfortably at home in the world. There have been times and places where groups of Christians have tried to turn Matthew 5–7 into a legal code, but far more often the church has heard Jesus's teaching as little more than lovely but unattainable idealism. "You have heard it said . . . but I say to you" is the shape of Christ's continuing call to the church. These words are more than an intensification of Torah, they are an intensified differentiation from all that the church hears about the customary way of life in its social and culture milieu. The Sermon on the Mount, as a concrete occurrence of the kingdom of God, of God's way in the world, is not a catalogue of how the church is to act but a representation of how the church is to be. Christ calls the church to be holy as God is holy, to be holy in the midst of the world.

The church's call to holiness is only secondarily a call to distinction from the world, however; it is primarily a call to be God's people, Christ's body, the communion of the Holy Spirit. The church does not seek ways to be different, but to be conformed to Christ. Conforming to Christ results in not being conformed to the world, but there are many ways of not being conformed to the world that have nothing to do with being conformed to Christ. Christ calls us to seek first the kingdom of God, to follow first in God's way. In that way, the church's holiness follows God's undeflected purposiveness in the world.

Called to Be Catholic—"The Time Is Fulfilled"

Christ's call to catholicity is heard at the beginning as "salvation prepared in the presence of all peoples" (Luke 2:29–32) and at the climax as the risen Lord interprets to us "the things about himself in all the scriptures" (Luke 24:27). Christ continues to call the church in his self-interpretation through Scripture, for it is only in knowing the fullness of the gospel that the church can know the fullness of salvation prepared for all peoples. Inclusivity measured by representational categories is far exceeded by the scope of the gospel. Apart from the whole of God's way in the world, even the church's most admirable attempts to institute inclusion will be oddly parochial.

The time is fulfilled now as God's undeflected purposiveness through Christ and in the Holy Spirit gathers the scattered peoples of the world. The great gathering is manifested at Pentecost, revealed in unmistakably inverse parallelism with Babel. Christ has not left us orphaned but has given us the Spirit of truth, the Spirit of the Father and the Son, who guides the church into all truth, into the whole truth. Now, when the time is fulfilled, in the last days, God pours out his Spirit on "all flesh . . . on sons and daughters, young and old, men and women, everyone who calls on the name of the Lord" (Acts 2:17–21). The gathering now proceeds *kat' holos*, according to the whole of God's way in Christ. Christ calls the church to listen for the sound of dividing walls of hostility crashing to the ground.

As the prophet calls out, "The Holy One of Israel is your Redeemer, the God of the whole earth he is called" (Isa 54:5), Israel and the church are encompassed within God's wider will for the whole earth. As John proclaims that Jesus Christ "is the atoning sacrifice for our sins, and not only for ours but also for the sins of the whole world" (1 John 2:2), we are encompassed within the Lord's saving grace for all. So the church is called to exhibit in its life the wholeness of the gospel for the wholeness of the whole world. Jew and gentile, slave and free, male and female, rich and poor, parents and children, young and old, Parthians, Medes, and Elamites, captive and blind, mourners, meek, and peacemakers—throughout Scripture Christ's call to the people of God is the call to be the whole people of God in the way of the whole gospel.

Called to Be Apostolic—"Believe the Good News"

Christ's clear call to apostolicity is heard in the familiar great commission: the risen Christ says, "All authority in heaven and on earth has been given to me. Go therefore and make disciples of all nations, baptizing them in the name of the Father and of the Son and of the Holy Spirit, and teaching them to obey everything that I have commanded you. And remember, I am with you always, to the end of the age" (Matt 28:18–20). Our familiarity with the great commission—even our labeling it "the great commission"—leads us to skip lightly past it, hearing it, if at all, as a warrant for the church's programmatic mission activities. What the church too often misses is its world-shattering proclamation of Christ's radical call to the church. Stanley Hauerwas says of Christ's call at the end of Matthew's Gospel,

> What has been hidden from the foundation of the world, what has been hidden from the wise, is now revealed by the Son. The God of Israel is the God of all nations. The disciples are now equipped to be sent to the nations, baptizing them into the death and resurrection of Jesus to make them citizens of his death-defying kingdom. Israel is not to be left behind, but rather its mission is now continued in a new reality called church. Through the church, all nations will learn to call Israel blessed.[11]

What has been obscured in the church, if not rehidden, is the present reality of the living Christ's call to go. When the great commission is reduced to a written text that merely encourages and validates whatever mission the church undertakes, its present tense is converted to past tense, and Christ's call to the church is muted.

"All authority in heaven and on earth has been given to me." The crucified and resurrected One is the *pantocrator*, the almighty Lord of all. The risen Christ who is Lord of the church is not only Lord of the church but of the world, so that the church's life is lived within the world's life. The call of this One to whom all authority is given comes to the church as command,

---

11. Stanley Hauerwas, *Matthew* (Grand Rapids: Brazos, 2006), 249.

not mere encouragement. The church is missional, not by nature, but by virtue of the Lord who calls it.

"Go therefore to all nations." Christ calls the church out of itself, sending the church into the world for the sake of the world. The call is voiced continually because the church is always tempted to settle into comfortable self-care. The command to Go comes to each congregation, to each judicatory, to each denomination. Each is joined to all as the whole church goes to all nations. "Going" takes many forms, from constant prayers to geographic travel, but not going is disregard of Christ's call.

"Make disciples, teaching them to obey everything that I have commanded you." Christ calls the church to many forms of witness. The church is called to serve the world's multiple needs for water, food, clothing, healing, education, safety, and dignity. Never neglecting these needs, the church's primary call is to make disciples, to proclaim the grace of Christ, the love of God, and the communion of the Holy Spirit so that the nations (i.e., all peoples) will follow God's way in the world.

"Baptizing them in the name of the Father and of the Son and of the Holy Spirit." The purpose of the church's commission is to incorporate persons into union with Christ. While this entails incorporation into the body of Christ, the church, it does not mean making them "members" of a particular church. In union with Christ, persons are called to discipleship, obeying Christ's commands.

"I am with you always." Christ's call to apostolicity—as the call to catholicity, holiness, and oneness—is personal, the beckoning of One who is with us now. Because the *Christus praesens* is personal presence, the church is not left on its own to fulfill abstract demands from a remote deity. Christ's calls to the church, summarized above, always come in specific form and always come with the promise of empowering presence.

CALLED TO BE THE ONE, HOLY, CATHOLIC, APOSTOLIC CHURCH

Christ calls the church to be one, holy, catholic, and apostolic. The *notae* are not ontological attributes of the church. Yet, declining to grant their ecclesial actuality does not contradict the creed or denigrate the church. On the contrary, understanding oneness, holiness, catholicity, and apostolicity as callings from the Lord of the church is the source of the church's confidence, confidence not in itself—in its wisdom, capacities, and capabilities—but confidence in the *Christus praesens* who has promised to be with us always, until the completion of the age. Because the Lord calls the church, the church knows what it is to be. Moreover, the church is able to know its calling because the Spirit gives it ears to hear. It is the church's vocation to be one, holy, catholic, and apostolic communion, and this calling can be pursued in the assurance that the living Lord has many things to say to us and that the Spirit of truth will guide the church into all truth (John 16:12–13). The church is both assured and encouraged: Let anyone who has an ear listen to what the Spirit is saying to the churches.

Wolfhart Pannenberg asserts that "In no other field has Christian theology given itself so unreservedly to a purely secular understanding of reality, detached from any connection with the reality of God, as in its handling of church history." He goes on to note that current accounts of the church's history interpret events and processes according to the canons of secular historiography, leaving the impression that, from the close of the apostolic age on, God has withdrawn from human history. "Today," says Pannenberg, "even theologians who stress the fundamental significance of God's activity in biblical presentations of the history of Israel and Jesus Christ treat with skepticism, or totally reject, a theological interpretation of the course of Christianity and the church."[12] Pannenberg's critique does not affect only the past history of the church, for it also concerns its present life. Absent an operative conviction that the grace of the Lord Jesus Christ, the love of God, and the communion of the Holy Spirit are living, active realities in the lives of the churches, ecclesial life becomes characterized by anxiety, obsession with technique, and self-rationalization. Central to all three characteristics is the habitual and fruitless assertion that somehow, in spite of appearances to the contrary, the church's inner identity really is unity, sanctity, wholeness, and fidelity.

In word and sacrament, in its inner communion, and in its participation in the *missio Dei*, the church is addressed by its Lord. Its response is not always congruent with its calling, however, and so it too often listens to the siren call of a social culture that beckons it to join the ranks of organizations that rationalize their existence according to the canons of secular success. And so, as with Israel, the church's calling includes the call to repent, to turn from self-justification to God's way in the world. From the Groupe des Dombes, to the Princeton Proposal, to *Ut Unum Sint*, to "Called to Be the One Church," deep repentance—confession, turning,

---

12. Pannenberg, *Systematic Theology*, vol. 3, 498–99.

conversion—has been seen as the necessary starting point for renewal of the gospel imperative to strive for the visible unity of Christ's church, for its holiness, catholicity, and apostolicity.

- "Our confessions have to 'make confession,'" says the Groupe des Dombes, "to move forward to admitting their limitations and inadequacies, even sins."[13]
- The Princeton Proposal declares that "we must examine our collective consciences and repent of actions, habits, and sentiments that glory in division."[14]
- John Paul II notes explicitly that "there is an increased sense of the need for repentance: an awareness of certain exclusions which seriously harm fraternal charity, for certain refusals to forgive, of a certain pride, of an unevangelical insistence on condemning 'the other side,' of a disdain born of an unhealthy presumption."[15]
- The Ninth Assembly of the World Council of Churches recognizes that "each church must become aware of all that is provisional in its life and have the courage to acknowledge this to other churches."[16]

Nearly a century ago, Karl Barth gave voice to the church's need to turn around, turning its back to the way things are, and following in the way of Christ who continues to say to the company of disciples, "Follow me."

If the Church were sufficiently humble to recapture its understanding of the communion of saints as the fellowship of sinners dependent upon forgiveness, and so be rid of that nervous, devastating, vigorous founding of new societies; . . . if it were courageous enough to keep its eyes fixed on its own theme, to abandon all striving after, attaining, and boasting about visible goals and successes; . . . if only the Church were directed wholly and altogether towards the unknown, living, free God,

---

13. Groupe des Dombes, *For the Conversion of the Churches* (Geneva: WCC Publications, 1993), 28.

14. Carl E. Braaten and Robert W. Jenson, eds., *In One Body Through the Cross: The Princeton Proposal for Christian Unity* (Grand Rapids: Eerdmans, 2003), 57-58.

15. John Paul II, *Ut Unum Sint* (Washington: United States Catholic Conference, Publication 5-050), ¶ 15, 20.

16. World Council of Churches, "Called to Be the One Church" (Geneva: WCC Publications), ¶ 7.

and would concentrate its preaching upon the cross of Christ—then the Church could be, unobservably and in a manner unheard of, the Church of Jacob, the Church of faith, and the Church of the righteousness of God.[17]

17. Barth, *Epistle to the Romans*, 367–68.

Chapter 11

HOPE FOR THE CHURCH

Then I saw a new heaven and a new earth; for the first heaven
and the first earth had passed away, and the sea was no more.
And I saw the holy city, new Jerusalem, coming down out of
heaven from God, prepared as a bride adorned for her husband;
and I heard a great voice from the throne saying, "Behold, the
dwelling of God is with humans. He will dwell with them, and
they shall be his people, and God himself will be with them."

Revelation 21:1–3, RSV, altered

"I just want to say one thing, though. If the Lord is more gracious than any of us can begin to imagine, and I'm sure He is,
then Doll and a whole lot of other people are safe, and warm,
and very happy. And probably a little bit surprised. If there is
no Lord, then things are just the way they look to us. Which is
really much harder to accept. I mean, it doesn't feel right. There
has to be more to it all, I believe."

"Well, but that's what you want to believe, ain't it?"

"That doesn't mean it isn't true."

Marilynne Robinson, *Lila*

Is there hope for the church? Of course there is hope, for the church is
the body of Christ, the people of God, the communion of the Holy Spirit.
Even at its lowest points, there has been, is, and will be hope for the church
because the saying remains as sure today as when it was first voiced: "If

we are faithless, he remains faithful—for he cannot deny himself" (2 Tim 2:13). That is why Christian hope is not hope for something; it is hope in someone—hope in "the God of hope" (Rom 15:13), hope in "Christ Jesus our hope" (1 Tim 1:1), hope that abounds "by the power of the Holy Spirit" (Rom 15:13). Hope for the church—the hope of the church—is lodged not in itself but in the one God—Father, Son, and Holy Spirit—who is hope's source, substance, and goal.

Christian hope in God runs up against different, culturally dominant ways of talking about hope, however, often resulting in churchly confusion. Hope is sometimes thought of as little more than a last resort when life becomes difficult and distressing: a distraught woman emerges from the intensive care unit where her husband lies connected to machines by tubes and wires. "How is he?" others ask, and she replies, "We must hope for the best." Too often, the church talks about hope only when success eludes it. Similarly, hope is regularly confused with wishing: "I bought ten Powerball tickets today," the man says. "I sure hope I win." Too often, church talk about hope is merely the expression of desire. Additionally, hope is commonly collapsed into optimism: politicians assure unemployed miners that "the coal mines will open again and prosperity will return." The church responds to membership losses and budget shortfalls by asserting that things will soon turn around and that better days are ahead. Christian hope, the hope of the church, is neither fallback, nor wishing, nor optimism.

Churches in North America and Europe now live in distressing circumstances. The evident decline in public interest and engagement produces an anxiety-driven sense of ecclesial need. Some churches respond by pining for a return to past glory while others imagine a future advance to restored prominence. Both outlooks emerge from neediness as forms of craving for the church's prospects to change for the better. Mired in ecclesial distress, some congregations and denominations fall back on wishful thinking while others engage in official optimism, but neither wishing nor optimism can provide a cure for churches' ills. Wishful thinking results in odd passivity as churches continue to conduct their lives as they always have, perhaps trying a bit harder, dreaming that a time will come when their fortunes will be reversed. Official optimism results in odd hyperactivity as churches generate a flurry of constantly changing goals, strategies, and programs, all in the conviction that finding the right technique will produce desired results. Both wishful thinking and official optimism grow in the soil of perceived depletion and of desire for restored institutional success.

Wishful thinking and official optimism are not tied to specific ecclesial forms or ideologies. They are present within both historic communions and newer churches, and they reside in both liberal-progressive and conservative-evangelical denominations and congregations. But none of it has much to do with "a living hope through the resurrection of Jesus Christ" (1 Pet 1:3). When wishful thinking does not lead to an ecclesiastical "winning lottery ticket," churches console themselves by sighing that they are not called to be successful, but to be faithful (confident that they are being faithful, of course). When official optimism does not lead to an uptick in market share and ecclesiastical "profit," churches scurry to adopt the latest management theory in the conviction that better technique and metrics will lead to a march from good to great.

It is true enough that the church is called to fidelity, not guaranteed success. It is also true enough that the church is called to order its common life and mission wisely. Yet the point of both faithfulness and wisdom is lost if their source and purpose is the church itself. The central ecclesiological question is, "Fidelity to whom? Who is the source of Wisdom?" Hope for the church and hope within the church are not matters of perception, as if the church should avert its gaze from unpleasant reality and project the vision of a bright future. Hope is not an attitude, as if positive thinking should replace grim analysis. Christian hope lies in its object, who is also its subject: the one God, known in creation, redemption, sanctification, and hoped-for consummation. God alone is the ground of Christian hope, the one in whom and toward whom the church's hope is directed. If hope is to be something more substantial than the projection of an ecclesial utopia, it must find its life in God and God's way in the world.

HOPING BACKWARDS AND REMEMBERING FORWARD

At the outset of his classic *Theology of Hope*, Jürgen Moltmann states that eschatology is the doctrine of Christian hope, "which embraces both the object hoped for and also the hope inspired by it."[1] Moltmann's aim is to orient Christian eschatology away from the future as such, toward the future in light of a definite reality in history: "the question whether all statements about the future are grounded in the person and history of Jesus Christ provides it with the touchstone by which to distinguish the spirit of

---

1. Jürgen Moltmann, *Theology of Hope* (New York: Harper & Row, 1967), 16.

eschatology from that of utopia."[2] For Moltmann, Christian eschatology is the doctrine of hope in Jesus Christ and his future. The firm ground of hope is the *missio Christi*. It is in the future of Christ that he is recognized as what he is, says Moltmann, "illuminated in advance by the promise of the righteousness of God, the promise of life as a result of resurrection from the dead, and the promise of the kingdom of God in a new totality of being."[3]

Moltmann is surely right that hope is grounded in history, and he is right that the resurrection of Jesus Christ is at the heart of the history of God-with-us. But the history of God-with-us is not confined to the crucified and risen Christ and his future. Christian hope, the hope of the church, is grounded in the character of God—Father, Son, and Holy Spirit—made known in the fullness of God's engagement with the world from creation through the present toward consummation. Both Israel and the church hope in the one who vows, "I will be your God, and you shall be my people." Hope is not exclusively focused on the future of the resurrected Christ, or linked only to eschatology.

Dietrich Ritschl, whose *Memory and Hope* was written at the same time but independently from Moltmann's *Theology of Hope*, binds hope and memory together more tightly. Ritschl maintains that "what the church can see concerning the past, she can also see in relation to the present and she can prepare herself for the future, so that past, present, and future appear in their relevance to Christ."[4] The different emphases of Ritschl and Moltmann are evident in the subtitles of their books: Moltmann's *On the Ground and the Implications of a Christian Eschatology* and Ritschl's *An Inquiry Concerning the Presence of Christ*. The one centers hope on Jesus Christ and his future while the other focuses memory and hope in the present Christ. While their approaches are complementary, Ritschl's may have more to contribute to the ground and implications of a Christian ecclesiology.

Ritschl views the present church in light of intertwined memory and hope: "Honest and concerned *memory* is possible because of the *hope* that decisive things in the relation between God and the world are still to come, and *hope* is possible because of what has already happened and of what is understood and accepted as a promise."[5] Theological reflection

---

2. Moltmann, *Theology of Hope*, 17.
3. Moltmann, *Theology of Hope*, 203.
4. Dietrich Ritschl, *Memory and Hope* (New York: Macmillan, 1967), 64.
5. Ritschl, *Memory and Hope*, 13.

on the memory of God's faithfulness and hope in God's enduring faithfulness invites the church to "hope backward" into memory and "remember forward" into hope. "Memory and hope are the dimensions of faith in the *Christus praesens*," says Ritschl, "and it is only because of the *Christus praesens* that these dimensions are open to our perception."[6] It is the presence of the living Christ that enlivens memory of God's "wonderful deeds" in the past, and engenders hope in God's consistent fidelity to his people until the completion of the age.

"The church," says Ritschl, "not only hopes because she *remembers* the promises, but she makes the accounts of Israel's and her forefathers' memory her own memory *because she hopes*, that is to say, she would not be 'interested' in memories and hopes of previous generations if she were not prompted to do so by her own hope."[7] Can it be that the church's current preoccupation with itself and its own diminishment grows from its lack of interest in the faith and life of previous generations? Inattention to the memory of God's presence with his people, embedded in both Scripture and tradition, results in the church replacing hope with wishful thinking and official optimism. Perhaps Ritschl's statements should not be understood as a description of what the church actually is and does but rather heard as the call of the living, present Christ to the church, a call to memory of God-with-us and hope in God-with-us.

Because Christian hope does not emerge from the church's need but from God's abundance, hope is not a last resort response to ecclesiastical, communal, or personal deficit. Hope is confidence in the overflowing love of God. This can be seen in the two New Testament letters attributed to Peter, for they display the church's hope as present confidence in God's abundance. Both begin with what must have been a common Christian salutation: "May grace and peace be yours in abundance." In the first letter, God's abundant grace and mercy lead immediately to the church's hope: "Blessed be the God and Father of our Lord Jesus Christ! By his great mercy he has given us a living hope through the resurrection of Jesus Christ from the dead." In the second letter, abundant grace and peace flow from "the knowledge of God and of Jesus our Lord" and flow into the remembrance of God's "precious and very great promises." The one letter looks forward, the other remembers; hopeful memory and remembered hope of God's abundant grace and peace empower the people of God in the difficult present.

6. Ritschl, *Memory and Hope*, 13.
7. Ritschl, *Memory and Hope*, 229.

It may be stating the obvious to say that hope in God is hope in God's way in and for the world. Hope for the church, the people of God, is sure, but it is not necessarily hope for the achievements and perpetuation of every denomination and congregation. The church in Hippo is no more, but the Catholic Church now lives on every continent. The day may come when the Presbyterian Church (USA) will live only in its billions of endowment dollars, but the churches it planted in Asia, Africa, and Latin America continue to grow in faith, hope, and love. Hope for the church and hope within the church is confidence that God is the God of a people and that the people of God will bear faithful witness until the fullness of time when God gathers up all things in him (Eph 1:10).

A MORAL THEOLOGY OF HOPE

The church's living hope is dynamic. Hope in God does not wait passively for God to do something; hope acts in specific ways because it is grounded in and directed toward the One who is Alpha and the Omega, the beginning and the end. The church's action is hopeful when it remembers the ways of God with the people of God and so anticipates future consummation when God will be all in all. Past and future, memory and hope live in the church's present. How, then, is the hopeful church called to live?

Moltmann says that "those who hope in Christ can no longer put up with reality as it is, but begin to suffer under it, to contradict it . . . for the goad of the promised future stabs inexorably into the flesh of every unfulfilled present."[8] Hope in the triumph of God's way in the world produces profound dissatisfaction with "the way things are," and so the church lives in correspondence with the purposes of God in whom it hopes. Brazilian theologian Rubem Alves proposes a reverse dynamic. For Alves, the way things are leads to "a shout of pain, anger, and refusal" that expands into "a symphony of negation," rejecting the present state of affairs. Alves contends that it then becomes "possible and necessary to search for those possibilities that are absent from the present. The consciousness then projects itself in the direction of the future, giving birth to hope."[9] For Moltmann, dissatisfaction with the way things are emerges in the light of hope; for Alves, hope emerges in the light of dissatisfaction with the way things are.

8. Moltmann, *Theology of Hope*, 21.
9. Rubem Alves, *A Theology of Human Hope* (New York: Corpus Books, 1969), 13.

Both Moltmann and Alves wrote a theology of hope, the one believing that hope engenders the refusal to put up with reality as it is, the other believing that the refusal to put up with reality as it is stimulates hope. Both approaches ring true, but Alves's approach raises an obvious question, "What hope does refusal of present realities engender?" Contradiction of the way things are opens myriad possibilities: Hitler's National Socialism is as conceivable as Mandela's democratic South Africa, terrorism as possible as Gandhi's nonviolence. The social, political, and economic plight of Germany in the 1920s and 1930s and the oppressive realities of apartheid South Africa both produced "shouts of pain, anger, and refusal." Shouts in Germany generated hope for the nation's rehabilitation, but that hope led to dictatorship, the extermination of six million Jews, and a World War. South Africa's pain and refusal generated hope for the end to apartheid, and that hope led to Nelson Mandela, Desmond Tutu, peaceful transition, and reconciliation commissions. Hope that emerges from negation is necessarily indeterminate.

Conversely, the approach of Moltmann (and Ritschl) is hope in God and God's way in the world, which lays bare the deformities of the present. Remembered hope and hopeful memory in God is determinate, not open-ended. Hope in God and God's way in the world exposes present reality as the weary way of the world. It is God's righteousness that exposes injustice, God's love that uncovers animosity, God's fidelity that unmasks duplicity. Hope in the righteous, loving, faithful God not only opens our eyes to reality as it is but prompts the church to determinate action in and for the world.

Grace to Us and Peace from God Our Father and the Lord Jesus Christ

The letter to the Ephesians begins with an impossibly long Greek sentence (Eph 1:3–14), mercifully divided into eight sentences and two paragraphs by English translators. The text should be read as one sustained declaration, however, not as two distinct topics and eight discrete thoughts, much less as twelve self-contained verses. Paul declares what God has done, the purpose of God's action, and the life of God's people within this matrix of memory and hope. Memory, hope, and the present flow over the church in a cascade of grace.

> Memory: "Blessed be the God and Father of our Lord Jesus Christ, who has blessed . . . chosen . . . destined . . . bestowed . . . redeemed . . . forgiven . . . lavished."

Hope: "for he has made known to us the mystery of his will . . . his purpose . . . a plan for the fullness of time . . . the purpose of him who accomplishes all things."

Memory and hope in the life of the church: "we who first hoped . . . heard the truth . . . believed in him . . . have been destined and appointed . . . to live for the praise of his glory . . . sealed with the promised Holy Spirit. . . the guarantee of our inheritance until we acquire possession of it."

At the heart of the matter is the mystery, the plan, the purpose itself: "to gather up all things in Christ, things in heaven and things on earth" (1:10). "Gather up" is the NRSV's translation of the compound Greek word *anakephalaiōsasthai,* which occurs only twice in the New Testament. Its breadth can be sensed in the various ways it is translated into English: "gather up" (NRSV), "unite" (RSV), "sum up" (NAB), "bring all things together" (CEB). The NRSV's "gather up" is an appropriate choice, for it best expresses the central biblical theme of God's ongoing action to gather the scattered. It is also consistent with its other New Testament use in Paul's letter to the Romans: "The commandments, 'You shall not commit adultery; You shall not murder; You shall not steal; You shall not covet'; and any other commandment are *anakephalaioutai* in this word: 'Love your neighbor as yourself'" (Rom 13:9). The NRSV translates "summed up" here, but this rendering may suggest that summation overrides particulars. Paul's meaning is more graphic, picturing the Decalogue's second table and all its multiple subsets gathered up into love of neighbor.

The memory of what God has done for us and the sure hope in God, whose purpose is to gather together all things in heaven and on earth, shape the church's calling: to live for the praise of God's glory. God's glory, known in grateful memory of his presence with and for his people, and known in the confident hope of his enduring faithfulness with and for creation, is praised as the church looks for the gathering of all things into communion with God. The church is called to hope backward as it discerns God's history of gathering the scattered through Israel and in Christ, and it is called to remember forward, acting out of its hope in the deep mystery of God's purpose made known in Christ. In the present, the church is called to live its God-given appointment and purpose: to love God with heart, soul, mind, and strength, and to love its neighbors in God's world as actively as it loves itself.

Love of God and love of neighbors are bound to one another, for the Lord's gathering of his people reconciles them to himself and reconciles them to one another in the fullness of *koinōnia*. The character of the church's calling to love God and others is evident in a central text from Paul's second letter to the church in Corinth. Paul writes to the Corinthians, and to us, that "in Christ, God was reconciling the world to himself" (or "God was in Christ, reconciling the world to himself"; 2 Cor 5:19). In Christ, God is *now* reconciling the world to himself, for Christ is not sequestered in the past and God's reconciling grace is not restricted to a moment in time.

Reconciliation is God's mission; God is the reconciler and humans are the reconciled. "For," says Paul, "if while we were enemies, we were reconciled through the death of his Son, much more surely, having been reconciled, will we be saved by his life. But more than that, we even boast in God through our Lord Jesus Christ, through whom we have now received reconciliation" (Rom 5:10–11). We, the enemy, were reconciled (passive) through Christ's death. Having been reconciled (passive) we will be saved, made whole, by his [risen] life. So we boast (better, we glory) in God through Christ, in and through whom we have now received reconciliation (passive). God's glory is praised as the church glories in God, not in itself.

The Service of Reconciliation

Reconciliation is God's work. And yet, astonishingly, God gives the *diakonia* of reconciliation to us, to the church (2 Cor 5:18). For whom is the church's service of reconciliation intended? Clearly, Paul has in view those who are not yet reconciled to God. God chooses to gather the scattered ones by making his appeal through the church. The church serves those who do not know God's reconciliation in Christ by representing that reconciliation in its own life. Its service is not only to speak about God's reconciliation of the world but also to display God's reconciliation by its evident love for God and its palpable love for others, both within and outside the church.

Little wonder, then, that Paul concludes his statements on the service of reconciliation with an urgent call—"we entreat you on behalf of Christ, be reconciled to God" (5:20). But hasn't Paul just told us that we *are* reconciled to God? The people of God, the body of Christ, the communion of the Holy Spirit, the church, has been reconciled and called to the service of reconciliation, but the church's response to its call is always ambiguous. We are the reconciled people who both live out and fail to live out our service of reconciliation. We are the community of the justified that tries to justify itself. We are God's ambassadors of reconciliation who remain divided among ourselves. We give glory to God and seek glory for ourselves. We are all of those things, but even in our evident equivocation we do not lose heart because we hope in the ever-present Christ who continues to call to the church, "Be reconciled to God."

Paul's prayer for the saints in Ephesus is his prayer for the church in all times and places (Eph 1:16–23): that the church will love God with heart, soul, mind, and strength, that "the Father of glory" will give the church a spirit of wisdom and revelation as it comes to know him more fully so that the church "may know the hope to which he has called us, what are the riches of his glorious inheritance among the saints, and what is the immeasurable greatness of his power for the church" (1:18–19, altered). In its worship, focused on Word and sacraments, and in its mission, focused by prayers of thanksgiving and intercession, the church is to be oriented by the praise of God's glory.

Loving God and loving neighbors are bound together. In an extended passage (Eph 2:11–22), Paul reminds the gentiles (and the church) that we were at one time "without Christ, alienated from the commonwealth of Israel, and strangers to the covenants of promise, having no hope and without God in the world." But now, says Paul, we who were once far off have been brought near by Christ, who "preached peace" to those who were far off and those who were near. Christ himself is our peace, who "has broken down the dividing wall of hostility" (RSV), reconciling both to God in one body, "bringing hostility to an end." There are no longer "strangers and aliens" but fellow citizens and members of "the household of God."

Do we think that Paul was only reporting on the Christ-established unity of Jews and gentiles in first-century Asia Minor? If so, the letter to the Ephesians, not to mention most of the New Testament, has little relevance beyond wistful awareness of an ancient, partially fulfilled ideal. Or can we hear Paul's words as living, partially fulfilled hope in God's "plan for the fullness of time, to gather all things in Christ, things in heaven and things on earth" (Eph 1:10)? If so, the church is called to live its service of reconciliation hopefully, seeking to live in accord with Christ who breaks down walls of hostility wherever they exist.

Walls of hostility exist within the church itself. Churches separate themselves from other churches, holding some nearer while keeping others far off, all the while content with ecclesial distance. Within the churches, racial, ethnic, gender, age, and class walls are constructed for the very purpose of keeping some farther away. High and low walls between church and world endure, keeping the world's social, cultural, political, and economic barriers out of sight.

But we know all of that. What the church is called to know better than all of that is the certainty that Christ breaks down walls, God gathers the scattered, and the Spirit is poured out upon all flesh. The church is called to live out its hope in the fullness of time when all walls will fall, all who are scattered will be gathered, and the multitude will live together.

Bibliography

PATRISTIC WRITINGS

Alexander of Alexandria. "Encyclical Letter." In *A New Eusebius*. Edited by J. Stevenson. London: SPCK, 1965.

Athanasius. "On the Incarnation of the Word." In *Christology of the Later Fathers*. Edited by Edward R. Hardy. Philadelphia: Westminster, 1954.

Augustine. "Tractates on the Gospel of John." www.newadvent.org/fathers/170180.htm.

Chrysostom. "Homily II on the Acts of the Apostles." In vol. 11 of *The Nicene and Post-Nicene Fathers*. Edited by Philip Schaff. Grand Rapids: Eerdmans, 1969.

Clement of Rome. "The Epistle to the Corinthians." In *The Epistles of St. Clement of Rome and St. Ignatius of Antioch*. Ancient Christian Writers 1. Edited by Johannes Quasten and Joseph C. Plumpe. New York: Paulist Press, 1946.

"Confession of the Arians Addressed to Alexander of Alexandria." In *Christology of the Later Fathers*. Edited by Edward R. Hardy. Philadelphia: Westminster, 1954.

"Epistle to Diognetus." In *Early Christian Fathers*. Edited by Cyril C. Richardson. Philadelphia: Westminster, 1953.

Irenaeus. "Against the Heresies, Book I." In *St. Irenaeus of Lyons*. Ancient Christian Writers 55. Edited by Walter Burghardt. New York: Newman Press, 1992.

John of Damascus. "Orthodox Faith." In *The Fathers of the Church*, vol. 37. Edited by Joseph Deferrari. Washington, DC: The Catholic University of America Press, 1958.

Justin Martyr. "First Apology." In *Early Christian Fathers*. Edited by Cyril C. Richardson. Philadelphia: Westminster, 1953.

Origen. "Against Celsus." In *A New Eusebius*. Edited by J. Stevenson. London: SPCK, 1965.

Tertullian. *Against Marcion*. www.newadvent.org/fathers/03124.htm.

———. "Apology." In vol. 3 of *Ante-Nicene Fathers*. Edited by Philip Schaff. Grand Rapids: Eerdmans.

———. "Prescription Against Heretics." In *Early Latin Theology*. Edited by S. L. Greenslade. Philadelphia: Westminster, 1956.

Vincent of Lérins. "A Commonitory." In *Nicene and Post-Nicene Fathers*, 2nd series, vol. XI. Edited by Philip Schaff. Grand Rapids: Eerdmans,1964.

OTHER WRITINGS

Alves, Rubem. *A Theology of Human Hope*. New York: Corpus Books, 1969.

Armstrong, Donald, ed. *Who Do You Say That I Am? Christology and the Church*. Grand Rapids: Eerdmans, 1999.

Auerbach, Eric. *Mimesis*. Princeton: Princeton University Press, 1968.

Barrett, C. K. *The Gospel According to St. John*. London: SPCK, 1962.

Barth, Markus. *Israel and the Church*. Eugene, OR: Wipf & Stock, 1969.

———. *The People of God*. Eugene, OR: Wipf & Stock, 1983.

Barth, Karl. *Church Dogmatics*. 4 vols. Edinburgh: T&T Clark, 1936–1969.

———. *Dogmatics in Outline*. Translated by G. T. Thompson. London: SCM, 1949.

———. *The Epistle to the Romans*. 6th ed. London: Oxford University Press, 1968.

———. *The Word of God and Theology*. London: T&T Clark, 2011.

Bell, Daniel. *The Economy of Desire: Christianity and Capitalism in a Postmodern World*. Grand Rapids: Baker Academic, 2012.

Beveridge, Henry, and Jules Bonnet, eds. *Selected Works of John Calvin: Tracts and Letters*. 7 vols. Carlisle: Banner of Truth Trust, 2009.

Bonhoeffer, Dietrich. *Christ the Center*. New York: Harper & Row, 1966.

———. *Sanctorum Communio: A Theological Study of the Sociology of the Church*. Translated by Reinhard Krauss and Nancy Lukens. Minneapolis: Fortress, 1998.

———. *Letters and Papers from Prison*. Vol. 8 of *Dietrich Bonhoeffer Works*. Minneapolis: Fortress, 2009.

Bosch, David. *Transforming Mission: Paradigm Shifts in Theology of Mission.* Maryknoll, NY: Orbis Books, 1991.

Braaten, Carl E., and Robert W. Jenson, eds. *In One Body Through the Cross: The Princeton Proposal for Christian Unity.* Grand Rapids: Eerdmans, 2003.

Buechner, Frederick. *Wishful Thinking: A Theological ABC.* New York: Harper & Row, 1973.

Buttrick, David. *Homiletic.* Philadelphia: Fortress, 1987.

Calvin, John. *Commentary on the Book of the Prophet Isaiah.* Vol. 4. Grand Rapids: Eerdmans, 1956.

———. *Commentaries on the Epistles of Paul to the Galatians and Ephesians.* Grand Rapids: Eerdmans, 1957.

———. *Institutes of the Christian Religion.* 2 vols. Edited by John T. McNeill. Translated by Ford Lewis Battles. Philadelphia: Westminster, 1960.

———. "Reply to Sadolet." In *Calvin: Theological Treatises,* edited by J. K. S. Reid. Philadelphia: Westminster, 1954.

Chaves, Mark. *American Religion: Contemporary Trends.* Princeton: Princeton University Press, 2011.

Cochrane, Arthur C., ed. *Reformed Confessions of the Sixteenth Century.* Louisville: Westminster John Knox, 2003.

Collins, Paul M., and Barry Ensign-George, eds. *Denomination: Assessing an Ecclesiological Category.* London: Bloomsbury/T&T Clark, 2011.

Dean, Kenda Creasy. *Almost Christian: What the Faith of Our Teenagers Is Telling the American Church.* Oxford and New York: Oxford University Press, 2010.

Dix, Dom Gregory. *The Shape of the Liturgy.* New York: Seabury Press, 1982.

Dulles, Avery. *Models of the Church.* Garden City: Doubleday, 1974.

Dunn, James D. G. *Jesus, Paul and the Law.* Louisville: Westminster John Knox, 1990.

———. *The Partings of the Ways Between Christianity and Judaism.* London: SCM, 1991.

———. *Romans 9–16.* Vol. 38 of *Word Biblical Commentary.* Waco, TX: Word, 1988.

Epstein, Isadore. *Judaism: A Historical Presentation.* Harmondsworth: Penguin, 1959.

Farley, Edward. *Practicing Gospel.* Louisville: Westminster John Knox, 2003.

Farrow, Douglas. *Ascension and Ecclesia.* Grand Rapids: Eerdmans, 1999.

Fitzgerald, Frances. *Fire in the Lake: The Vietnamese and the Americans in Vietnam.* Boston: Little, Brown and Company, 1972.

Fox, Robin Lane. *Pagans and Christians*. San Francisco: Harper & Row, 1986.

Fredriksen, Paula, and Adele Reinhartz, eds. *Jesus, Judaism, and Christian Anti-Judaism*. Louisville: Westminster John Knox, 2002.

Frei, Hans W. *The Identity of Jesus Christ: The Hermeneutical Bases of Dogmatic Theology*. Expanded edition. Eugene, OR: Cascade, 2013.

Frymer-Kensky, Tikva, et al., eds. *Christianity in Jewish Terms*. Boulder: Westview Press, 2000.

Fuchs, Lorelei F. *Koinonia and the Quest for an Ecumenical Ecclesiology*. Grand Rapids: Eerdmans, 2008.

Fulkerson, Mary McClintock, and Marcia Mount Shoop. *A Body Broken, A Body Betrayed: Race, Memory, and Eucharist in White-Dominant Churches*. Eugene, OR: Cascade, 2015.

Goldstein, Phyllis. *A Convenient Hatred: The History of Anti-Semitism*. Brookline, MA: Facing History and Ourselves National Foundation, 2012.

Gregory, Brad S. *The Unintended Reformation*. Cambridge: Harvard University Press, 2012.

Groupe des Dombes. *For the Conversion of the Churches*. Geneva: WCC Publications, 1993.

Guder, Darrell L., ed. *Missional Church: A Vision for the Sending of the Church in North America*. Grand Rapids: Eerdmans, 1998.

Gunton, Colin. *Intellect and Action*. Edinburgh: T&T Clark, 2000.

Hall, Douglas John. *Thinking the Faith: Christian Theology in a North American Context*. Minneapolis: Augsburg, 1989.

———. *Confessing the Faith: Christian Theology in a North American Context*. Minneapolis: Fortress, 1996.

Hardy, Edward R., ed. *Christology of the Later Fathers*. Philadelphia: Westminster, 1954.

Hauerwas, Stanley. *Matthew*. Grand Rapids: Brazos, 2006.

Hays, Richard B. *Reading Backwards: Figural Christology and the Fourfold Gospel Witness*. Waco, TX: Baylor University Press, 2014.

Healy, Nicholas. *Church, World and the Christian Life: Practical-Prophetic Ecclesiology*. Cambridge: Cambridge University Press, 2000.

Hollinger, David A. *After Cloven Tongues of Fire: Protestant Liberalism in Modern American History*. Princeton: Princeton University Press, 2013.

Hurtado, Larry. *Why on Earth Did Anyone Become a Christion in the First Three Centuries?* Milwaukee: Marquette University Press, 2016.

Husbands, Mark, and Daniel J. Treir, eds. *The Community of the Word: Toward an Evangelical Ecclesiology*. Downers Grove, IL: InterVarsity Press, 2005.

Hütter, Reinhard. *Suffering Divine Things: Theology as Church Practice.* Grand Rapids: Eerdmans, 2000.

Janssen, Allan J., and Leon van den Broeke, eds. *A Collegial Bishop? Classis and Presbytery at Issue.* Grand Rapids: Eerdmans, 2010.

Jennings, Willie James. *The Christian Imagination: Theology and the Origins of Race.* New Haven: Yale University Press, 2010.

Jenson, Robert W. *Systematic Theology.* 2 vols. New York: Oxford University Press, 1997.

Jinkins, Michael. *The Church Faces Death: Ecclesiology in a Post-Modern Context.* New York: Oxford University Press, 1999.

John Paul II. *Ut Unum Sint.* Washington: United States Catholic Conference, Publication 5–050.

Johnson, Luke Timothy. *The Creed: What Christians Believe and Why It Matters.* New York: Doubleday, 2003.

Kärkkäinen, Veli-Matti. *An Introduction to Ecclesiology.* Downers Grove, IL: InterVarsity Press, 2002.

Kinnamon, Michael, and Brian E. Cope, eds. *The Ecumenical Movement: An Anthology of Key Texts and Voices.* Geneva: WCC Publications, 1997.

Kittel, Gerhard, and Gerhard Friedrich. *Theological Dictionary of the New Testament.* 10 vols. Grand Rapids: Eerdmans, 1971.

Kreider, Alan. *The Change of Conversion and the Origin of Christendom.* Harrisburg: Trinity Press International, 1999.

———. *The Patient Ferment of the Early Church.* Grand Rapids: Baker Academic, 2016.

Lathrop, Gordon. *Holy Things: A Liturgical Theology.* Minneapolis: Fortress, 1993.

Latourette, Kenneth Scott. *The First Five Centuries.* Vol. 1 of *A History of the Expansion of Christianity.* London: Eyre and Spottiswoode, 1952.

Leith, John H., ed. *Creeds of the Churches.* 3rd ed. Louisville: John Knox Press, 1982.

Lippy, Charles H. *Being Religious, American Style: A History of Popular Religiosity in the United States.* Westport: Praeger, 1994.

Lohfink, Gerhard. *Does God Need the Church?* Collegeville: Liturgical Press, 1999.

Luther, Martin. "On the Councils of the Church." In *Martin Luther's Basic Theological Writings.* 2nd ed. Edited by Timothy F. Lull. Minneapolis: Fortress, 2005.

MacIntyre, Alasdair. *After Virtue: A Study in Moral Theory.* 2nd ed. Notre Dame: University of Notre Dame Press, 1984.

Miller, Vincent J. *Consuming Religion: Christian Faith and Practice in a Consumer Culture*. New York: Continuum, 2008.

Minear, Paul S. *Images of the Church in the New Testament*. Philadelphia: Westminster, 1960.

Moltmann, Jürgen. *The Church in the Power of the Spirit*. New York: Harper & Row, 1977.

———. *Theology of Hope*. New York: Harper & Row, 1967.

———. *The Way of Jesus Christ*. San Francisco: HarperSanFrancisco, 1990.

Morrison, Charles Clayton. *The Unfinished Reformation*. New York: Harper & Brothers, 1953.

Morse, Christopher. *Not Every Spirit*. New York: Trinity Press International, 1992.

Neuhaus, Richard John. *The Naked Public Square: Religion and Democracy in America*. Grand Rapids: Eerdmans, 1984.

Neusner, Jacob. *From Politics to Piety: The Emergence of Pharisaic Judaism*. Englewood Cliffs, NJ: Prentice Hall, 1973.

———. *Judaism in the Beginning of Christianity*. Philadelphia: Fortress, 1984.

Niebuhr, H. Richard. *The Social Sources of Denominationalism*. New York: Living Age/Meridian, 1960.

Noll, Mark. *The Scandal of the Evangelical Mind*. Grand Rapids: Eerdmans, 1994.

Norris, Kathleen. *Amazing Grace*. New York: Riverhead Books, 1998.

Novak, David. *Talking with Christians: Musings of a Jewish Theologian*. Grand Rapids: Eerdmans, 2005.

Ochs, Peter. *Another Reformation: Postliberal Christianity and the Jews*. Grand Rapids: Baker Academic, 2011.

O'Donovan, Oliver. *The Ways of Judgment*. Grand Rapids: Eerdmans, 2005.

Olin, John C., ed. *A Reformation Debate: John Calvin and Jacopo Sadoleto*. New York: Fordham University Press, 1966.

Pagels, Elaine. *The Gnostic Gospels*. New York: Vintage Books, 1979.

Pagels, Elaine, and Karel L. King. *Reading Judas: The Gospel of Judas and the Shape of Christianity*. New York: Penguin, 2007.

Pannenberg, Wolfhart. *Systematic Theology*. 3 vols. Grand Rapids: Eerdmans, 1998.

Presbyterian Church (USA). *The Book of Confessions*. Louisville: Office of the General Assembly, 2002.

———. *The Confession of 1967*. Inclusive Language Version prepared by the Office of Theology and Worship. Louisville: Congregational Ministries Publishing, 2002.

————. *The French Confession of 1559*. Louisville: PCUSA, 1998.

————. *Selected Theological Statements of the Presbyterian Church (U.S.A.) General Assemblies (1956–1998)*. Louisville: Office of Theology and Worship, 1998.

Radner, Ephraim. *The End of the Church: A Pneumatology of Christian Division in the West*. Grand Rapids: Eerdmans, 1998.

Ratzinger, Joseph. *Called to Communion: Understanding the Church Today*. San Francisco: Ignatius Press, 1996.

————. *Church, Ecumenism, and Politics: New Endeavors in Ecclesiology*. San Francisco: Ignatius Press, 1987.

————. *Pilgrim Fellowship of Faith: The Church as Communion*. San Francisco: Ignatius Press, 2005.

————. *Principles of Catholic Theology: Building Stones for a Fundamental Theology*. San Francisco: Ignatius Press, 1987.

Ratzinger, Joseph, and Vittorio Messori. *The Ratzinger Report*. San Francisco: Ignatius Press, 1985.

Richey, Russell E. *Denominationalism Illustrated and Explained*. Eugene, OR: Cascade, 2013.

Ricoeur, Paul. "The Metaphorical Process." *Semeia: An Experimental Journal for Biblical Criticism* 4 (1975): 75–106.

————. *The Rule of Metaphor*. Toronto: University of Toronto Press, 1977.

Ritschl, Dietrich. *Memory and Hope*. New York: Macmillan, 1967.

Robinson, J. A. T. *The Body: A Study in Pauline Theology*. Vol. 5 of *Studies in Biblical Theology*. London: SCM, 1952.

Rosenthal, Gilbert S. *A Jubilee for All Time: The Copernican Revolution in Jewish-Christian Relations*. Eugene, OR: Pickwick, 2014.

————. *What Can a Modern Jew Believe?* Eugene, OR: Wipf & Stock, 2007.

Russell, Letty. *Church in the Round: Feminist Interpretation of the Church*. Louisville: Westminster John Knox, 1993.

Ruthven, Jon. *On the Cessation of the Charismata*. Sheffield: Sheffield Academic, 1993.

Sanders, E. P. *Jesus and Judaism*. Philadelphia: Fortress, 1985.

————. *Paul, the Law, and the Jewish People*. Philadelphia: Fortress, 1983.

Schleiermacher, Friedrich. *The Christian Faith*. Edinburgh: T&T Clark, 1928.

————. *On Religion: Speeches to Its Cultured Despisers*. New York: Harper & Brothers, 1958.

Seitz, Christopher. *The Character of Christian Scripture: The Significance of a Two-Testament Bible*. Grand Rapids: Baker Academic, 2011.

Stark, Rodney. *The Rise of Christianity*. New York: HarperOne, 1997.

—————. *What Americans Really Believe: New Findings from the Baylor Surveys of Religion*. Waco, TX: Baylor University Press, 2008.

Stern, Chaim, ed. *Gates of Prayer: The New Union Prayerbook*. New York: Central Conference of American Rabbis Press, 1975.

Stevenson, J., ed. *A New Eusebius*. London: SPCK, 1965.

Taylor, Charles. *A Secular Age*. Cambridge: Belknap Press of Harvard University Press, 2007.

Thompson, Bard, ed. *Liturgies of the Western Church*. Philadelphia: Fortress, 1961.

Tillard, J.-M. R. *Church of Churches: The Ecclesiology of Communion*. Collegeville, MN: Liturgical Press, 1992.

Tillich, Paul. *Systematic Theology*. 3 vols. Chicago: University of Chicago Press, 1963.

Torrance, T. F. *Royal Priesthood*. 2nd ed. Edinburgh: T&T Clark, 1993.

van Buren, Paul M. *A Theology of the Jewish-Christian Reality, Part 2: A Christian Theology of the People Israel*. New York: Harper & Row, 1983.

Vischer, Lukas, ed. *The Church in Reformed Perspective*. Geneva: Centre International Réformé, 2002.

Webster, John. *Holiness*. Grand Rapids: Eerdmans, 2003.

Weil, Simone. *The Need for Roots*. London: Routledge, 2002.

—————. *Selected Essays, 1934–1943*. London: Oxford University Press, 1962.

Welker, Michael. *What Happens in Holy Communion?* Grand Rapids: Eerdmans, 2000.

World Council of Churches Faith and Order Commission. *The Church: Toward a Common Vision*. Faith and Order Series 214. Geneva: WCC Publications, 2013.

World Council of Churches. *The Theology of the Churches and the Jewish People*. Geneva: World Council of Churches, 1988.

—————. "Called to Be the One Church." Geneva: WCC Publications, 2006.

Wright, N. T. *Justification: God's Plan and Paul's Vision*. Downers Grove: IVP Academic, 2009.

Wuthnow, Robert. *Christianity in the Twenty-first Century*. New York: Oxford University Press, 1993.

Zizioulas, John D. *Lectures in Christian Dogmatics*. London: T&T Clark, 2008.

Index of Authors

Alexander of Alexandria, 28
Alves, Rubem, 214–15
Armstrong, Donald, 38
Auerbach, Erich, 135
Augustine, 2, 13, 47–48, 120

Babinsky, Ellen, 54
Barnhardt, Wilton, 189
Barrett, C. K., 101
Barth, Karl, xvi, 36, 39, 49, 59–60, 118, 119, 138, 190, 193–94, 207–8
Barth, Markus, 158
Battles, Ford Lewis, 2, 36
Beha, Christopher R., 42, 173
Bell, Daniel, 18
Berger, Peter, 173
Beveridge, Henry, 8, 92
Bonhoeffer, Dietrich, 5, 105, 106, 113
Bonnet, Jules, 8, 92
Bosch, David, 192
Braaten, Carl E., 207
Bromiley, G. W., 190
Buechner, Frederick, 119, 123
Burghardt, Walter, 33
Buttrick, David, 61

Calvin, John, xix, 2, 6–9, 13, 15, 36, 43, 44, 46, 48, 51, 55, 57–58, 91, 92, 112, 119–20, 121–22, 132, 134
Chadwick, Henry, 185

Chase, Frederick, Jr., 70
Chaves, Mark, 4
Chrysostom, 109
Clement of Rome, 12
Clifford, Catherine E., 79
Cochrane, Arthur C., 63
Collins, Paul M., 77
Cope, E., 66, 81

Dalferth, Ingolf, 21
Dean, Kenda Creasy, 39
Dix, Dom Gregory, 59, 185
Dulles, Avery, 86
Duncan, David James, 104, 167
Dunn, James D. G., 142–43, 157
Dykstra, Craig, ix–xi

Ensign-George, Barry, 77–78, 79
Epstein, Isadore, 131

Farel, Guillaume, 6
Farley, Edward, xv, 50
Farrow, Douglas, 108
Faulkner, William, 6
Feuerbach, Ludwig, 38–39
Fitzgerald, Frances, 75
Fox, Robin Lane, 176, 181
Fredriksen, Paula, 139
Frei, Hans W., 106, 111, 113
Friedrich, Gerhard, 87–88

Frymer-Kensky, Tikva, 152, 159
Fuchs, Lorelei F., 65, 66
Fulkerson, Mary McClintock, 58

Gibbs, Eddie, 176
Goldstein, Phyllis, 133
Greenslade, S. L., 33
Gregory, Brad S., 9
Groupe des Dombes, 79, 206-7
Guder, Darrell L., 168, 198
Gunton, Colin, 26

Hall, Douglas John, 92, 167-68, 170
Hardy, Edward R., 28
Hauerwas, Stanley, 204
Hays, Richard B., 135-36
Healey, Nicholas, 5
Heurtley, C. A., 30
Hippolytus, 185
Hollinger, David A., 175
Hurtado, Larry W., 182
Hütter, Reinhard, 97

Irenaeus, 32-34, 127
Isaacson, Walter, 19

James, P. D., 22
Janssen, Allan J., 83
Jennings, Willie James, 10, 129, 153
Jenson, Robert W., 134, 207
Jerome, 51
Jinkins, Michael, 187
John of Damascus, 70
John Paul II, Pope, 207
John XIII, Pope, 146, 149
Johnson, Luke Timothy, 35, 36
Justin Martyr, 127, 179, 181

Kärkkäinen, Veli-Matti, 12
King, Karel L., 30
Kinnamon, Michael, 66, 81
Kittel, Gerhard, 87
Knox, John, 45
Krauss, Reinhard, 5
Kreider, Alan, 176, 178, 182, 183
Kundera, Milan, 124

Kuyper, Abraham, 13-15

Lathrop, Gordon, 164
Latourette, Kenneth Scott, 176, 182
Leith, John H., 43, 64
Levine, Amy-Jill, 139
Lippy, Charles H., 39
Lohfink, Gerhard, 159-60
Lukens, Nancy, 5
Lull, Timothy F., 2, 45, 93, 101
Luther, Martin, 2, 6, 7, 45, 54, 93, 101, 170

MacIntyre, Alasdair, 16
Manheim, Ralph, 38
March, W. Eugene, 152
Marcion of Sinope, 126-28
Marga, Amy, 60
McNeill, John T., 2
Messori, Vittorio, 3
Miller, Vincent J., 20
Minear, Paul S., 85-86
Moltmann, Jürgen, 3, 96-97, 102, 105, 113, 114, 211-12, 214-15
Morrison, Charles Clayton, 76
Morse, Christopher, 40

Nebelsick, Harold, 118
Neuhaus, Richard John, 168-69
Neusner, Jacob, 142
Niebuhr, H. Richard, 77
Noll, Mark, 169-70
Norris, Kathleen, 27
Novak, David, 153

Ochs, Peter, 153
O'Donovan, Oliver, 75
Olin, John C., 6
Ondaatje, Michael, xvii
Origen, 178
Orwell, George, xiii

Pagels, Elaine, 30
Pannenberg, Wolfhart, 197, 206
Parker, T. H. L., 39
Parkinson, C. Northcote, 198-99

Philipps, J. B., 144
Pontius Pilate, 180
Presbyterian Church (USA), 10–11, 149–50, 164
Pringle, William, 51
Putnam, Robert, 4

Radner, Ephraim, 8–9, 135
Ratzinger, Joseph, 3, 49, 65, 67, 125
Reid, J. K. S., 7, 55, 91, 122
Reinhartz, Adele, 139
Richardson, Cyril C., 178, 179
Richey, Russell E., 4
Ricoeur, Paul, 90
Ritschl, Dietrich, 111, 113–14, 212–13, 215
Robinson, J. A. T., 88, 89
Robinson, Marilynne, 62, 85, 209
Roof, Wade Clark, 4
Rosenthal, Gilbert S., 146, 163
Roth, Philip, 145
Russell, Letty, 3

Sadoleto, Jacopo, 6–8, 15
Sanders, E. P., 142
Schaff, Philip, 109, 179
Schleiermacher, Friedrich, 13–15
Seitz, Christopher, 129, 135
Shoop, Marcia Mount, 58
Small, Joseph D., 54, 67, 83, 146
Stanislavski, Constantin, 50
Stark, Rodney, 38, 176, 178–79, 181
Stern, Chaim, 166

Stevenson, J., 28, 178, 180

Taylor, Charles, 25, 171–74
Tertullian, 33–34, 35, 127, 179–80, 181, 183–84
Thompson, Bard, 132
Thompson, G. T., 49
Tillard, J.-M. R., 65
Tillich, Paul, 3
Torrance, T. F., 107, 110, 190
Tyler, Anne, xvii

Updike, John, xiii, 1, 35

van Buren, Paul M., 133
van de Beek, Abraham, 15
van den Broeke, Leon, 83
Vanhoozer, Kevin, 50
Vidal, Gore, 27
Vincent of Lérins, 30–31, 33

Webster, John, 191
Weil, Simone, 25
Welker, Michael, 121
Wilken, Robert Louis, 162, 176
World Council of Churches, 11–12, 65–66, 80–81, 82, 149, 207
Wright, N. T., 38, 156
Wuthnow, Robert, 4

Zwingli, Ulrich, 7

Index of Subjects

Accidental Tourist, The (Tyler), xvii
African Americans, 10
Anabaptists, 2–3
Anglican Communion, 64
Anti-Semitism, 126, 133, 141, 148, 149
Apostles' Creed, 34, 37, 73
Apostolic Tradition (Hippolytus), 185
Apostolicity: the church's call to,
    204–5; the domesticated church and
    deficiency of, 197; God as apostolic
    (and the *missio Dei*), 192; and the
    great commission, 204–5. *See also*
    Mission/missiology
Arian controversy, 27–28
Ascension of Christ: church doctrine
    of, 106–12; and the resurrection,
    108–12; the risen Christ and paradox
    of, 111–12
Asian Americans, 10
Augsburg Confession, Preface to, 64

Baptism, 46, 47, 53–55, 61, 98, 110, 120–
    23; and the ascension, 110; Calvin on,
    44–45, 46, 122; and catechumens of
    the early church, 32; and the church
    as body of Christ, 98; ecclesial racial-
    ism and exclusion through, 55; and
    the Holy Spirit, 53–55, 61, 98; Jesus's,
    55, 98; New Testament baptismal

texts and images, 53; Paul on the
    church's baptismal identity, 98; and
    real presence of Christ, 120–23; typi-
    cal North American services, 53, 98
Barmen Declaration. *See* "Theological
    Declaration of Barmen"
Baylor University's 2008 Survey of
    Religion, 38–39
Black Protestant churches, 10
"Blueprint ecclesiologies," 5
Body of Christ, the church as, 85–103;
    and baptism, 98; a body knit together
    in Christ, 184; Christ's wounded/cru-
    cified body, 91–93; and the church's
    cross-bearing, 100–102; and the Holy
    Spirit, 96–103; and the incarnation,
    97–98; Luther's theology of the
    cross, 92–93; metaphor and meta-
    phorical language, 90; and ministry
    of Jesus/of the church, 99–100; and
    New Testament treatment of the
    church, 85–103; other images and
    models of the church, 85–86; Paul's
    appeal for church unity, 93–96;
    Paul's body of Christ texts, 87–96;
    Paul's theology of the body, 89–90;
    and the resurrection, 102–3; and the
    temptation of Jesus Christ, 99
Buddhism, 2, 146

232

"Called to Be the One Church" (World Council of Churches), 66, 206–7

Catholic Church: Eucharist in, 78, 122; and the fractional church, 196; moral teachings, 169; and the people of God, 124–25; Reformation and, 2–3, 6, 8, 47, 164; theologians on *koinōnia*/communion ecclesiology, 65, 67; Vatican II statements on relationship of Jews and Christians, 146–49

Catholicity: the church's call to inclusion and, 203–4; the fractional church and deficiencies of, 196–97; God's, 191–92

Celsus, 178

Christian Faith, The (Schleiermacher), 14

Christianity in Jewish Terms (Frymer-Kensky et al.), 158–59

Christian Scholars Group, 153

Christology, 104–23; Bonhoeffer on, 105, 106, 113; call and response Christology/ecclesiology, 113–18; and celebration of the sacraments, 118, 120–23; doctrine of the ascension, 106–12; historical Jesus studies, 106, 108; identity of Jesus Christ, 105–6, 113; paradox of the real absence/presence of Christ, 106–8, 111–12; proclamation of the Word of God, 118–19; the real presence of Christ in/with the church, 106–8, 118–23; union with Christ, 121–22

Church, contemporary: Barth on inadequacy and the need for change, 193–94, 207–8; as body knit together in Christ, 184; call to apostolicity, 204–5; call to catholicity and inclusion, 203–4; call to holiness, 201–3; call to unity among the people of God, 200–201; common hope, 186–87; common religious profession, 185; conforming to the world and society, 195–96; consumer-driven market forces and commodification of, 18–21; critiques and indictments for failures, 193–99; denominational divisions and the absence of ecclesial *simplicitas*, 194–95; domesticated (deficiency of apostolicity), 197; as the emerging Christian minority, 182–87; fractional (deficiency of catholicity), 196–97; proclamation of the word of God in, 167–87; proclivity to self-justification in the face of critique, 198–99; repentance by, 164–65, 205–8; and the secular age, 170–75, 182–87; unity of discipline and communal life, 186; wishful thinking and official optimism, 210–11

Church (defining), 1–21, 22–41; as body of Christ, 85–103; Calvin on, 2, 6–9, 13, 43, 44–46, 92; and Christian commonality, 22–25; the credibility of the gospel, 15–18; ecclesial fragmentation/pluralism, 6–9; ecclesial racialism and exclusion, 9–11, 55, 58; ecclesial sin, 117–18, 137–38, 164–65, 194; ecclesiology as theological doctrine of, 3–6, 21; Faith and Order Commission's common vision, 11–12; idealized theological descriptions, 3–4; *koinōnia*/communion ecclesiology, 62–84; Kuyper's ecclesiology of the true church, 14–15; language for, xix–xx, 1–2; Luther on, 2, 101; notions of the "invisible church," 12–15; Pannenberg on church history, 206; pastors' attention to, 5–6; Ratzinger on, 3; Schleiermacher's conceptual categories of, 13–14; sociological constructs and actual churches, 4–5, 25; theological meanings and differing conceptions of, 2–3. *See also* Church, contemporary; Early church

Church of Churches: The Ecclesiology of Communion (Tillard), 65

Church, The: Toward a Common Vision, (Faith and Order Commission), 11–12

Colonialism, legacy of, 9–11

Commonality, Christian, 22–25; the church's common hope, 186–87; the church's rule of faith and common religious profession, 185; sociological/theological accounts of, 25

Communion. *See* Congregational communion; Eucharist (Lord's Supper); *Koinōnia*/communion ecclesiology

Congregational communion, 75–76, 80–82; "The Lund Principle," 80–82; prayer for other congregations, 80; "we-ness" and *koinōnia*, 75–76

"Connectional" churches, 64

Consensus Tigurinus, 7

Consumer-driven church life, 18–21

Consuming Religion (Miller), 20

Council of Chalcedon, 26

Council of Constantinople, 26, 31, 73

Council of Ephesus, 26

Council of Nicaea, 26, 27, 32, 73

Covenants: covenantal identity in Torah, 131–32, 136, 142–43, 161, 165; covenant fidelity, 161–62; covenant of Sinai, 130–32; and Genesis creation saga, 130; God's covenant with Abraham, 130, 152, 156, 157–58, 159; keeping, 137; Old Testament as Scripture of, 130–33, 134, 137, 138–39

Creedal tradition, 26–41; Apostles' Creed, 34, 37, 73; the church's foundational creed ("one, holy, catholic, apostolic church"), 188–208; confession of faith in one God, 28–30, 38–39, 191–92; the early church, 26–34; and the gathered congregation, 44, 62, 104–5; local creed-like summaries of belief, 32–34; Nicene Creed, 26–41, 73, 190, 191–92; Nicene legacy and core Christian identity, 34–41; Nicene rule of faith, 31–41; non-creedal churches, 26; rejections of false doctrines, 36–38; and Scripture, 35–36

Cross: the church as the wounded/crucified body of Christ, 91–93; the church's cross-bearing, 100–102; Luther on ecclesial cross-bearing, 101; Luther's theology of the cross, 92–93; the New Testament Passion narratives, 100–101

Cyprian, bishop of Carthage, 180

Dabru Emet: A Jewish Statement on Christians and Christianity, 153

Denominations: and communion ecclesiology, 74–79, 83; divisions and denominationalism, 76–79, 83, 174, 194–95; divisions and the absence of ecclesial *simplicitas*, 194–95; divisions and the secular age, 174; Ensign-George on, 77–78, 79; exclusivity, 64; interdenominational civility and ecumenical indifference, 17–18; judicatories, 83; marketing and "church shopping," 18–21; Niebuhr on denominationalism, 77; Reformation-era mutuality between, 64; structures and ministry of *episcopé*, 79; as term, xix–xx; triumphalism, 17

Dutch Reformed Church, 14, 64

Early church: Arian controversy, 27–28; care for the sick and dying, 180–81; catechumens, 32, 185; celebration of the Eucharist, 56–57, 137; common hope, 186–87; communities and relationships between, 63, 177–81; creedal tradition, 26–34; expansion in the first three centuries, 175–82, 184–87; as *kyriakos* ("belonging to the Lord"), 43; local creed-like summaries of belief, 32–34; loving care extended to pagans and other Christians, 179–81; Marcion's rejection of the Hebrew Scriptures, 126–28; Paul's body of Christ texts and appeal for unity in, 93–94; proclamation of the gospel in, 50, 175–82, 184–87; proclamation through existing social networks, 181–82; religious organizations, 178–79; Roman Empire context, 176–82; rule of faith and common religious profession, 185; unity of discipline and communal life, 186. *See also* Nicene Creed

Ecumenical movement, 23, 65–67, 78–79

"Epistle to Diognetus," 177–78

Eucharist (Lord's Supper), 46, 47–48, 55–58, 61, 120–23, 164; the bread as body of Christ, 91; Calvin on, 7, 44–45, 46, 55, 57–58, 122; Catholic Church, 78, 122; churches that restrict access, 58; daily/monthly rites, 55; early church, 56–57, 137; as God's gift for God's people, 164; Great Thanksgiving prayer, 54, 137; and *koinōnia*, 70, 110; New Testament eucharistic texts and patterns, 56; Orthodox liturgy, 164; and the real presence of Christ, 47–48, 120–23; theological differences, 47–48

Evangelical Lutheran Church in America, 19

Evangelicals, American, 169–70

Faith and Order Commission, World Council of Churches, xiv, 11–12, 65–66, 80–83

"Flood Prayer" (Luther), 54

French Confession of 1559, 54

Gates of Prayer: The New Union Prayerbook (Stern, ed.), 166

Gathering: the gathered congregation, 44, 62, 104–5; gathering and sending, 58–61; Old Testament references to the gathering of the scattered people, 159–60

Gaudium et spes (Vatican II), 65

Gender inclusive language, xvi–xix

"Gifts and Calling of God Are Irrevocable, The" (Commission for Religious Relations with Jews of the Pontifical Council for Promoting Christian Unity), 148

Global South, church of, 187

Gnostic Gospels, 30

God: American belief in, 38–39; as apostolic (and the *missio Dei*), 192; Barth on knowledge of, 39, 190; catholicity of, 191–92; covenant with Abraham, 130, 152, 156, 157–58, 159; Feuerbach's critique of anthropological notions and popular religiosity, 38; fidelity of, 138–39; gender-inclusive God language and pronouns, xvii; holiness of, 191; judgment of, 138, 194; love of, 192, 213–14; love of God and love of neighbors, 216–17, 218; Nicene Creed and confession of faith in, 28–30, 38–39, 191–92; popular culture and understandings of, 39; singularity and simplicity (oneness), 190–91; as the source and ground of the church, 189–90. *See also* Proclamation of the Word of God

Gospel and Our Culture Network, 168, 198

Gospel of Judas, 30

Groupe des Dombes, 206–7

Heidelberg Disputation, 92–93

Hinduism, 146

Hispanic Americans, 10

Holocaust and Nazi Germany, 105, 126, 133, 146, 215

Holy Spirit: articles of the Nicene-Constantinopolitan and Apostles' Creed, 73; and the ascension, 109–10; and baptism, 53–55, 61, 98; the church and the gifts of, 95–96; and the church as body of Christ, 96–103; and the church's cross-bearing, 100–102; and the incarnation, 97–98; *koinōnia*/communion as the work of, 73–74; and the ministry of Jesus and the church, 99–100; and the resurrection, 102–3; and temptation of Jesus Christ, 99

Hope, Christian, 186–87, 209–19; common hope in the early church, 186–87; and confidence in the love of God (first and second letters of

Peter), 213–14; love of God and love of neighbors, 216–17, 218; Moltmann on eschatology as the doctrine of, 211–12; a moral theology of, 214–19; Paul's letters on memory and, 215–17, 218; Ritschl on memory and, 212–13; the service of reconciliation, 217–19; the shared hope of Jews and Christians, 152; wishful thinking and official optimism by contemporary churches, 210–11

Humanism, exclusive, 173

Images of the Church in the New Testament (Minear), 85–86
Incarnation of Christ, 97–98
Institutes of the Christian Religion (Calvin), 36
In the Beauty of the Lilies (Updike), xiii
In the Skin of the Lion (Ondaatje), xvii
Invisible church, 12–15; Calvin's distinctions between visible and, 13; Kuyper's ecclesiology of the true church, 14–15; Schleiermacher's conceptual categories, 13–14
Islam, 146, 183
Israel, modern state of, 146, 152, 163–64; and God's promise of the land, 151–52, 163–64; Six-Day War and the occupied territories, 149; Yom Kippur War, 149. *See also* Jews and Christians, relationship between

Jews and Christians, relationship between, 145–66, 183; bound in shared hope, 152; Christian biblical translation and portrayal of the Jews/ Hebrew language, 139–41; covenant fidelity and covenant obligations, 161–62; deepening Christian ecclesiology through attention to the Old Testament and Israel's history, 159–66; ecclesiological understanding of, 152–59; God's promise of the land, 151–52, 163–64; journal articles and statements of Christian scholars, 153;

Paul's image of the root and branches (tree of Israel), 157; Paul's images depicting, 157–58; Paul's letter to Romans on God's righteousness/ human unrighteousness, 154–57, 193; the people of God (and what it means for the church), 159–61, 165–66; the Pharisees and inaccurate Christian stereotypes, 141–43; place and community, 162–64; Presbyterian Church (USA)'s 1986 document on, 149–52; rejecting supersessionism, 133, 139, 150; Vatican II's *Nostra Aetate*, 146–49
John the Baptist, 98, 100, 116, 183
John's Gospel, prologue to, 51–52
Julian, Emperor (the Apostate), 180–81

Koinōnia/communion ecclesiology, 62–84; Catholic theologians on, 65, 67; communion among believers, 69–70; communion and mutual sharing of resources, 72–73; communion and reconciliation, 71–72; communion in the truth of the Gospel, 70–71; congregational communion, 75–76, 80–82; denominations and ecclesial communion, 74–79, 83; and the Eucharist, 70, 110; the Holy Spirit's work of, 73–74; "The Lund Principle," 80–82; and the modern ecumenical movement, 65–67, 78–79; prayer for other congregations, 80; Ratzinger on, 65, 67; Reformation-era mutuality between denominations, 64; Tillard on, 65; Vatican II documents, 65; the word *koinōnia* and New Testament texts, 64, 67–74

Lilly Endowment's survey of American congregations and pastoral leaders, 41
Logos, 51–52
Lord's Supper. *See* Eucharist (Lord's Supper)

Lumen gentium (Vatican II), 65, 124–25
"Lund Principle, The" 80–82
Lutheran-Episcopal "Called to Common Mission," 67
Lutheran-Reformed "Formula of Agreement," 66–67

Mandela, Nelson, 215
Marketing, denominational, 18–21
Memory and Hope (Ritschl), 212–13
Missio Dei (mission of God), 192
Mission/missiology: the domesticated church and diminished mission, 197; the great commission and the church's call to apostolicity, 204–5; missional theology, 167–68. *See also* Proclamation of the Word of God
Mitzvot (commandments), 132
Models of the Church (Dulles), 86

Naked Public Square, The (Neuhaus), 168–69
National Study of Youth and Religion, 38–39
Native Americans, 10
New Testament: accounts of Jesus's calling of the disciples, 116–17; baptismal texts and images, 53; Christian reclaiming of, 139–44; as Christian Scripture, 143–44; the church as body of Christ in, 85–103; eucharistic texts and patterns, 56; *koinōnia* in, 64, 67–74; Passion narratives, 100–101; Paul's body of Christ texts, 87–96; Pharisees in, 141–43; translations, 139–41
Nicene Creed, 26–41, 73, 190, 191–92; confession of faith in one God, 28–30, 38–39, 191–92; and early church's local creed-like summaries of belief, 32–34; legacy and core Christian identity, 34–41; and rejections of false doctrines, 36–38; rule of faith (*regula fidei*), 31–41; and scriptural tradition, 35–36
Nostra Aetate (Vatican II's Declaration on the Relation of the Church to Non-Christian Religions), 146–49

Old Testament, 125–39, 159–66; and Christian ecclesiology, 159–66; Christian reading and reclaiming of, 129–39; covenant of Sinai, 130–32; covenantal identity in Torah, 131–32, 136, 142–43, 161, 165; figural readings, 135–36; Genesis creation saga, 130; God's covenant with Abraham, 130, 152, 156, 157–58, 159; Israel's history and faith of the Jewish people, 125–26, 133, 136; Marcion's heretical rejection of, 126–28; marginalization of, 128–29; prophetic texts, 128; reading as Christian Scripture, 133–39; references to the gathering of the scattered people, 159–60; retaining designation of Testament, 128–29; as Scripture of covenants, 130–33, 134, 137, 138–39

Pastoral leaders: Lilly Endowment's survey of vocational satisfaction, 41; task of attention to church/understanding the church, 5–6
Pentecostalism: ecclesial racialism and racial exclusion, 10; and the Holy Spirit, 97–98; and mainline Protestant churches, xix, 3, 8, 97; and meaning of church, 3
People of God: the contemporary Church's call to unity, 200–201; images, 124–26, 137; metaphor, 125; what it means for the church to be, 159–61, 165–66. *See also* Jews and Christians, relationship between
Pharisees, 141–43
Presbyterian Church (USA), xiv, 214; *Confession of 1967* and theme of reconciliation, 10–11; denominational marketing, 19; interdenominational civility and denominational loyalty, 17–18; theological statement on doctrine of the Trinity, xviii–xix; "A

Theological Understanding of the Relationship between Christians and Jews," 149–52

Princeton Proposal, 206–7

Proclamation of the Word of God, 45, 48–52, 61, 167–87; Barth on, 49; Calvin on, 44–45, 48–52; and the Church of the Word and sacrament, 45, 48–52, 61; in the contemporary church, 167–87; in the early church, 50, 175–82, 184–87; "out-church" preaching, 61; and the real presence of Christ in/with the church, 118–19; Scripture and, 50–52, 118–19; in the secular age, 174–75, 182–87

Protestant churches: "connectional churches," 64; contemporary mainline, 138, 169, 175; denominationalism, 16–17, 23, 77–78; Eucharist in, 55–56; on exile, 138; historic Black, 10; the "invisible" church, 12–13; liberal, 175; and meaning of church, 3; Pentecostals and, xix, 3, 8, 97; preaching in, 49, 122; and relationship between Christians and Jews, 149–50; sacramental minimalism, 122–23; and the secular age, 169, 175; and Vatican Council II, 149. *See also* Reformation, Protestant

Racialism, ecclesial, 9–11; and sacrament of baptism, 55; and sacrament of the Eucharist, 58

Reconciliation: and communion ecclesiology, 71–72; hope for the church and the service of, 217–19; Presbyterian Church (USA)'s *Confession of 1967*, 10–11

Reformation, Protestant, 6–9, 23; Calvin and the celebration of the Eucharist, 7, 55; Calvin on ecclesial fragmentation, 6–9; and the church of the Word and sacrament, 44–46; disputes on the shape of the church, 2–3; mutuality and relationships between congregations and denominations, 63–64; reformers on sin and repentance, 164; *sola scriptura*, 35–36; Swiss, 7, 42–43

Reformed-Pentecostal Dialogue, xiv

Resurrection of Jesus Christ: and the ascension, 108–12; and the church as body of Christ, 102–3

Rule of faith (*regula fidei*), 185; early church, 185; Irenaeus on, 32–33; Nicene, 31–41; Tertullian's rendition, 33–34, 35

Sacraments, 44–48, 53–58, 61, 120–23; Calvin on, 44–45, 46, 48, 55, 57–58, 120, 121, 122; Christology and, 118, 120–23; ecclesial racialism and exclusion through, 55, 58; Protestant minimalism, 122–23; and real presence of Christ, 47–48, 120–23. *See also* Baptism; Eucharist (Lord's Supper)

Sacred Obligation: Rethinking Christian Faith in Relation to Judaism and the Jewish People, A (Christian Scholars Group), 153

Scandal of the Evangelical Mind, The (Noll), 169–70

Scientology, "church" of, 146

Scots Confession (1560), 45, 63

Scripture: biblical studies and discipline of theology, xv–xvi; Calvin on the life of the church and, 119; the church as body of Christ in, 85–103; creeds and, 35–36; *koinōnia* in, 67–74; and Nicene rule of faith, 35–36; people of God in, 125–26, 137; proclamation of the Word of God, 50–52, 118–19; Reformation's *sola scriptura*, 35–36; on the visions of the ascended Christ, 109–11. *See also* New Testament; Old Testament

Second Helvetic Confession, 48–49

Secular Age, A (Taylor), 171–74

Secularism/secular age, 170–75, 182–87; denominational divisions, 174; laments for the marginalization of religion in public life, 168–71; morality and moral goals, 172; Neuhaus on absence of religion from American public life, 168–69; nonreligious lives and nonreligious descriptions of reality, 172–73, 174–75; proclaiming the gospel, 174–75, 182–87; and Protestant churches, 169, 175; Taylor on, 171–74

Sermon on the Mount, 101, 142, 179, 202

Shape of the Liturgy, The (Dix), 59

Short Treatise on the Lord's Supper (Calvin), 7

Sin, church, 117–18, 137–38, 164–65, 194

Six-Day War (1967), 149

Solipsism, ecclesial, 62–63

South Africa's apartheid system, 117, 215

Supersessionism, 133, 139, 150

Synod of Dort (1618–1619), 64

Temptation of Jesus Christ, 99

Ten Commandments, 131, 132, 216

Ten Theses of Berne (1528), 42–43

"Theological Declaration of Barmen," 37, 43

Theology, discipline of, xv–xvi

Theology of Hope (Moltmann), 211–12

Trinitarian language, xviii–xix

Triumphalism: denominational, 17; pretense of the triumphant church, 91–92

Tutu, Desmond, 215

Unitatis redintegratio (Vatican II), 65

"Unity of the Church as Koinonia, The: Gift and Calling" (World Council of Churches), 65–66, 82

Ut Unum Sint (John Paul II), 206–7

Vatican Council II, 65, 124–25, 146–49

What Happens in Holy Communion? (Welker), 121

Word and sacrament, the church of. *See* Proclamation of the Word of God; Sacraments

World Alliance of Reformed Churches, 117

World Communion of Reformed Churches, xiv, 64

World Council of Churches (WCC): Assembly in Porto Alegre, Brazil (2006), 66; "Called to Be the One Church," 66, 206–7; Canberra assembly statement "The Unity of the Church as Koinonia: Gift and Calling" (1991), 65–66, 82; Faith and Order Commission, xiv, 11–12, 65–66, 80–83; *koinōnia*/communion ecclesiology, 65–66, 80–83; World Conference in Lund, Sweden (1952), 80–81; World Conference in Santiago de Compostela (1993), 66

World Missionary Conference in Edinburgh (1910), 65

Yom Kippur War (1973), 149

Your God Is Too Small (Phillips), 143

Index of Scripture References

OLD TESTAMENT

Genesis

1–11	130
1	24, 51–52, 130
2	130
3	130
4	130
6	130
8:11	130
8:21–22	130
12:2	130
17:5	130
17:16	130
26:2–5	130
28:13–17	130
35:9–13	130

Exodus

6:5	131
6:7	131
19:5–6	131, 161
19:6	191
19:8	131
20:2	132

Leviticus

19:2	191
26:12	44, 125

Numbers

15:19–20	157

Deuteronomy

4:32	144
5:2–3	131
5:6	132
7:6	133
7:6–8	124
26:5	144
28:9–10	202
30:3–4	159

Judges

2:2	133
21:25	132

1 Kings

8:34–35	137

Psalms

65:6	144
137:4	163

Isaiah

2:2–4	186
2:2–4, ESV	177
11:12	165
11:12–13	160
40:5	52
42:6	125, 133

49:6	125
49:15	xix
52:13–53:13	135
54:5	203
55:10–11	104

Jeremiah

3:12	199
3:14	199
17:1	138

Hosea

10:9	137
11:9	191
11:9, TNIV	xviii

Amos

2:4	138
2:6	138
8:11	194

NEW TESTAMENT

Matthew

3:11	98
4:18–22	116
5–7	202
5	100
5:6	57
5:17	141
12:18	100

240

14:19	56
26:26–29	56
27:50	101
28:16–20	53
28:18–20	204
28:19	102
28:19–20	32, 120

Mark
1:10	98
1:15	99, 199
1:16–20	116
2:13–28	143
2:17	143
2:19	143
2:27	143
6:30–8:21	57
6:41	56
8:27–29	105
8:34–35	101
14:22–25	56

Luke
2:29–32	203
4:18–19	99, 192
4:43	192
5:1–11	117
6	100
7:18–23	183
7:22	100
10:22	xviii
13:29	57, 58
22:14–23	56
23:46	101
24:27	203
24:30–31	56
24:36–49	91

John
1	51–52
1:1–2, RSV	51
1:14	52
1:14, RSV	51, 201
1:18, RSV	201
1:35–42	117
1:41	125

3:17	199
4:22	157
6:11	56
12:12–13	56
14:16–17	74
14:26	74
15:26	192
15:26–27	74
16:8–11	74
16:12–13	206
16:13–15	74
17:1	200–201
17:1–3	201
17:11–23	200
17:21–23	122
19:14–16	141
19:30	101
20:21	192
20:22	73, 74, 98, 102
20:24–29	91
21:9–17	103
21:18	102

Acts
1–2	110
1:5	98
1:15–26	109
2:1–13	74, 109
2:12	97
2:14–36	109
2:17	98
2:17–21	203
2:32	105
2:37–41	110
2:37–42	53
2:42	110
6:7	176
7	111
7:55	111
9	111
9:5–6	111
9:31	176
10:44–48	53
12:24	176
15:19	161
16:5	176

19:20	176
22:6–11	111
23:11	111
28:30–31	176

Romans
1:4	102
2:12	154
3:1	154
3:3–4	154
3:5	156
3:22	156
3:23	155–56
5:10–11	217
6:1–11	53
6:4	48
6:5	92
8:9–10	102
9–11	154–55, 193
9:4	193
9:4–5	154
9:6	154
9:14	155
10:4	140–41
10:14	41
10:14–15	167
11:1	155
11:11	155
11:11–12	156
11:15	156
11:16	157
11:25–26	156
11:28	140
11:29	133
12	87
12:3	94
12:4–5	88
12:4–6	94
12:5	85, 95
12:6	95
12:6–8	96
12:10	94
12:18	94
13:9	216
15:13	210
15:25–27	73

1 Corinthians

1:9	68
1:10	93
10:1–4	53
10:16	48
10:16–17	42, 69
11	56
11:23–26	56
12	87
12:3	112
12:4–6	95
12:7	95
12:12	88
12:12–13	53
12:13	92, 98
12:21	94
12:25	94
12:26	24
12:27	88, 95
13:5	94
15:1–3	22
15:23–24	112

2 Corinthians

4:5	20
4:7	21
5:18	217
5:19	217
5:20	217
8:3–4	72
8:9	73
9:13–14	72
9:13–15	62
13:13	68
13:14	67–68

Galatians

2:9	71
3:26–29	53
3:27–28	55
3:27–29	98

5:25	98
6:1–2	72
6:6	72

Ephesians

1	87
1:3–4	202
1:3–14	215
1:10	109, 214, 216, 218
1:16–23	218
1:18–19	218
1:22–23	88
2:2	165
2:11–14, RSV	145
2:11–22	218
2:12	154, 158
2:19	166
2:20	166
3:9–10, RSV	188
4	87, 94
4:2–3	94
4:4	95
4:4–6	88
4:7	96
4:7–13	112
4:15–16	88, 184
5:11	71

Philippians

1:3–5	69
1:7	68
1:27	195
2:1	68, 83
2:1–2	95
2:1–5	72
3:5	154
3:10	68

Colossians

1	87
1:17–18	89
1:24	89, 94

2:11–15	53
3:16	48

1 Timothy

1:1	210

2 Timothy

2:13	210
2:14	xiii

Philemon

4–6	71

Hebrews

1:1–2, RSV	159
4:12	48, 114
4:14	114
4:15	114
9:14	101
13:8	103
13:12–13	59, 93, 103

1 Peter

1:3	211
2:9	1, 137, 158, 161
2:10	137, 166
3:18–22	53
4:12–13	91

1 John

1:1–3	82
1:3	69, 162
1:5–7	71
2:2	203

Revelation

3:16	194
5	91
19:9	56
21:1–3, RSV	209
22:2	165
22:17	53